96/99

Our Town Oak Park

Our Town Oak Park

WALK WITH ME, IN SEARCH OF
TRUE COMMUNITY

Ken Trainor

Ken Trainor

Streetlight Books

Copyright © 2023 by Streetlight Books

All Rights Reserved.

ISBN: 978-1-958943-44-1 (Print), 978-1-958943-45-8 (eBook).

Library of Congress Control Number: 2023904667

Edited by Kevin Theis, Ft. Raphael Publishing Company

Front Cover Design by Paul Stroili, Touchstone Graphic Design, Chicago

Cover Artwork by Mitchell Markovitz, www.facebook.com/artmitchmarkovitz

PRAISE FOR "OUR TOWN OAK PARK"

Ken Trainor's thirty-year stroll through Oak Park takes us into the lives of its residents, to the benches and pathways of its parks, and the challenges and inspiration of a town working overtime to create COMMUNITY – not community as in a geographically defined set of coordinates, but a sense of place that nurtures and sustains its residents. If you are from this town, these essays will paint a picture that feels familiar. If home is elsewhere, this intimate peek into an extraordinary village, just west of Chicago, will draw you in for more.

Rebekah Levin
Social justice activist

Our Town Oak Park - Walk with Me, in Search of True Community is about us, for us. This collection of short essays is like finding love letters at the bottom of a sock drawer. They are familiar but new, old yet young. They cover life's spectrum: the grand, the small, the joyful, the sad. He has put into words the collective thoughts of our better selves. This is a book you will read many times.

McLouis Robinet
Scientist, retired from Argonne Labs

In a world that embraces the latest social media craze or digital device, Ken Trainor unplugs and invites his readers to celebrate a simple, low-tech stroll around his hometown, joining him on his walks as a way to discover fascinating stories around the corner or through the next shop window. In fact, the sidewalks, homes and places of Oak Park are themselves characters in his very own staging of "Our Town." But while many of us can walk with him, few are as capable at seeing, listening, and discovering the fascinating villagers who make this community the eccentric, unique, cantankerous, and inspirational place it is for so many of us.

This walking writer uncovers the details and turns the phrases that make his last 30 years on the local journalism beat come to life with poetry and passion. I know of no other book so "Pedestrian Friendly"!

Frank Lipo
Executive director, Historical Society of Oak Park & River Forest

Contents

Foreword   xi

1. Prelude   1
2. Spring   15
3. Day in the Life   25
4. Growing Up   32
5. Ceremonies & Celebrations   57
6. Summer   91
7. Characters with Character   102
8. Settings   133
9. Tourism   154
10. Autumn   186
11. Scenery   196
12. Walkabouts   226
13. Time Capsule   243
14. Winter   278
15. Eulogies   286

Postlude   339

To Marty
and the long walks to forever

Foreword

Welcome to our town

Walk with me — to the heart of Oak Park, a community like no other, yet like all others. Travel the pathways of our town, mining meaning from the everyday, finding extraordinary in the ordinary, at the intersection where unique meets universal.

Each of us has a town, a neighborhood, a subdivision, a municipality, a church congregation, a home enclave — a community. It consists of our experiences, connections, and lifestyles. Each of our towns is different from everyone else's, even if we share the same geography, the same municipality. My town. Your Town. It's when we get to the heart of things, the crucible that forges the bond, that we find Our Town.

It's a long walk to Our Town, by many paths to one goal, one destination: true community.

Does a community have a soul?

If we're talking about a collection of individuals, each representing an iceberg of consciousness in an ocean of unconsciousness, then the collective's soul is greater than the sum of its individuals, the "parts" constantly changing, departing, arriving, returning, renewing — evolving.

Many parts, one whole. Many hearts, one soul. Many paths, one home.

The ever-shifting nature of, in Oak Park's case, the 52,000-plus individuals comprising it, makes this community a dynamic, ever-evolving entity — who we were, who we are, and who we will be.

The unifying thread is true community — finding it in the journey of everyday life, unearthing it in the day-to-day, the face-to-face, the moments of beauty, the longing to be better than we were, the striving to be better than we are, and, as Thornton Wilder wrote in his play, *Our Town*, prizing the smallest details and events of daily life.

What is "community"? More than merely living next to one another. It is the alchemy that takes place when we interact; we become better individuals when we intersect.

Our town is an ongoing experiment to see if a mere collection of individuals can "integrate," be diverse yet whole, to the benefit of everyone. And if one community can accomplish this, then all communities can.

"We" are headed somewhere. "We" are not some static set piece, some staged play, some museum diorama. You and I are part of a greater whole yet to come. We're getting there, moment by moment. You'll find many such moments in this book.

Welcome to *Our Town Oak Park*, based on chronicles written over three decades in the local newspaper, *Wednesday Journal of Oak Park-River Forest*.

This book is written with an appreciative bow to *Our Town*, the 1938 Pulitzer Prize-winning play by Thornton Wilder about Grover's Corners, a fictional village in New Hampshire. *Our Town* is, in the view of many, the Great American Play — not some simplistic, sentimental, cultural cliché, as many misread it, but a profound, groundbreaking work that Edward Albee, author of *Who's Afraid of Virginia Woolf?* (and no sentimental slouch by any stretch) described as "one of the toughest, saddest, most brutal plays I've ever come across — and so beautiful."

Except for the "brutal" part, this book is loosely inspired by *Our Town*, which features, among much else, a time capsule; a detailed geological and anthropological summary; a full moon hanging high overhead, coldly watching the proceedings, remarked upon by several of the characters during Act 1, who are stirred by its "terrible," "wonderful" light; and a letter with far-reaching ripples, sent from the local minister to a sick young girl, addressed to her at "the Crofut Farm, Grover's Corners, Sutton County, New Hampshire, United States of America, Continent of North America, Western Hemisphere, the Earth, the Solar System, the Universe, the Mind of God."

Oak Park, meanwhile, anchored in the middle of the Midwest, was once described by local newspaper editor Otto McFeeley, an occasional walking partner of Frank Lloyd Wright and Carl Sandburg, once upon an earlier century, as "the Middle Class Capital of the World."

Going back further, the first European-American residents, Joseph and Betty Kettlestrings in 1833, settled on land vacated by the Potawatomi Nation at the insistence of the United States Army, following the trumped-up land grab known as the Black Hawk War of 1831 and the subsequent Treaty of Chicago in 1833.

Our town was built on a geological wrinkle, a remnant of shoreline of the vast body of water now known as Lake Michigan, as the glaciers receded following the last Ice Age. This lip gave the town its original name, Oak Ridge, and — after incorporating the east-central neighborhood known as Ridgeland — eventually became known as Oak Park.

The village grew rapidly following the 1871 Chicago Fire, when the charred and scarred were looking to get the hell out of Dodge — or at least dodge the City of Big Smolders. Conveniently, Oak Park was connected by rail, as it is still, due west from Chicago's lakefront. Because the high ground that Oak Park occupies separates two watersheds (one leading to the Mississippi River/Gulf of Mexico and the other to the Great Lakes/St. Lawrence Seaway/Atlantic Ocean), our barely perceptible ridge qualifies as a continental divide.

Among the new arrivals to Oak Park were both sets of grandparents of Ernest Hemingway, who was born and raised here at the beginning of the 20th century. Contemporaneously, Frank Lloyd Wright began his solo architectural career here, you could say, in earnest.

In a remarkable cultural convergence, the Wright Home & Studio was located directly across Chicago Avenue from Oliver Wendell Holmes School, which Hemingway attended (and lived a block north of), so the two were in close proximity for a few years but probably never interacted, though young Ernie likely heard about Frank, based on the flamboyant architect's racy reputation and the fact that a Wright-designed home was built across the street from the house on Kenilworth where Hemingway grew up.

A decade later, Edgar Rice Burroughs moved here and began publishing his Tarzan novels, so Oak Park can legitimately boast two of the bestselling American authors, as well as the greatest architect, of the 20th century.

Just saying.

In the early 1950s, Oak Park citizens voted out a corrupt political machine and voted in a new form of government at the behest of the Village Manager Association, a good-governance revolution that changed the course of village history, fostering a commitment to Fair Housing, followed by a half-century of managed-integration efforts, making this village a model of openness and stable diversity in a sea of segregation.

That was the setting into which I was born in 1952 — and from which I departed in 1970, following high school, then returned 20 years later in 1990 when I began writing for the local newspaper. Like a re-awakened Rip Van Winkle, I found a very different community from the one I left. Better in most respects. These essays chronicle my rediscovery (the year each piece was published is marked at the outset, although most have been revised and updated to indicate subsequent changes, which slightly distorts the chronological order).

What I discovered over a span of three decades is that this is not your average, inclusive, equity-aspiring, ever-evolving, welcoming community. So why does the title of this book allude to a play set in a small town in New England more than a century ago?

Because *Our Town* shows the way — from the local to the universal.

As Donald Margulies says in his Foreword to my well-thumbed, used paperback copy of *Our Town*, picked up one August morning during the annual Friends of the Oak Park Public Library Book Sale in the cafeteria of Oak Park and River Forest High School: "The perfection of the play starts with its title. Grover's Corners belongs to all of us; it is indeed *our* town, a microcosm of the human family, genus American. But in that specificity, it becomes all towns. Everywhere. Indeed, the play's success across cultural borders around the world [translated into 80 languages] attests to its being something much greater than an American play: It is a play that captures the universal experience of being alive."

Our Town Oak Park aims for that same "rainbow's end": capturing the experience of being alive — in one middle-sized, middle-class, home-ruled, Midwest town at the beginning of the 21st century.

So thank you, Char Thomas — whose name is inscribed on the inside cover of the play — for disposing of your copy when you did. I try to re-read it every summer.

Our Town provides a template for every town — a lens through which to view all our towns. It focuses on family, community interconnection, young love that turns into true love, culminating in a wedding and, just when you think you're heading toward happily ever after, along comes a third act in a graveyard so devastating it's hard to sit through, but which is necessary ultimately in order to, as the playwright put it, "find a value above all price for the smallest events in our daily life."

My hope is that, in reading this book, you will find meaning and value in Oak Park's daily life, too, and by extension — if you don't happen to live in Oak Park — in the events and daily details in your town, however small or large that might be.

Grover's Corners is not exactly like Oak Park — and yet, in essential ways, it is. Oak Park is not exactly like your town — and yet it is, in essential ways

And I believe it is critical to the very survival of our nation, the sum total of our towns, that this be true.

Our Town, then, is a metaphor, a destination, our goal — finding our way to "true community," a many-layered process. The deeper you go, the closer you get to "Our Town" and the realization that there exists a kind of heaven on Earth here, though we rarely recognize it. Not for long anyway. "Oh, earth, you're too wonderful for anyone to realize you!" exclaims the main character, Emily, in ecstatic frustration, at the end of the play. But we do catch glimpses of it in daily life. Treasures above all price. It has been my mission to find these, and I have collected them here.

This has been both a personal and collective journey. Oak Park has worked hard over the past 70 years to foster true community. Not some blissful utopia. Moving toward true community is hard work, but worth the struggle. We have a long way to go, but we've left a trail of efforts behind us. We're pointing the way. Other communities may go even further. Some already have in certain respects, which is good because we need as many inclusive, equity-aspiring, ever-evolving, good-governing, welcoming communities as possible.

My own long walk has lasted 32 years. Returning to Oak Park, covering the town for the local newspaper, I got to know people I probably never would have met otherwise. I listened as they talked about their remarkable lives. Everyone, I soon learned, has a story and everyone's story is worth telling. Cumulatively, those stories tell who we are — in our living, loving, and dying.

Ever so slowly, I discovered, here in our town, a place of deep belonging.

I found my way back home.

Ernest Hemingway, reportedly, was not keen about coming back to Oak Park once he became a citizen of the wider world. Thomas Wolfe (not from here) famously wrote a book titled, *You Can't Go Home Again*, by which he meant "to lose the earth you know for greater knowing; to lose the life you have, for greater life; to leave the friends you loved, for greater loving; to find a land more kind than home, more large than earth."

But I did go home again — in the sense that Ursula Le Guin described in her novel *The Dispossessed*: "You shall not go down twice to the same river, nor can you go home again. ... [But] you can go home again, the General Temporal Theory asserts, so long as you understand that home is a place where you have never been."

This town, then, is a place you and I have never been, a place that keeps changing, evolving, opening ... ripening. It differs from the time I wrote these words to the time you read them, a place whose changing face I have known and chronicled for the last three decades: Oak Park, Cook County, Illinois, United States of America, Continent of North

America, Western Hemisphere, the Earth, the Solar System, the Universe, the Mind of God.

It is a good place. A place I once called, and now again call, home. My town. Your town. Our town. In these pages, as in the play by that name, you will find a time capsule, geography, community interconnection, true loves, and final resting places.

And, of course, morning and moonlight and everything in between.

Let's begin.

1

Prelude

"I would like to know what that play would look like today, if Wilder were writing today about the average American experience in a small town. I have no idea where that would go now. It would certainly be something different."

Paul Newman
Playing the Stage Manager in "Our Town"
Westport Country Playhouse, 2002-03
From "Another Day's Begun – Thornton Wilder's 'Our Town' in the 21st Century"
By Howard Sherman

Who we are (2013)

But you know and I know there never was reason to hurt
When all of our lives were entwined to begin with
Here in Spoon River...
The morning is heavy with one more beginning
Here in Spoon River...

Michael Smith, *Spoon River*

Waking to a rainy morning was soothing. As beautiful as Friday and Saturday were — low humidity, clean skies, clarified sunlight, comfortably cool — this cloud-cast Sunday felt needed.

A light but steady, day-long rain soaked the parched earth. How exquisite, how nourishing and sustaining that must be for all rooted, and unrooted, living things.

On Friday, I drove two hours west to White Pines State Park, where a young Oak Park couple was married outdoors on as perfect a wedding day as has ever been ordered and delivered. Later, under bright stars and a glowing half-moon, Evan and Missy were encircled, blessed and feted, and danced to their hearts' delight.

I left them to their midnight bonfire because I had a 6:30 a.m. date with donuts at Farmers Market, a cherished local tradition. Once a summer I serve coffee and OJ to the remarkably large number of people who are up and about before 9 a.m. on a weekend morning.

This was no ordinary Saturday. It was prime time for vegetables, midway through September, one of our best weather months.

A young father came through the donut line with two young children, including a boy no more than 5, who was singing "Oh What a Beautiful Morning" from *Oklahoma*. He knew the words ("All the cattle are standing like statues ...") and sang on key, artlessly. He wasn't showing off. I don't think his father was even paying attention. What will this kid be like in 10-15 years?

I work this shift for a local service organization that makes scholarships available (thanks in part to dollars raised by these donut sales) to help fund higher education for young women.

I enjoy the "cycles." Young couples, with young kids in tow or in strollers, come under the tent looking a bit weary and craving caffeine. These parents were young children in 1990 when I moved back to town. Their parents are now my age and looking more relaxed. Life seems to fit them — or they fit life. They've been through enough cycles to have confidence in the reliable succession of seasons, years and decades. They know what gives way to what.

The year is aging — a cycle so familiar we have it memorized. Farm produce has its cycle as well. Foodies load their reusable bags as they have all summer, as they have for many summers and autumns before that.

We are, in our way, as rooted as the plants that produced this bounty — "our lives entwined to begin with, here in Spoon River," as songwriter Michael Smith put it.

Or as I prefer to think of it, here in "Our Town," as Thornton Wilder, by way of the Stage Manager, described it in his classic American play:

"This is the way we were: in our growing up and in our marrying and in our living and in our dying. ... It's like what one of those Middle West poets said: You've got to love life to have life, and you've got to have life to love life. ... It's what they call a vicious circle."

Cycles and circles. Not so vicious really.

This is the way we are, here in Spoon River, here in Our Town, here in Oak Park, here in Everytown in the early decades of the 21st century.

With a few more soakings like last Sunday, the grass will green up again and demonstrate its stubborn persistence deep into autumn. But by then we'll stop noticing because the littering leaves will blanket it, and besides, we'll be pulled inside by the warm, well-lit, ornamented, pumpkin-spiced interiors of holiday fellowship.

But for the moment, it's still glorious late summer. The young couple who got married on Friday may or may not birth children, but their life together will bear fruit in any number of ways and that will be cause for further blessings and celebrations and encirclements. And many others who declare their lives joined will contribute offspring to the next cycle.

Not everyone stays, of course. Many migrate and root elsewhere. But some left elsewhere and rooted here. On Saturday, I detected a cornucopia of accents from other regions and other lands.

The cycles continue with soothing predictability, yet each is new and fresh — like the donuts at Farmers Market, which have become a symbol of this Saturday morning ritual. Sweet circles that symbolize our cycles.

Yes, this is who we are.

Embracing the hassle (2013)

There are many things to love about Oak Park. For one, the citizens are progressive. Not many towns this size in the United States, I'm guessing, have so dominant a progressive majority. Even the conservatives here are broad-minded. They're willing to live in a freer-thinking enclave and some actually read the local newspaper even though certain weekly sermons certain outspoken homilists frequently infuriate them. Which may mean we have the most open-minded conservatives in the entire country.

We have our share of libertarians, New-Agers, and sundry other non-mainstreamers. Respecting diversity doesn't mean much, after all, unless you have diversity on hand to respect. Oak Park isn't an easy place to pigeon-hole. We differ, but we talk to one another. I love that.

I love Oak Park's social conscience. A Day in Our Village, the annual festival in Scoville Park the first Sunday in June, is dense with booths promoting worthy causes. They represent our "social infrastructure." People here care, they're involved, and they bring skills to bear on their activism. Housing Forward, the homeless shelter (and homelessness prevention) program, is a shining example.

This is also one of the country's loveliest towns. People come from all over the world to see the Wright homes, but the Victorians and other non-Prairie-style houses are also worth admiring. We live in a virtual movie set. People around the country fantasize about the kind of housing stock on display here. When they get here, ostensibly to see Wright's Prairie-style architectural treasures, their fantasies spring to life. Mine did. Wander up and down Forest or Kenilworth avenues (in the Wright Historic District) and listen to the tourists. Residents have invested an enormous amount of money restoring their Victorians and foursquares and brick bungalows, resulting in a genuine showcase. The challenge is not taking all this for granted.

And then, of course, there are the trees. Driving my mother-in-law from the city to Oak Park one day, she looked out the window, and sighed, "Mature trees!" We've become accustomed to living in an "urban forest," but if you go out on the 13th floor deck at the Brookdale retirement facility (or one of the other tallish buildings in town), you'll sigh too over the seemingly unbroken canopy of green (for two-thirds of the year). We (and the squirrels) owe so much to people who had the foresight to plant so many trees so long ago — and to those who replaced the trees we lost to Dutch elm disease and the emerald ash borer with other leafy varieties.

I love that we raise more than our share of smart, talented kids, who are comfortable with diversity and have strong values; then we unleash them on the world. We're making a contribution.

I love that we have (or had) many smart, cultured, creative people living here who have accomplished much already (author Caroline Myss, the late actor John Mahoney, illustrator Chris Ware). The list is long, and who knows how many others are working furiously on achievements still to come.

I love the intersections — literal and figurative. I live in an apartment overlooking what I call "the intersection of life." Sometimes the cars waiting at the stoplight blast rap, sometimes rock, and sometimes even Broadway musicals. Recently my living room filled with the sound of Julie Andrews singing, "It's May! It's May! The lusty month of May!" We're even musically diverse.

I love the longstanding tradition of block parties. They started as a tool for fostering community connection, block by block. Village government actively promoted them in the 1960s as a way to welcome and integrate newly arriving families of color and widen the comfort zone of white families. As the Village Diversity Statement puts it, we need to do more than live next to each other. We need to get to know one another. Interaction is the best way to build trust. It's also the best way to create great memories for our kids as they grow up — together.

One day, as I waited to cross the Oak Park Avenue and Lake Street intersection, I found myself next to a kid wearing the uniform of a particular PONY League youth baseball team. He was heading up to Lindberg Park on his bike for a game. I said, "I played for that team in

1966 and used to ride *my* bike to that park." Looking startled and full of wonder, he said, "Really?" then was off. We are a town of confluence, coincidence, connectedness and continuity.

But we also have the Oak Park-River Forest, Oak Park-Austin, Oak Park-Berwyn/Cicero, Oak Park-Forest Park, Oak Park-River Forest, Oak Park-Elmwood Park, and Oak Park-Galewood intersections. We're surrounded by interesting, and differing, communities. If no one is an island, no community is either.

American society still too often segregates, but Oak Park works at integrating, though not always successfully because sustaining diversity takes effort. Voices must be heard — singles, families, seniors, teens, gays, straights, Blacks, Whites, Christians, Jews, Muslims, Buddhists, immigrants, tourists, animal lovers, commuters, homeowners, apartment dwellers, condo owners, the homeless, rich, poor, middle class, motorists, pedestrians, bicyclists, merchants, consumers, progressives, conservatives, moderates, men, women, gender fluid, people in need of various levels of assistance, and people to assist them. We have a full spectrum. That's a lot to integrate — and navigate.

We're more than the sum of our parts. We're the quilt, the stew, or whatever collective metaphor you choose. We merge then differentiate, differentiate then merge. But we rarely divide. We contend, compete, conflict, cooperate, rub the wrong way, rub the right way, overlap, mesh, miss, and eventually come to terms.

It's a lot of work. Not everyone is up to it. But looking at the end result that is Oak Park, I think it's worth the complications. In fact, that could be our village slogan:

Living here is worth the hassle.

What makes Oak Park so cool? (2019)

Is our town cool? Apartment Therapy, which bills itself as "the leading independent home site, designed to inspire anyone to live a more beautiful and happy life at home," in May 2019 named Oak Park one of the 24 "Coolest Suburbs in America." That's cool.

The website explains, "Apartment Therapy hopes to emphasize that the quest for a home, and community, with more space doesn't necessarily mean the sacrifice of cultural relevance."

According to the Oak Parker who wrote our entry, "When city-dwellers think of the suburbs, boring homogeneity might be what incorrectly comes to mind." But Oak Park "offers suburban perks, while maintaining the diversity and eccentricity of urban life."

Diversity, eccentricity and cultural relevance — sounds about right.

The writer touted our status as Illinois' first "municipal arboretum," our pro-active stance on diversity in the 1960s, "launching an organization [the Oak Park Regional Housing Center] to sustain and improve the village's racial diversity."

She cites Wright and Hemingway, of course, under "What the suburb is known for," and names the Hole in the Wall soft-serve ice cream shop on South Oak Park Avenue near the expressway as a "Hidden Gem," the Oak Park Public Library as the "Place that makes you happy to live here," Farmers Market (and donuts) as a "Favorite activity for families," Live Café and Creative Space (now Brewpoint Café) as "Favorite hangout for young professionals," Lake Street (anchored by the Lake Theatre) as "Favorite teen hangout," Book Table as "Favorite local bookstore," Wise Cup as "Favorite place to get coffee," Kinslahger as "Favorite bar when you want to be around people," Lindberg Park as "Favorite alone spot," summer concerts in Scoville Park as "Favorite free cultural thing to take part in," Lively Athletics as "Favorite boutique," the fiesta mole at New Rebozo (since moved to Forest Park) as "Signature food," Taylor Park as "Most walkable area," Buzz Café for "Favorite brunch," Oak Park

Conservatory (especially in winter) for "Favorite free activity," Sugar Beet Co-op as "Favorite grocery store," BFit Fitness and the sledding hill stairs at Barrie Park as "Favorite place for a workout," the Oak Park Arts District and Val's halla Records as "Favorite place to take an out-of-towner," MicroBrew Review as "Favorite annual event," Alioto's Gift Shop as "Favorite home store," George's Restaurant as "Favorite local diner," the Garden Club's annual walkabout as "Favorite house/garden walk" (which is saying something in a suburb that offers more housewalks per capita than probably any other), Ridgeland Common as "Favorite dog park," and Brown Elephant as "Favorite resale and antique store."

Being diverse and eccentric, we can quibble about particular choices, but this is a good starting point for discussion (which is sure to occur). Part of that discussion is: Do all of these really qualify as "cool"? It depends, of course, how you define cool, an ever-elusive quicksilver characteristic.

The 1936 Lake Theatre marquee, for instance, is still functioning, at no small expense and effort. In 2017, according to Classic Cinemas' co-founder Willis Johnson, they spent $5,734 on maintenance alone. That's because "the marquee is important," Johnson said. "It's a symbol of downtown vitality." The marquee has since been refurbished to give it a more modern "digital billboard" look. And the movie palace it adorns is also air-conditioned.

That's cool.

Frank Lloyd Wright's homes are visually inventive, as evidenced by "The Wright Triangle," three of his homes in close proximity: the Japanese-style Hills-DeCaro house; the Moore-Dugal house, an unusual blend of English Tudor with Mayan influence; and across Forest Avenue, the prow-shaped Heurtley house façade (pointing back at the other two). All of this just down the street from Wright's Home & Studio, which might have been dismantled and shipped to Japan in the 1970s, were it not for John Thorpe and a group of dedicated volunteers, who acquired and restored the structure and launched Oak Park's tourism industry.

That's cool.

The tongue-in-cheek signs at the small-but-mighty pharmacy near the corner of Home and Madison are cool. My favorite is "Sears Pharmacy – The Pillar of Oak Park." Exaggerated to be sure, but with a grain of truth. Indie shops are indeed the mini-pillars of Oak Park, and Sears is one of the best examples.

The Pagan Festival at Mills Park is cool (also odd), as is the Violano Virtuoso, a mechanical music marvel inside Pleasant Home (manufactured by Herbert Mills whom the park is named for). The violano is a hybrid of violin and piano innards. You have to see it and hear it to believe it.

Hemmingway's Bistro in the Write Inn combines intentional misspellings of Oak Park's two cultural giants. Hemmingway's needed the extra "m" to keep from running afoul of the Hemingway family estate, which guards the legacy of their famous patriarch. Write Inn not only prevents the same difficulty with the Wright Trust, but also serves as a nod (and invitation?) to Oak Park's many literary connections. That's cool, but what's really cool is dining at the bistro on a sunny morning with light pouring through the tall windows, giving the place a "Moveable Feast," Parisienne feel, of which, we like to think, Papa himself would have approved.

Rick's Rickshaw rides were cool (until bon vivant entrepreneur Rick Carter died in 2022), as is Thursday Night Out in the summer for dine-arounds on Marion Street in the Downtown Oak Park business district.

Declaring ourselves a "Nuclear Free Zone" was/is cool (we took down the much-mocked signs, but we're still nuke-free).

The Love Locks on the sides of the Oak Park Avenue and Marion Steet railroad underpasses are cool and very romantic (the idea sparked by Hemingway's connection to Paris), as are the colorful original paintings by local artists brightening the inset panels of the train embankment all the way from our western to our eastern border, thanks to a program sponsored by the Oak Park Area Arts Council.

The Oak Park Public Library is cool, as previously mentioned, because the 2003 building is the only one built in the last quarter-century worthy of our vaunted architectural heritage — and the only one whose roof simulates a mountain range.

But the many Little Free Libraries all over town are likewise cool.

Wrap-around porches are cool — cooler still when people actually use them. Maya del Sol is cool because it's owned by former Mayor-del-Sol Anan Abu-Taleb, a Palestinian-American who married the neice of John Gearen, the village president who ushered in Oak Park's Fair Housing era in the 1960s. Talk about pedigree. Anan lives in John Gearen's former home in the only village where, to paraphrase Barack Obama, a story like his is even possible.

But the question remains: How cool is Oak Park? If you asked Oak Parkers, they would probably roll their eyes or fix you with an incredulous look. Residents, by and large, pay no attention. Instead, we complain about the paucity of parking. We call ourselves "Oak No Park."

Our bad-mouthing keeps us from getting a big head.

Oak Park is so cool it doesn't even know it's cool.

How are we doing? (2014)

Getting off the CTA Green Line last week, I met a friend I haven't seen in a long while. Our sons played youth baseball together back in the 20th century. We endured the hard, aluminum bleachers at Lindberg Park during PONY League games in the chill of a Midwestern spring as we encouraged our offspring to master a game we never quite mastered.

Hadn't seen this friend for 15 years, then ran into him at A Day in Our Village, an event where you can learn more about Oak Park in one afternoon than anyplace else. I'm always amazed by how many people come from out of town to this thing — as if they were shopping for a hometown.

Three months later, we meet again. This is the kind of place where, sooner or later, you're likely to run into people you know.

Just before we parted, he asked, "How is Oak Park doing?"

I thought back: On Friday night, I attended a lecture at Frank Lloyd Wright's Unity Temple by Michael Dowd, a visiting Unitarian minister who promotes "Religious Naturalism," which contends there is no conflict between religion and science. "Ecology is the new theology," he said to a crowd of over 100, including out-of-town participants in the Climate March, held in Chicago, who were being hosted by members of the congregation. Climate change is the ultimate moral issue of our age, Dowd said.

"Our present course leads to certain catastrophe," he added, yet our political situation makes it impossible for us to change that course.

"We are stuck between the impossible and the unthinkable."

What do we do about it?

"It's everyone's job to make the impossible possible," he concluded.

Making the impossible possible — sounds like a good slogan for Oak Park, and maybe the rest of the country, not to mention the rest of the planet.

On Saturday, the weather was just too beautiful to stay indoors. I walked to Mills Park, which has recently been renewed, refreshed and restored, along with the rest of Oak Park's parks.

I came across, of all things, a cricket match. An expatriate Englishman, who lives across the street, assembled a group of friends, adults and kids, to experience one of baseball's precursors. How cosmopolitan we have become, I thought, with multiple languages heard regularly on our streets and now, cricket, which, like baseball, has become an internationally popular sport.

Downtown was crowded and busy, as it is most weekend evenings. We are developing, little by little, into a nightlife hub. Economic activity is a welcome sign in a business district that saw its share of downturns in the last third of the 20th century.

The following morning, I heard out my window a cheery "Good morning!" called at some distance, judging by the volume. Suddenly this felt like a small town again. There are times when we act like a municipality and times when we feel like a small village. Our well-being may hinge on our ability to maintain a balance between the two.

I attended services at two extremes of religious ritual: Unitarian-Universalists (their slogan is "Come as you are") and Catholics (in effect, "Come as we'd like you to be"). The Unitarians talked about taking the path of risk and the choir sang a spirited, multilayered Swahili anthem, accompanied by seven drummers drumming (djembes to be precise). Meanwhile, St. Catherine-St Lucy Church, which I haven't attended since the age of 6, welcomed back Sr. Teresita Weind, exiled in the early 1990s for not accepting her womanly place (in other words, second class). During the intervening years, Teresita became the head of her order, now lives in Rome, and is even more widely respected than she was when she was leading services at St. Kate's, but on this homecoming Sunday, she preached — humbly and eloquently — about the long road to reconciliation. The archdiocese didn't like her sermons 23 years ago. Now they should hire her to teach the men how to do it. She would never say something so snarky, of course. Instead, she encourages patience and perseverance because, as she put it, reconciliation takes as long as it takes.

But in the end it's worth the effort because God's gift to us is a deeper peace, which she proceeded to sing about beautifully.

Teresita is a living, breathing psalm and spiritual balm. Wonder why the higher-ups couldn't see it.

That afternoon, a number of us gathered to help one of our fellow employees here at the paper. He and his family were forced from their home in the middle of the night by a terrible fire. Much was damaged or destroyed and they had this one day to pack the remainders and move to temporary storage and lodging. A severe disruption and dislocation. So the call went out and helping hands appeared. They have a long road ahead.

How are we doing?

Well, we're a community where you can walk everywhere and meet people you know. We're a place that refreshes its parks, not just its computers. Our urban forest is sunlit, soothing and sheltering.

We live in a town other people fantasize about calling home, a great place to be from, return to, or just visit, judging by all the visitors — and all the businesses, complaining every step of the way about what sticklers village hall staff are about regulations, but who keep applying to open up here nonetheless. Nobody comes here to be trendy, which makes us the epitome of anti-cool. We take the path of risk. We face the moral issues of the day and work to make the impossible possible. And we welcome those who come here to remind us to keep on doing just that. We are cosmopolitan townies, an urban village, where Unitarian choirs sing Swahili anthems and Catholics never give up on the promise of reconciliation. We're not too sophisticated to shout out a cheery good morning and not afraid to organize a game of cricket in the park. And when people need help, they call and we respond. But there is a long road ahead for all of us.

And we have people who have been here 30 years who are awake and care enough to ask, "How is Oak Park doing?"

What a good question.

So, Oak Park, how are we doing?

2

Spring

The calendar starts and ends in winter, which seems odd. A case can be made that the year should close with the end of winter and begin with the arrival of spring since that's when life re-awakens and the cycle begins again. We should be governed by the equinoxes not the solstices — balance instead of extremes.

That's not likely to change, but for me the year begins in March.

Winter cleanses the palate. Spring elates. Summer overloads. Autumn mellows, ripens, fades. It signals the end of the cycle of life. Winter prepares us for the coming vernal resurrection.

The familiarity is reassuring, even with climate change disrupting the patterns. We develop muscle memory about the year as it unfolds, peaks, fades and refolds.

The seasons are a dress rehearsal for our own life revolutions, the stages we pass through as we age, which are staggered, allowing each of us to review and preview the changes as our paths cross.

Communities also go through "seasons." Trends run their course; new trends begin. Demographics change. Towns grow older, then younger. Shop closings and openings remind us of life's impermanence, and condition us to accept the larger changes that are inevitable.

It is a privilege to observe the seasons, year after year, from a single vantage point, in the same meeting places, with many of the same people and traditions. We return indoors when the light flees and the winds punish, and then we greet each other when the sun's returning warmth draws us out again, eager to reconnect with one another.

Welcome, spring.

Spring in its step (2022)

Late-winter's march into spring has begun as February gives way, unwillingly, to its successor season. Winter's clenched teeth have stopped chattering, and unmasked smiles are visible after a two-year pandemic pall. Not wishing to be fooled again, we venture out, hesitantly looking over our shoulders, no false sense of security this time, no fooling us twice.

The odds seem finally in our favor. Even pandemics come to an end. Winters too. And when those two endings coincide, my, my. That's some beginning.

A pre-spring, morning-long rain rinses soot from evaporating snow. Temps rise into the 40s. Windy. The air no longer hurts. Grey turbulence roils the sky, the accumulated, dense cumulus weeping its excess across the newly exposed landscape following a month-long coverlet of icy white.

Flower bulbs down below are bathed in waves of snowmelt. Daffodil shoots throw caution to the wind. "If not now, when?" they seem to say. Frozen ground turns to mud, though tiny ice floes still cling to the parkways, like micro-glaciers, dark with dirt.

Rain ministers its cold-water cleansing. The world is awash. Braided rivulets follow curbed channels, streaming toward slotted sewer covers, eager to join the cascading cataract and underground torrent.

Meanwhile, at the end of every down-sloping branch of tree and shrub, droplets hang, suspended between cling and surrender, awaiting the irresistible pull of gravity. Dangling from last year's decaying crabapple clusters and new, ambitious buds, hundreds of greyblue droplets shine like tiny ornaments, celebrating the new season, freed at last from frigidity's rigidity.

You could easily miss these adornments, hunched beneath an umbrella, eyes downcast, hurrying to escape the damp affront. An old adage contends, "Some people feel the rain. Others just get wet."

Like droplets, we too hang between heaven and earth, sickness and health, awaiting our summons, an invitation we can't refuse, too preoccupied perhaps to notice that the world around us has been refreshed. But afflicted as we are, sick and tired of sickness, it is still possible to re-enter the beautiful world that surrounds, just waiting for us to pay attention.

March arrives and we yo-yo between 69 degrees and snow. The black locust tree across the street has long languished in the icy shadows as the sun's arc, formerly bent low in the southern sky, inched north up the horizon. Now the morning sun finds an opening between the old church and school, and bastes this tree with the brightest flashlight in our corner of the universe, super-luminous, exposing every wrinkle in the patterned bark. But even a light this strong can't reach the opposite side, and the trunk casts its long shadow down the street, a defiant tail against the growing glow.

Sunlight spills on walkway and parkway and street, curb and gutter, nicks and cracks, lava flows of tar and patchwork repairs, illuminating every flaw in pavement's decay. Light has banished night, yin to shadow's yang.

Mornings trend sunnier now, free of the overcast that often fills the afternoon sky. A clean slate, baptized with sinless sunsplash. Give us this day our daily resurrection. Today is yesterday redeemed.

A shining tree in the morning is a welcome portent, nourishing hope, even though the rest of the day may have other ideas.

Birds, clearly approving, lift praise songs, their morning psalm to our warming star.

Daylight Salvation Time is just around the corner. Two years ago, we locked down. Now faces emerge from lowered masks. Shadow remains, but light is contending.

Have we turned the corner?

Will we meet our mask-optional future face to face?

With a little luck, and a little common sense, a new day might just be dawning.

Slow dancing with a Midwest spring (2009)

Spring is here.
Why doesn't my heart go dancing?
Spring is here.
Why isn't the waltz entrancing?
Why doesn't the breeze delight me?
Why doesn't the night invite me?
Spring is here.
Spring is here
I hear.

Rodgers and Hart

Spring in the Midwest is an acquired taste. To enjoy spring in this part of the country, patience must be cultivated. Spring is the ultimate backslider, the weather constantly reverting to its wintry ways. Two steps forward, one step back. Sometimes one step forward, two steps back.

Charles Kuralt once described spring in Charleston, South Carolina, as arriving "in a showy rush." There is no such rush in the Midwest. Spring takes its sweet time.

It is the diametric opposite of high-speed internet. Spring is like a wave in super-slow motion — or the slow swelling that leads to that wave. It is inexorable and can't be contained once set in motion, but it feels absolutely no sense of urgency.

Spring arrived last Sunday, but by the time you read this it will have likely departed. It will arrive again — and depart again — several more times. Some years, it seizes the stage all to itself, but usually it shares the bill with winter, the freeloader, which always overstays its welcome.

Spring has stage fright. It is shy and unassuming, and just about the time it finally settles in, summer is there to tap it on the shoulder and give it the hook.

The first signs are easy to overlook, but you can find them, even in the dreary grey of a frigid March: a lovely patch of snowdrops blooming in Austin Gardens, witch hazel bushes blossoming in front of the Frank Lloyd Wright-designed Frank W. Thomas house where Forest Avenue bends into Ontario Street, crocuses on the south side of the rowhouses near the 19th Century Club, the sun positioning itself at the end of every street as it sets, midway on the horizon, taming its bi-polar tendencies momentarily in favor of balance, giving us 12 full hours of daylight.

Hands come out of gloves, jackets are wrapped around waists like shed skins.

Squirrels nose through leaves, scouring the dirt, looking for last November's buried nut stashes. The earth softens with the release of frost, pregnant with resurrected root systems, vital vegetation, and God knows how many awakened worms, sifting through the spongy topsoil.

Overhead, the tips of tree branches produce new matter exponentially. The breeze has a hint of tenderness in it, following months of astringency. Dog delirium is rampant as smells, unimaginable to us, swell sensitive nostrils, the great outdoors being the ultimate canine entertainment medium.

The squirrel guy arrives in his khaki vest and begins feeding his bushy-tailed disciples like a secular Francis of Assisi. A young woman wheels her brother with cerebral palsy, into the clearing, ties the family dog to a tree, and sets up a small picnic. Sharp, nasal, high-pitched voices pierce the quiet, as kids slide past on bikes and scooters.

Hurry has gotten the hint and left the premises — though some walkers continue to set a brisk pace. A Frisbee group forms a foursquare. The disk flutters, wobbles, and dives like the proverbial wounded duck.

Spring is grudgingly flamboyant with its passive/aggressive, approach/avoidance style.

The season must be taken on its own terms. It does no good to expect more or demand consistency. It is a creative genius, subject to its own laws and flaws. It won't be rushed. It refuses to conform.

Expect only one thing of spring: its inevitability. It will arrive ... and depart ... and arrive ... and depart.

We always hope for spring ever after, the same way we want happiness.

But spring and happiness are first cousins, romantics of the worst sort and therefore totally unreliable and unpredictable.

There will be days that make us positively giddy with delight. But it might take them a while to settle in and stay.

To enjoy spring in these parts, dress for winter. Too many dress by the calendar. If it's spring, they think, we should be able to wear shorts. Then they gripe about the cold.

In general, overdress till mid-June.

Spring is a notorious tease. Thirty-degree temperature swings are the norm. Don't take it personally; it's no one's fault. Spring is maddening, but only if you expect more than the season is willing to give. Impatience will be punished, each setback infuriating. Winter was long enough. Aren't we entitled to some relief?

It took a long time to realize that spring isn't about us. It's about the world wide web of grass and the carefully prescribed schedule of blossoming: crocus and scilla, hyacinth and daffodil, forsythia and tulip, magnolia and crabapple and pear, iris and peony.

Spring doesn't care that you want to go to the beach. It knows the grass likes 43 degrees and drizzle.

Sometimes it seems as if spring will never come, but it comes anyway. Buds swell, barren branches thicken with growth, grass greens, the vanguard leaves of future flowers breaking the newly thawed soil.

People complain that spring is too short, but what they really mean is that its peak is too short. The season itself is long and leisurely.

Spring says, "Slow down. The heat will be here soon enough. Enjoy the subtlety, the extended anticipation, the coming forth, the colors, the scents, the mystery of it all. So much is ahead. Savor this beginning. Look at the earth awakening. The world is coming alive again."

It took many years to slow down enough to appreciate this season, ever so incremental in its unfolding. Winter has lost its grip, no matter how often the rain turns slushy.

There's nothing fancy or showy about a Midwestern spring.

Spring is here. My heart is beginning to dance ... oh so slowly.

May makes its case (2014)

It's difficult to say what time of year is best. January is the calm following the holiday hurricane, as daylight incrementally lengthens in the wake of the winter solstice. I relish the snugness of the February cocoon; the first brave protrusions of erupting crocuses in March, the sun setting, dead center on the western horizon, in perfect balance at the spring equinox; the sudden elongation of light into the evening following Daylight Saving Time; Easter, when the theological Resurrection enjoys an objective correlative in the season's rebirth; the blossom bonanza in April; the leafing of trees in early May; the lush lawns, brilliant roses, and lingering daylight deep into a June night; the peak-summer sultriness of July and August; the hazy, mellow sunlight of September; the explosion of color in October; the moody darkness of Halloween; the inviting warmth of Thanksgiving; the starry wonder of the winter solstice and the luminous rebuttal of Christmas.

Every time of year has something to recommend it, not the least being that each lasts so short a time, yet can be counted on to return again. Variety and continuity — not a bad deal this cycle of seasons.

But May, when it's right, would finish near the top of most lists.

Johnny Cash composed his anthem to Ireland, "Forty Shades of Green," in 1961 after an enchanting visit to the Emerald Isle. I thought of it, wandering the village last Sunday in the full glory of early May. There must be 40 shades of green in Oak Park and River Forest now.

The catalogue is unfolding, not all of it green: Tulips, daffodils, dandelions, rhododendrons, hyacinths, bleeding hearts, scilla siberica, spring beauty, magnolias, crabapple, ornamental pear, forsythia, redbud, dogwood — even lilacs and lilies of the valley are poised and ready to issue their intoxicating fragrance.

It's touch-and-go for tree blossoms each spring. A blustery day at the wrong time can decimate these painted ladies. It was blustery last week and the week before, but somehow, spring perseveres.

The deciduous trees are also flowering right now. Though not as showy, maples bear a lighter shade of green, a lovely contrast to the deeper green of grass and tulip leaves.

The air is full of fragrance and pollen, which means my nose (newly reawakened from its wintry slumber) and eyes are full of it. Watering, itching and sneezing are how I relate to spring. Spring is nothing if not ironic. I worship what I'm allergic to, but suffer I must because this is the glorious time of year.

Also the most unsettled, even turbulent, time. Maybe "dynamic" is the better term. Fertile to the point of fecundity. It's all in how you look at things. I look dazzled.

In Austin Gardens, the park district has posted small signs, close to the ground, identifying the various patches of wildflowers — rue anemone, trout lily, mayapple, red trillium — exotic names for unusual flowers that could easily be overlooked if you didn't know there was a treasure trove at your feet in the wooded section of this hidden oasis.

Spring is notoriously stingy in this part of the country, but May is when it peaks, with its wide array of tulips (waning), irises, bridal veil, Korean spice viburnum, and heavy-headed peonies. Trees shed seeds by the truckload, and the streets fill with birds, darting to and fro, feasting on this reproductive orgy while dodging the murderous fenders of passing autos.

There is no spring delirium like the euphoria in the upper Midwest because we are accorded so few perfect days that, when they arrive, people are dazed by the grandeur of it all.

We shouldn't set holidays by the calendar. We should wait for perfect days and declare them holidays — by consensus.

If only life could be so simple.

Actually life is that simple, though we disguise it in complicated clothing, which is why we too often overlook what it offers. We long for more when life is presenting its best right under (and currently in) our noses.

Unhappiness is the belief that life, in its current condition, isn't good enough. I don't mean man-made life with its poverty, injustice, and violence — all the nasty stuff we can't seem to solve.

I mean life itself, being alive, a life worth living, those rare moments when you find yourself saying, "It doesn't get any better than this."

If that's enough, you're one of the lucky ones. If you keep asking, "Is that all there is?" then you've joined the ranks of the restless, spreading dissatisfaction.

I often find myself with a foot in each camp.

Which may explain why satisfaction and dissatisfaction have little correlation with wealth or poverty, illness or health, success or failure. It may be due to body chemistry, but if there's a secret to happiness, it's not asking more of life than life is capable of giving.

The problem with happiness is that it isn't exciting enough. Happiness is closer to stillness, which may be why it escapes our notice. Those who meditate would say stillness is the gateway to inner contentment, and when you reach contentment, you're in proximity to happiness.

I come closest when I'm outside in the warm sunshine, my face lifted to the sun, doing my best impersonation of a peony.

Or as poet Naomi Shihab Nye writes:

"Since there is no place large enough to contain so much happiness, you shrug, you raise your hands, and it flows out of you into everything you touch. You are not responsible. You take no credit, as the night sky takes no credit for the moon, but continues to hold it, and share it, and in that way, be known."

Most of the year it's either too hot or too cold around here, but when it's right, nothing is more marvelous than May.

Get out and wander.

Even if it makes you sneeze.

3

Day in the Life

What a day this has been, what a rare mood I'm in ...
All the music of life seems to be like a bell that is ringing for me ...

Lerner & Loewe
Brigadoon

If life is an odyssey, each day is a pilgrimage.

Most pilgrimages have a destination. Pilgrims aim for the ending, preferably the happily-ever-after sort. However, the destination of life's odyssey, we know only too well, is dying. We don't know what's on the other side of death's door. Might consciousness continue on in some fashion? That is humanity's unanswerable question and our great longing.

Asking the question, however, is important. It is to wonder, as Chardin said, whether we might be spiritual beings having a human experience instead of the other way around. So each day is a pilgrimage, beginning with light invading bedrooms or a clock radio bursting forth with the urgency of developments in the wider world. We traverse each day, paralleling the sun's arc overhead, which is sometimes clouded, sometimes aflame. Drawn by dawn, destined for dusk and beyond, to deep sleep's carnival of dreams, each day is a journey within the larger odyssey.

We set out with daily goals, meeting challenges with determination, and encountering delights with mindful awareness — if circumstances and time grant us the luxury of such awareness. We are the monks of our monasticism, planting seeds, tending them, loving where we can, praising where we find reason, helping where needed, laughing at the world's comedy — or our own — staying present in someone's life, easing pain where possible, wondering about the lives and burdens and delights of fellow pilgrims, regarding each day as a gift, feeling the upswell of gratitude, bestowing our gifts in return, paying attention to what begs to be noticed.

Each day ends with a string of pearls passing before our inner eyes, a necklace of memories, meaning to be mined.

We may reach our mecca or help someone reach theirs, treading lightly on the path, welcoming other pilgrims without getting in their way. And at day's end we ask, "What could I do better?"

Give us this day our daily plans: But let them be flexible, making room for surprise, embracing adventure when we dare. Forgive us our changing moods and minds. And may our trespasses lead to greater wisdom and our mistakes to atonement.

Beginnings and endings, and in between, we go places. Pilgrim's progress. Moving forward toward ... something. Walking — the body's act that messages the mind. We trace a "route," however random, however many right and left turns, however many steps forth and back.

Walking mirrors the inner "travel" our longing craves. We may not know where "there" is, may not recognize it when we arrive. If we arrive. Maybe going is all there is. Maybe it's enough.

Looking far ahead, the parallel lines of the sidewalk converge to a single point we will never reach, are in no hurry to reach.

The pilgrim's path.

A day in our village (2010)

Passing the tents in Scoville Park on this 37th "Day in Our Village," the word that seems to fit best is "adjacency." In a landlocked town, everything is "next to" everything else. You can't separate or segregate. Segregating is when the problems start — or when they start to fester.

Adjacency fosters connection. Scoville Park is adjacent to the eye-catching, still-new public library directly west. To the north, the park is adjacent to First Baptist Church. To the east is the old Oak Park Club, now private condos, but once upon a time a "country club," which may have been exclusive, but it was right in the middle of Oak Park — next to everything.

To the south is the modern, prairie-style Masonic building, "Scoville Square," and the very old-world looking, orange-brick, stair-step building that some say was modeled on the town hall (Rathaus) in Frankfurt, Germany. Old World meets New World at a single intersection.

The intersection of Lake Street and Oak Park Avenue is the community "epicenter," where an informal pedestrian parade takes place on beautiful weekend days, such as this first Sunday in June, perfumed by linden blossoms, and all observable from the large picture windows of the bakery/coffeeshop (then Red Hen, currently Courageous Cupcakes) that affords the best view of this crossroads. From the stools that line these "windows to the world," you can sit with a cup of tea or coffee and study Oak Park's "adjacency agency" in the village green of Scoville Park, fronted by the Horse Fountain, which anchors the entry plaza where commuters, students and sundry passersby wait for buses or stop to rest.

Once the private estate of early settler James Scoville, when the family was ready to move on (1912), did they sell the property to some enterprising entrepreneur, looking to make a killing on the real estate market? No, they sold it to the newly instituted park district, and a century hence, during our annual "booth fest" event, we get to appreciate their foresight. If you need a memory refresher, stop by the Historical Society tent and find out why "Scoville Institute" is engraved near the entry of the adjacent library (James Scoville established the first library in Oak Park on that spot, next to his estate).

A Day in Our Village is an "expo" of local organizations, booths crammed side by side, so residents, non-residents, and prospective residents get a sense of all this village offers. Walking along the avenue sidewalk, you can see Friends of Oak Park Dogs, next to the 19th Century Club, next to the Pleasant Home Foundation, next to the Secular Jewish Community and School, next to the West Suburban Special Recreation Association, next to West Suburban Temple Har Zion, next to the Ernest Hemingway Foundation, and on and on.

From this perch across the street, you can see many shades of skin, young and old, new parents and empty-nesters, stroller-pushers and dog-walkers, coffee-sippers and water-guzzlers, the fancy and the plain, the fit and rotund (and every body in between), shade-lovers and sun-worshipers, Sox fans and Cub fans and hockey fans, liberals and conservatives and libertarians, rich and poor and whatever's left of the middle class, nicotine addicts and caffeine addicts and sugar addicts and media addicts and fresh-air addicts, four-wheelers and two wheelers and two-leggers, the church-going and the church-leaving, same sex and opposite sex, the bused and trained and driven, individuals and couples and four-somes and small herds, wired and wireless, tattooed and tanned and sunscreened and carefully covered, hand-holders and hands filled, the flip-flopped and well-heeled, the graceful and the waddlers, the hurried and the amblers, buttoned-up and buttoned down and unbuttoned, capped and helmeted, shaved and shorn and bald, the unshaved and the breeze-blown, the staged and spontaneous, and even two girls with identical yellow T-shirts, one with SROO on the back and the other HROO.

There is room for everyone at the intersection of Oak Park and Scoville Park on this Sunday — the SROOs, the HROOs and the rest — all living next to one another, as they do every day in our village. It is our adjacency agency: Living next to one another leads to closer connections, which leads to a stronger community.

A night in our village (2013)

A midweek night out, a village waiting to be discovered.

On the second floor of the Oak Park Public Library, in the Veterans Room, which doubles as this village's cultural center, the Historical Society of Oak Park-River Forest hosted *Our Village*, a two-person play, penned and performed by Kevin Bry, co-starring Diane Pingle.

Bry is a local attorney whose career had no success whatsoever in suppressing the creative side of his personality. He even produced a comic-book version of this play. You can see him starring in Open Door Theater's current production of *Superior Donuts*.

As a creative presentation of our rich cultural past, *Our Village* is quite engaging. A fictional exchange of letters between Ernest Hemingway and his mother, it is worth the price of admission (or would be if they had charged admission).

Afterward, I walked to a reception that followed an unusual tri-board meeting, during which the District 97 and District 200 school boards, plus the Oak Park Village Board of Trustees, approved a unique intergovernmental agreement to fund the efforts of the Collaboration for Early Childhood, which works with children, 5 and under, their parents, and early educators to level the playing field by the time those kids — especially those from low-income, resource-restricted backgrounds — enter our school system.

The payoff could be enormous, and Oak Park's pioneering effort on this front may someday be hailed as historic.

I took the long way to the reception, strolling up to Chicago Avenue under a full, luminous moon, the same one that shined on Hemingway and Frank Lloyd Wright. The same one that will someday shine on our at-risk 5-and-unders as they graduate from high school and head to college — not a single one left behind (we hope).

The same moon was shining on our paramedics and firefighters, as they raced past me, lights flashing, sirens screaming, to Kenilworth, where they stopped on either side of an at-risk young woman, maybe 14 or 15, sitting on the parkway next to a driveway, clutching her book bag and looking dazed.

The neighbors on either side of the driveway stood on their porches and watched as a firefighter bent over and gently asked her, "Are you OK?" It takes a village sometimes to protect our at-risk kids.

The situation seemed well in hand, so I proceeded to Frank Lloyd Wright's Beachy House a block west, one of the many residential works of art in which families are raised. Here, thanks to the hospitality of Carollina Song and Alec Harris, Early Childhood Collaboration board members, elected officials, and numerous other champions of a more pro-active response to educating our kids, gathered to celebrate the aforementioned course-setting vote.

For some, it was one of the last votes before leaving their respective boards. For others, this vote set the stage for their imminent tenures. The home's beautifully designed rooms hummed with best intentions. No dreamers here. Local governance grinds that out of you.

Everyone on hand seemed to recognize this was a risk worth taking, and understood they might well be part of something tide-turning. They didn't just grip and grin and disappear. They stayed and savored and looked as if they were eager to work together. Also on hand were newly elected River Forest Village President Cathy Adduci and her Oak Park counterpart, Anan Abu-Taleb.

Carolyn Newberry Schwartz and Eric Gershenson, who have done more to launch this Collaboration and keep it aloft than most, looked half-thrilled, half-humbled, and half-terrified (which is three halves, but it was that type of evening). It was also an evening where people shed their roles and simply enjoyed each other's company.

As I walked home under that same full moon, risen higher and brighter, it all stretched ahead of me, under me, behind me — past, present, and future.

Our village.

4

Growing Up

"Ah, youth is wasted on the wrong people!" says the curmudgeonly neighbor in the Frank Capra film, *It's a Wonderful Life*, when George Bailey dawdles too long, beating around the hydrangea bush on his walk home with Mary following a most eventful senior prom. "Why don't you kiss her?" asks the exasperated bystander from his rocking chair on a nearby porch. But life intervenes.

Personally, I think youth is wasted on exactly the right people. Youth is meant to be wasted. And there is no better time and place to do so than the incubator known as "school days." Our offspring go in as children and emerge as young adults. There is nothing quite like it, short of a butterfly chrysalis.

In Act 2 of *Our Town*, the stage manager interrupts preparations for the wedding of Emily Webb and George Gibbs to examine how their imminent betrothal came to be.

"You see," he says to the audience, "we want to know how all this began — this wedding, this plan to spend a lifetime together. I'm awfully interested in how big things like that begin."

But before he visits "the conversation they had when they first knew ... they were meant for each other," he says, "I want you to try and remember what it was like to have been very young. ... Will you remember that please?"

Then before presiding over George and Emily's wedding, he concludes, "Every child born into the world is nature's attempt to make a perfect human being. Well, we've seen nature pushing and contriving for some time now. We all know that nature's interested in quantity, but I think she's interested in quality, too."

So is every parent and every child we launch into the world from the springboard of our schools.

But first, let's remember what it was like to be young ...

Fly balls for Father's Day (2004)

They'll watch the game and it'll be as if they dipped themselves in magic waters. The memories will be so thick they'll have to brush them away from their faces.

Field of Dreams

My son gave me a Father's Day gift last weekend. He asked me to hit him some fly balls.

That may not sound like your idea of the perfect present, but he couldn't have asked for anything dearer to my heart. It's an activity — a ritual really — that we've been re-enacting since he was 9.

It takes place at Rehm Park, just south of the Eisenhower Expressway, in the open meadow, ringed by the public pool on the north, tennis courts on the east, a row of deciduous trees to the south and the playground to the west. Rehm on a lovely summer afternoon is a busy place — but not in the meadow, which is usually an oasis of tranquility.

It's just long enough to bat fly balls to the leather-wrapped hand of a willing outfielder.

For most baseball fans, the iconic father-son bonding activity is playing catch — as depicted in the final scene of the film *Field of Dreams* — a lovely image, and we both love the film, but playing catch gets old pretty fast.

Over the years, my son and I have sustained our bond with fly balls, among more traditional ways. I enjoy smacking a baseball and watching it soar high and long; he enjoys running them down and smothering them with his oversized Chipper Jones-model mitt. I hit dozens of fly balls each time we go. Once I get in the groove, it's a very soothing activity. And he can't get enough. I usually have to put up the white flag, in fact, to get him to leave.

Rehm is the perfect place for all this. It's a pretty park, and the playground and pool are abuzz with activity. Throw in e.e. cummings' "blue true dream of sky," dotted with billowing cumulus, and suddenly several lives are flashing before my eyes.

There is the life with my son as he has grown older and more graceful. He glides under the ball now where once he pounded and lunged. There is my own childhood in this very park, this neighborhood, this town. The village still exists, though that era is no more. While the ball follows "gravity's rainbow" (title of a Thomas Pynchon novel), these memories acquire a pleasing particularity. Even the sunshine regains its innocence, resurrecting images of Mickey Mantle and Willie Mays in their prime, the Good Humor ice cream truck bells jangling down my once-upon-a-time street — just a few blocks from here — while Jack Brickhouse calls a game on a sunny afternoon from Wrigley Field.

Memories of life with my father also join the parade: His 30-year youth baseball coaching career (Suburban Bank) started on this field (known as South Park then) when I was just 7 and scared to death, standing in the batter's box, staring down that hard, red-stitched ball.

And finally, there is life as it leisurely unfolds this very day, with kids leaping off diving platforms, a group of teens playing "footbag" on the tennis courts, neighbors trading stories from their folding chairs while sponging some sun. A capless kid in a baseball uniform stands on the paved path, silently watching our exchange. When a couple of young women stroll by, my outfielder's energy level noticeably picks up, inspired to make an impression.

But the real pleasure here is in the rhythm. Ball after ball takes a nearly identical path to his glove, then bounces lazily back to my hand from his lobbed relay. The author Mihaly Csikszentmihalyi calls this "flow," or the state of "optimal experience" — relaxing, repetitive motion, requiring just enough skill to be satisfying.

My childhood and my son's converge in the pleasing present.

Time, momentarily, is tamed.

We are together in the eternal now of Father-Son Day.

Erik's Deli - Where kids eat, roam, and grow (2005)

On Monday night, kids eat free at Erik's Deli, and lately I've been eating there on Mondays, too, before going back to the office to write an article for the next day's deadline.

The free food, of course, draws families, but this place has always drawn families because of its friendly informality.

Like many, we came to this storefront on Oak Park Avenue, just north of the train tracks, frequently during the 1990s as my son was growing up. Meeting other families we knew was a good bet.

Things haven't changed much. Tables merge, boundaries blur and, before long, all the kids might be at one table while all the adults are sitting at the next. Kids migrate from one table to another. Dining decorum is fluid to say the least. Family membranes are permeable. There is freedom to move — with the kind of unself-conscious comfort usually reserved for living rooms.

Erik's is short on formality, long on familiarity. The decor simulates an outdoor patio. Four of the tables sprout large Coca Cola umbrellas ... inside ... the place to be should the sprinkler system ever get activated. This is as outside as inside gets.

The conversation is animated and even musical — a symphony of high and low tones. Kids sit sideways in their chairs or lean forward, butts in the air, while they munch and mingle. Some forsake chairs altogether and stand as they eat.

Parents swap stories, kids schmooze, families plan, catch up on the events of the day, discuss homework, extend advice, coordinate, assess.

One girl follows her dad to the ice cream counter chanting, "Where is Argentina on the map? Where is Argentina on the map?"

Watching a family settle in at their table is like watching military maneuvers — logistics, teamwork — as puffy, pastel coats are shed and slung across the backs of chairs. It is reassuring to see family members laughing together or engaged in animated conversation, face to face, only inches at times separating noses. Adult arms drape casually across young shoulders or chair backs.

If you want to see what happy families look like, this would be the place.

The 1990s seems not so long ago, a bright, hopeful time. We anxiously watched our children ripen (and their appetites grow). Coming here is a walk back in time. My position in the community has changed, the child-rearing stage of my life now past.

But I enjoy seeing younger parents traveling the same path I did. Time marches on, and we march right along, with nary a backward glance at the skins we shed, the roles we surrender, until something like this catches our attention.

This past Monday, while kids ate free at Erik's and parents took a break from the kitchen, my son turned 21, his childhood officially over. We were lucky. So was he. Oak Park in the 1990s was a good place to grow up.

We'll always be active parents. But it's his show now. We're rooting for him. We're his roots.

I miss those days, but I don't feel compelled to remind these parents to savor what they have right now.

They're savoring it.

They just don't know it yet.

Erik's Deli closed in 2010.

All they want to do is matter (2018)

A lovely day for a rally — blue skies, temps climbing into the 50s, the weather tipping, perhaps, finally, into spring itself, and our kids letting it be known they're not going away, tipping us, perhaps, finally, into change itself. Rallying our flagging spirits.

Middle-school kids, 14 and under, organized this public plea to reduce gun violence, an event with style, substance, and serious intent. Adults on hand to show support, but kids definitely running the show.

As for the setting, they chose well: Scoville Park greening nicely after a cold, wet week. Instead of a march, they set up stations circling the park's gentle slope, which forms a natural amphitheater.

At the park entry, Oak Park Avenue and Lake Street, we were asked to sign a "guest banner" and then a petition for state Sen. Don Harmon, who was on hand to receive it, some 500 signatures strong.

Orange was the color of the day, the color hunters use to signal "Don't shoot!" so they aren't mistaken by fellow hunters for fair game. Now it's the adopted color of the anti-gun violence movement. "Don't shoot" is the message directed toward those who hunt people of color and children in schools, and to politicians who, at least on the national level, refuse to pass common-sense legislation regulating guns, no matter how many mass shootings underscore the urgency.

Orange was also the official color of the village logo for many years, back when we had a handgun ban, noted former village clerk Terri Powell, who says not enough Oak Parkers know that voters resoundingly approved that prohibition in a referendum in 1984. For many years, the handgun ban was a source of village pride for the vast majority of residents here — until the Supreme Court's conservative majority overturned it in 2008.

Students at one of the stations kneel to fill out postcards or write letters. Names and addresses of local representatives are provided, as is the mailing address of one Wayne LaPierre, of NRA of America.

"Be respectful," cautions one of the parents, "so they take you seriously."

Orange "We are with you" postcards are destined for Marjory Stoneman Douglas High School in Florida, Columbine High School in Colorado, or Great Mills High School in Maryland, the latter being the site of the latest school shooting. In four years we won't even remember it. Our attention and empathy spans are short.

Poster boards are loosely taped to trees, inviting responses, written on pastel-colored post-it notes. The prompt "I want ..." elicits "the NRA to value kids more than guns," "to feel safe in my school," "to end gun violence," and a host of similar sentiments. "I use my voice because ..." engenders "to be silent is deadly" and "others don't have that chance anymore."

Statistic sheets with graphics line the table at the park entrance: On an average day, 96 Americans are killed with guns; on average, 13,000 gun homicides take place each year in the U.S.; on average each month, 50 women are shot to death by intimate partners in the U.S.; seven children and teens are killed with guns in the U.S. on an average day; Black men are 13 times more likely than White men to be shot and killed by guns.

These kids have been doing their homework.

The organizers, a group of 14-year-old girls, turn on the mic and call for 13 minutes of silence for the victims of the massacre at Columbine High School, which took place 19 years ago this day. "Since those 13 have been silenced forever," says one girl, "the least we can do is be silent for 13 minutes." All wear T-shirts that read "Protect People, Not Guns" and with each victim's name read aloud, an orange balloon is released into the air. A light breeze blows several into the trees behind the stage but, defying the odds, they work their way through the dense mesh of budding branches and find release.

Metaphors abound for anyone seeking them.

The girls are eloquent beyond their years. It's tough being endangered and then ignored by our leaders, says one, "when all we've ever wanted to do was matter."

"Why do children have to be the adults?" ponders another.

Yet another says much has changed since Columbine in 1999, "but you can still walk up and buy an assault rifle."

A helicopter from one of the Chicago news channels circles overhead.

Celine Woznica of Moms Demand Action praises the Julian principal who "let this happen." She turns to a group of kids and says, "You guys have changed this whole movement. We're so proud of you."

They've certainly focused the conversation. They're speaking out because adults stopped believing change was possible. Kids are helping us believe again. They're not going away.

You couldn't ask for a better educational experience than an event like this.

And the kids, no doubt, learned a lot, too.

* * *

Unfortunately, four years, and many more mass killings later — including the grocery store in Buffalo, New York; the school in Uvalde, Texas; and the July 4th Parade in Highland Park, Illinois, and many more by the time this book is published — nothing has changed.

To the protectors of the rights of mass murderers, our kids still don't matter.

Not your average high school musical (2013)

I dreamed a dream of days gone by
When hope was high and life worth living.

Les Miserables

Of all the traditions in your average American community, few are as poignant as the high school musical. Boundless energy and enthusiasm meet an art form designed to give full-throated expression to our dreams and longings.

But Oak Park and River Forest High School is not average. Your average high school doesn't put on *Les Miserables*.

Which is the challenge the Theater Department faced the last two weekends. It would be hard to exaggerate the sheer unvarnished brass it must have taken for Michelle Bayer and her cohorts to attempt an under-age, amateur production of *Les Miz*. Yet there they were last Friday night, all 108 cast members (plus crew, plus pit orchestra), decked out in period costume, belting out number after number and doing justice to each.

Justice, of course, is the operative word in this operatic musical. There is the obsessive, letter-of-the-law quest for "justice" as embodied by Inspector Javert, who succeeds only in upholding and perpetuating a system of injustice, in direct conflict with the high-minded rebellion of angry men (and child and woman) at the barricade. And all of the above are in conflict with the personal and interpersonal hunger and thirst for justice that characterizes the odyssey of Jean Valjean.

Big themes, big numbers, big set, big production.

And big audience. If you haven't been to the high school for some time, there is simply no way to brace for the solar flare of unleashed energy. Despite accompanying my son through his adolescence here, after more than a decade away from the high school scene, it still seems un-fathomable that human beings can live at this level of excitability without exploding — and that's just the audience before the lights went down in the auditorium and the curtains parted.

I wish every voter in the district could experience this power surge from time to time just to remember what it's like being young and why it's important for the formerly young who pay taxes to support them.

The arts help channel some of that energy. Even the most disgruntled voters who insist we're throwing too much money at our schools, might change their mind after seeing this production.

All of the lead male roles (except for the bad guy) were ably played by African American students, which was a refreshing change.

With John Clay III as Valjean, it seems the soul of a Broadway veteran has somehow transmigrated to the body of a high school senior. Where Hugh Jackman noticeably strains to hit the high notes of "Bring Him Home" in the recent film version, Clay pulls it off onstage with evident ease.

Stage presence and poise match his voice. Taking a character through an entire adult life span would challenge a mature 30-something, but a high school senior?

All the voices were strong in this production, right down to the ensemble.

John Clay III as Jean Valjean

From polished productions to the good old high school try, what musical theater does best is chronicle the hopes, ideals and dreams of its characters as they navigate the pitfalls and upswings of life. Doing so with hopeful, idealistic dreamers whose adulthood stretches before them is a wonder.

As an adult spectator with more rear view than road ahead, I find these rites of passage both powerful and poignant.

Whether these soon-to-be adults eventually fulfill their promise, settle comfortably into a niche, or aim high and come up short, they won't soon forget this night, this production, their fellow cast members, this audience erupting in full, hormonal acclaim after each number.

Younger members of the audience this night may be busy concocting dreams of their own — like pre-teen Mary Elizabeth Mastrantonio, who went on to fame in films, watching her older sister perform on this very stage, thinking to herself, "I can do that." And she did that and more.

While youth looks ahead to all that life has to offer — and all they have to offer life — more than a few adults in the audience, I would guess, are casting back to their own "once upon a time." Few of us would willingly return to the emotional maelstrom of adolescence and yet … every once in a very long while, it feels really good to be reminded.

Some of us might be tempted to go back for just one more day.

Or even one day more.

John Clay III made his Broadway debut in "Choir Boy" in 2019.

An audience of one on an October afternoon (2017)

On an Indian-summerish, mid-autumn, late-afternoon with the setting sun basting the orange brick of Oak Park and River Forest High School in the background, under blue skies airbrushed by winged cirrus, I came upon the Huskies Marching Band, or the Marching Huskies, or whatever moniker they proudly march by.

And proud they should be as the director and the conductor (who looked young enough to be a student) stood on their high platform and put the players through their paces. Section by section, they worked, while idle instruments — large brass bellows, for instance — rested on the turf, the instrumentalists schmoozing quietly nearby, awaiting further directions.

The grass in this still-natural portion of the grounds was green from last week's liberal drenching, the turf having drained just enough to support the hoofers above — for this is not so much a "marching" band but, at the moment anyway, a tango band, as the full contingent strikes up "Libertango," a composition by Astor Piazzola, the Bach of Tango. Members in shorts and T-shirts glide rather than pound, instruments playing the players instead of the other way around. Or so it seemed and sounded.

These are high school kids, right? I needed to remind myself — 14 to 18 years old? The sounds did not jibe with my expectations of adolescent proficiency, the familiar unripe discordances erupting here and there, understandable and easily forgiven. None of that was happening, as far as I could hear.

Purple and white flags whirled in the confident hands of the color guard. One inspired youth ran about with flags splayed to the sides like wings, as if about to take flight, which he did, in a manner of speaking, breaking free of the group and enjoying momentary liftoff, at least in spirit.

Parents pulled up in SUVs to drop off tiny, shoulder-pad-reinforced football players, who scurried to a separate portion of the field for practice, taking no evident notice, though surely these tykes heard their immediate elders — children themselves so recently — playing tunes with panache and soaring with emotion as their feet kept the beat.

Talk about multitasking.

The selections followed a Spanish theme, castanets and marimba in full flourish as girls in colorful flamenco outfits began to dance, in modified fashion, since the soft sod could never amplify the kind of gunshot stomping this dance tradition is famous for.

Not to hyperbolize all this, but ... oh hell, why not? When "Bolero" began and the afternoon deepened, and the ghosts of thousands of young hopefuls who have gamboled and drilled, tackled and sprinted, played and paraded, practiced and performed on this same consecrated ground for decades made their echoes almost tangible, this all felt like the culmination, not just of a "season" but of all that has always been worthwhile about high school. Gathered, in communion with one another and their music, simultaneously talented and fun-loving, practicing for God knows what. Their last home game? Some national competition at Disney World? Who cares really?

It's not about the competitions and halftime shows. Oh, they provide the motivation, incentive, and structure, surely, but what matters is not the audiences and judges or even the high bar this director clearly sets. When it flows, it's about transcendence. This was the pure thing itself. This is why we send kids to high school, to sit through all those classes — to develop their gifts, all so they might experience moments when they let go of self-doubt and self-questioning and just flat-out play. This is the bliss we all yearn for, and here they were experiencing it before turning 18: The tonic of total tonality.

What a gas! And all for the benefit of an audience of one (as far as I could tell, looking around).

As far as I was concerned, this was the real show.

When it was over, the director opened his arms wide as if to encompass them with appreciation or approval or whatever it is he uses to motivate them — or maybe just for the sheer audacious fun of it, yet rising to meet his standard. Who knows?

Like any institution, this high school has its ups and downs. Most of our institutions, you might have noticed, are having a lot of downs these days. All the more reason to celebrate the upswings.

That's how it feels to hear the OPRF Gospel Choir sing or Orchesis dance. That's how I feel when I attend the annual musical. And that's how I feel now about the Marching, Tangoing, Uplifting Huskies.

It doesn't mean we can postpone courageous conversations on tough topics forever. This doesn't make up for whatever shortcomings need to be addressed. That's also part of high school (and every other institution, for that matter).

But there's only one thing to say about what I witnessed last Thursday afternoon:

Thanks, I needed that.

America to Me: Not there ... yet (2018)

Let America be America again/Let it be the dream it used to be/America never was America to me.

Langston Hughes

The new 10-part documentary series on a year in the life of OPRF High School, *America to Me*, gets off to a strong start. The first two episodes, shown at the Lake Theatre on Aug. 13, are consistently absorbing. If the other eight match that intensity, then director Steve James and his crew have really accomplished something.

If you go in with preconceived notions, the experience may be something else entirely. If you're already convinced that White people will be unfairly blamed for all the challenges Black students face at OPRF, if you assume the series will "reflect badly" on this important community institution and "tarnish" its reputation, you'll miss a lot. And I've heard some of those rumblings.

If, on the other hand, you can let go of unconscious biases and conscious fears, this series will take you somewhere. Somewhere important.

It gives a clear-eyed view of life at OPRF High School in its many and varied dimensions, which is often edifying and uplifting.

It humanizes students of color, who for many, I suspect, have just been statistics in our ongoing discussions of the achievement gap. These kids have a lot to say. They're worth listening to, and they're kids you can root for.

It manages to make the viewer hopeful and uncomfortable — in equal measure, perhaps the ultimate measure of a successful documentary.

It shows teachers and administrators working hard to make connections with students, not all of whom are highly motivated. It shows the faculty and staff doing the hard work of trying to make OPRF a more welcoming place, not just for students who are easy to reach and teach, as has too often been the case in the past.

Students share plenty of insight. As Charles Donalson, who excels at Spoken Word poetry, puts it, "Everything is made for White kids because this school was made for White kids, because this country was made for White kids." The problem, in other words, is systemic. It's not "their" job to fit into "our" school. We need to create a new school system, where everyone fits in, a school made for all kids.

In one class, the teacher has his students write down areas where they have not been successful. At the end of each statement, he has them add the word "yet." For the most part, the school comes off looking quite good — not because it is "succeeding" but because it admits it isn't … at least not yet.

In *America to Me*, the word "yet" is another word for hope.

The team of four filmmakers, each of whom followed three students for an entire school year, is headed by Steve James, 33-year Oak Park resident whose kids went through the public schools here. James is also a critically acclaimed filmmaker with a ton of experience, including *Hoop Dreams*, so he's perfect for this task. The crew amassed 1,300 hours of footage, he said, covering school, home and what goes on in between.

One of the most interesting students is Ke'Shawn Kumsa, the kind of kid who drives a lot of teachers crazy: extremely intelligent, extremely charismatic, hates school. Ke'Shawn is the type of kid who will probably be either very successful or very unsuccessful and underscores what one of his teachers says — that their job has real life-or-death urgency.

Yet Ke'Shawn poses the central question of the series (thus far). He says, sarcastically, "I don't know what makes Oak Park so special," then looks directly into the camera with disarming sincerity as if to say, "I don't know. What makes Oak Park so special?"

What would you tell an African American student like Ke'Shawn? Why are we so special?

We could say we're special because we want to decrease, and ultimately eliminate, the achievement gap. But we've been saying that for two decades while pursuing it with a glass-half-empty lack of enthusiasm, which smart kids like Ke'Shawn see through in a second.

Our history of passing the Fair Housing Ordinance, and our half-century record of welcoming and managing diversity makes this village unusual, but not necessarily "special."

Part of what makes us special is accepting, even embracing, the challenges of educating a racially diverse student population. And part of it is recognizing that we aren't doing a good enough job at it and that we need to make more progress. Not many school systems get even that far. Are we really working to improve or are we satisfied with how far we've come? The former is "special." The latter is not.

Are we willing to face up to the racism inherent in any institution "made for White kids" or will we defend, consciously or unconsciously, White privilege while paying lip service to leaving no child behind? One is special. The other is not.

Do we see our Black kids *and* White kids as "our kids" or do we really see Black kids as "somebody else's problem"? One is special. The other is not.

Ta'garista, Those Things That Are Best — isn't that still OPRF's motto?

Filming for this series took place three years ago. I wonder if Ke'Shawn and all the other students featured have a better idea of what makes Oak Park so special.

If not, is that their fault or ours?

At the moment, what makes us special is that our high school board and administration allowed this amazing project to move forward, giving filmmakers remarkable access, and giving students a chance to have their say, even at the risk of the school "coming off badly."

Judging by the first two episodes, OPRF comes off as a remarkable institution with remarkable students, teachers, security personnel, and administrators who are trying to address at least some of the challenges facing a diverse educational institution — and not being afraid to hold themselves up for the world to see in all their glorious imperfection. That's special.

We're not there ... yet.

If the majority of Oak Park and River Forest residents actually watch this series in its entirety and discuss it and take it to heart and allow it to enact an ageless persuasion, a genuine conversion, then we might just get there yet.

Or as poet Langston Hughes put it: *O let America be America again/The land that never has been yet/And yet must be.*

Yet, another word for hope.

Fashion forward ... or backward? (2014)

Why are OPRF High School's graduation dresses so important to people? (And why is there never a controversy about what the guys wear?)

The latest dress debate resulted from the fact that nationally-known fashion prodigy Tavi Gevinson wore a short skirt at graduation. Some claimed — incorrectly — that she was the only one. Our photographer reported seeing several other short skirts but didn't take photos of them because it never occurred to him something like this would be a controversy. Shows how level-headed he is. But for some online obstinates, this is *extremely* important.

According to their comments, Tavi was the only one who skirted the rules, so to speak, so she must have received special consideration, being famous already at a young age and also the daughter of Steve Gevinson, District 200 board member, who delivered the most dangerous and divisive speech in the history of commencement ceremonies (in their not-so-humble opinion).

Not only was Tavi *not* the only grad to wear a short dress, this wasn't even the first year it happened (which Tavi, as a fashion influencer, may be disappointed to hear). We have the photos from last year's commencement to prove it.

Neither is this the first controversy involving graduation dresses. Back in 1998, Genevieve York-Erwin (now a litigation attorney with Cooley LLP in Manhattan) chose not to attend graduation at all if she had to don a dress. But the world somehow didn't end and the following year, the high school, showing admirable flexibility and diplomatic skills, amended the dress code to add white pant suits as an option.

The high school evidently amended the code again to allow short skirts as long as they are semi-covered by a long, open "wrap," so Tavi violated the (amended) rules, some critics insisted, by eschewing (or maybe just discarding) the wrap. What if everyone started flouting amended rules? Where would we be then?

Presumably we'd arrive at another amendment. And the republic, not to mention our villages, would once again, somehow, survive.

I can hear the wailing and gnashing of teeth. Where will it all end? Well, more than likely just above the knee. I doubt we'll ever have graduates wearing '70s-style hot pants, though you never know. If necessary, we can always fall back on the default setting — caps and gowns — which could even be white if people feel strongly enough [which is, in fact, what eventually happened].

Tradition is something many feel strongly about. Some believe traditions should never change (like Tevye the milkman in *Fiddler on the Roof*, which, coincidentally, was the musical this year at OPRF). Others feel just as strongly that tradition should evolve — like Tevye's daughters, you'll recall, and Steve Gevinson's daughter, come to think of it, and Gevinson himself, whose talk was titled, "A great, evolving tradition."

A lot of people were offended that he dared to pair the words "evolving" and "tradition." He was talking about more substantive issues than women's apparel, but he might as well have been talking about long white dresses, which seem a sacred tradition to some.

For the rest of us, long dresses are merely a quaint reminder of a more formal, elegant era — and there is something to be said for "unifying" the overall look of the class — but should this be where we draw the (hem)line? It depends, I guess, on what final message we want to give our graduates as we send them off into the world. After 18 years of raising and educating them and turning them, we hope (Steve Gevinson's expressed hope, too), into independent thinkers, do we want our final collective value statement to be that uniformity is prized above all else?

Or is it that rules, while important, must be flexible, with room for individual alterations?

We are, after all, launching them into a world that will change drastically by the time they're our age and, as both Gevinsons pointed out (one with a verbal statement, one with a fashion statement), they grew up in an evolving community (excuse me, two evolving communities because River Forest has also been transformed, both towns having changed with the times and arguably for the better). So we prepared our children well.

They accept diversity, not to mention change, as the way of the world — not adherence to rules for the sake of adhering to rules. A careful look around the sea of graduates on June 1 revealed that some young women wore white while others wore off-white, so we have altered our very definition of "uniformity."

We don't all need to look alike. That was what our kids learned on the first day of school, especially when it comes to skin pigmentation, and it should be our final message as we send them into a wider world that is ever adapting and evolving, not always — but usually — for the better.

The online commenters are in full fury over this, but they're always in full fury. It's their defining characteristic. Let them fume. The real question is what it has always been: When is it better to hold fast to the rules and when is it better to show some flexibility? Call it Tevye's dilemma.

OPRF made the right call, which isn't a surprise.

They are, after all, a great, evolving institution.

Choking up at Commencement (1994)

In a society with too few rites of passage, this is an exception. Not that those undergoing the passage approach it with any great reverence. Eighteen-year-olds, by and large, aren't capable of that yet, but give them time. Even the most jaded former 18-year-old in the stands probably felt something last Thursday evening. Life has a way of increasing our capacity for reverence.

The early June sun heads toward the horizon, but still shines brightly on the proceedings. Young men in suits, young women in white dresses process onto the football field, accompanied by stirring strains of Elgar's "Pomp and Circumstance," played by the school orchestra.

Those of us watching from the bleachers know what they're in for. To the graduates, the future is all tantalizing possibility. They haven't closed off myriad options like we have. The choices before them may be daunting, but also more than a little dazzling, a bouquet, dizzying in its array.

Not all of these hopefuls will "make it big," according to traditional (inadequate) measures of "success." A few will succeed beyond their wildest dreams. Most, however, will fall in the comfortable or not-so-comfortable middle. Life grades on a bell curve. Do most adults lead lives of quiet desperation, as Thoreau contended? At the least, most of us quietly — or not-so-quietly — learn to live with diminished dreams. The dreamers down on the field this evening, however, are ablaze with unlimited potential.

A critic once said reading this town's local paper each week was "the triumph of hope over experience" (praising with faint damnation), and that best describes a high school graduation, where hope always triumphs over experience. With a few sad exceptions, human beings seem incapable of despair. So every June we replay this pageant of hope and optimism, and most of us are taken in, in spite of our own experience.

Some in the stands grouse about the lack of decorum by the grads on the field, but they're outside, and I love the fact that these kids can't contain their joy. There may be more concentrated happiness at a high school graduation than anywhere else on Earth. So let them bat their beachballs and bellow at their friends and wave wildly to their family members in the stadium stands. It would be far worse to witness a graduating class bored by pomp and circumstance.

Names are called, hands shaken, diplomas clutched and waved overhead as they return to their seats.

Parents in the stands wave back with unabashed delight. The pride is palpable, affirmations matching graduates' hunger to feel affirmed. Nowhere else can you see so clearly that parenting in our community is working.

Four years is a long time in an adolescent's life. The difference between a 14-year-old and an 18-year-old is breathtaking. At commencement, they take their first collective gulp and move on, launched beyond the safe harbor of home, out into whatever awaits them. The school graduates them, but so too do their parents and likewise their community. The majority won't settle here after college. Americans are too mobile for that kind of continuity. But we've had our impact, for better or worse — probably both.

It's as if we have collectively given birth.

As the ceremony ends and the Class of '94 lingers long on the field below in the gathering twilight, mingling with family and friends, I can't help wishing they could be this happy forever. Parents, the only ones down there with much perspective, are busy taking some of the most important photos of their children's lives.

The ones with the brightest smiles.

5

Ceremonies & Celebrations

Celebrations take many forms. The calendar incorporates our default settings:

New Year's Day, Martin Luther King Jr.'s Birthday, Valentine's Day, Mardi Gras, St. Patrick's Day, Easter, Mothers' Day, Memorial Day, Fathers' Day, Juneteenth, Independence Day, Labor Day, Yom Kippur, Halloween, Thanksgiving, Hanukkah, Divali, Christmas, Kwanzaa, New Year's Eve. More are included as our culture widens its embrace.

Ceremonies mark formal occasions — weddings and baptisms, birthdays and anniversaries.

But there are other reasons for celebrating, spontaneous eruptions, some public, some private. We need to celebrate. It's good for us. The presence, or absence, of celebrations is a measure of our mental health.

A community defines itself by how it celebrates, how often it celebrates, and whether it celebrates at all. Celebrations offer opportunities to come together, to make the community visible to its component individuals. Celebrations reaffirm our bond.

Oak Park has block parties, progressive dinners, Day in Our Village, Thursday Night Out, the July 4th parade and fireworks, Sunday night concerts and movies in Scoville Park.

If a community never gathers, it can't celebrate. We need to see one another, interact, connect. Otherwise, we're little more than a "bedroom community."

Celebrations, like flowers, come in many varieties. Some are perennial, some annual, some are one-offs.

The following is a celebratory, ceremonial sampler:

From many foods, one feast (1998)

With "potluck" you don't know what you're going to get. Life isn't a box of chocolates. Life is potluck, which may not be the best for "me," but is a lot better for "us."

And you're bound to find something you like — especially with more than 200 dishes to choose from.

That was the situation a week ago Sunday at the Andersen Recreation Center, a lovely stretch of green space nestled among single-family homes on Hayes Avenue just north of Division in the northeast corner of the village. Beneath a gorgeous spreading survivor elm, the Festival of Potluck Foods had plenty of pots (plus Tupperware, aluminum pans, wooden bowls, and platters) and more than its share of luck.

Good weather for one thing — if you like your late-summer Sundays good and warm, that is — but luck is also something you make. It's the point where preparation meets opportunity, as Vince Lombardi used to say, in a completely different context.

Ricky Sain, Rebekah Levin, Jim Boushay

It takes a lot of preparation to pull something like this off, starting with Jim Boushay and Ricky Sain, who birthed this notion and watched it grow to the point where it has pretty much taken over their lives.

Yet so much of this is informal. Boushay says over 300 people helped — ranging from "the five-minute phone call to the many hours spent on one task over several weeks," he noted during welcoming remarks. He sees this as nothing short of reaffirming "the practical value of our nation's motto, E Pluribus Unum," which Boushay amends to read, "from many foods, one feast." Once again this year, he added, everyone proved "the whole is greater than the sum of its parts."

And there are plenty of parts. A table piled high with 600 plates, forks and cloth napkins awaits the potluck attendees on the far side of an arch formed by rainbow-colored balloons. The serving tables, fortunately, are located inside the rec center because of the pesky late-summer bees and because you don't want people sweating into the casseroles.

Rose Jones, the official greeter, stands at the door. "Guess I can't have one of everything," jokes one of the feasters. "Yes you can," Jones replies, "if you hurry."

One buffet grazer observes, "The concept is too simple for many people to grasp." That concept, according to Sain and Boushay, is "good eating at the big meeting," with as much emphasis on meeting as eating. Boushay won't allow name tags. "We have to tell each other our names," he said.

The only ID cards are attached to the foods themselves, and there is a cornucopia of choices to tempt even the most experienced buffet veteran: Spicy Zucchini Stew (Vegan), Vegetarian Chile, Eggplant Appetizer, Vegetable Biryani, Artichoke Dip ("I tried it before I got in line," Amy Williams confesses), Shrimp Salad, Ma's Bayou 'Taters, Mustard Curry Chicken with Brown Rice, Smothered Pork Chops, Chicken Mole, South African Pickled Fish, and those are just a few of the items that got people salivating. The dessert table alone features 36 items.

And almost all of it homemade (a few cheated and went to Whole Foods). "It's like a U.N. tasting," observes Tammy Green, who keeps the serving tables from descending into total chaos. "This is so good," she enthuses. "It's like an old-fashioned church supper. If more communities would do this ..." She leaves that thought for the rest for us to fill in.

"Where do we start?" asks one dazzled attendee. "Where do we stop is the question," corrects his companion.

Outside, some 17 dining tables accommodate the feast-ivities in the shade of that old elm. Picnic blankets fill in the empty spaces. The crowd is remarkably diverse — old and young, Black and White, gay and straight, a truly inclusive gathering. Jim Boushay's ex-wife is here. Even his ex-in-laws are here.

Beth Swaggerty, master of ceremonies, says she got involved the way everyone does. "Jim hunted me down," she says. On a small stage, a succession of musicians and singers perform, followed by "Dr. Boom," whose claim to fame, says Geoff Binns-Calvey, the actual performer/perpetrator, is "blowing up food." Kids love it.

Boushay tells the assembled multitude, "You are the real heroes and heroines," but this wouldn't have happened without this dynamic duo. He says they're hoping to pass the torch to some consortium who can keep the event going and maintain its spirit of generosity and goodwill. Then they can get their life back.

We wish them potluck.

Jim Boushay died in 2011. He and Ricky Sain organized a total of 12 annual potlucks.

Homecoming for Unity Temple (2017)

> *A home is not simply a building; it is the shelter around the intimacy of a life. Coming in from the outside world and its rasp of force and usage, you relax and allow yourself to be who you are. The inner walls of a home are threaded with the textures of one's soul, a subtle weave of presences. If you could see your home through the lens of the soul, you would be surprised at the beauty concealed in the memory your home holds. When you enter some homes, you sense how the memories have seeped to the surface, infusing the aura of the place and deepening the tone of its presence. Where love has lived, a house still holds its warmth. Even the poorest home feels like a nest if love and tenderness dwell there. Conversely, the most ornate, the grandest homes, can have an empty center. The beauty of a home is ultimately determined by the nature of its atmosphere, by the texture and spirit of those who dwell there. A house is like a psyche in the patterns of spirit it absorbs and holds. The art of memory is its secret weaving, how it weaves together forgotten joy and endured sorrow.*

John O'Donohue
Beauty

The message board outside proclaims this month's worship theme, "Surprised by Joy," but it's doubtful anyone at the first Sunday service in Unity Temple in two years is surprised by the joy of coming home after such a long absence.

The congregation relocated to United Lutheran Church on the north end of town and took pride in packing the pews of that great barn of a church, beneath the towering presence of one of the largest back-wall crucifixes in the village. Very different from the home they turned over to construction crews in June of 2015. The bare brick of United Lutheran's walls speak to a more austere spiritual orientation, where worshipers see the backs of heads as they face forward, the only faces visible being speakers at the lecterns, or the choir on the side as it struggled to overcome the smothering acoustics of the place.

The Lutheran congregation was as welcoming and generous as Unitarians could have aske. and they were grateful, It wasn't the same but, feisty, independent souls that they are, these free-thinkers insisted their home was wherever they worshipped, the congregation being more important than where they congregated.

Whereas United Lutheran is a traditional cruciform (cross-shaped) church, high-ceilinged, with a long aisle from sanctuary to the front door, the Frank Lloyd Wright-designed Unity Temple is a giant cube, blending horizontal and vertical, with two balconies rising above the main floor on three sides and a lower-level cloister where the choir clusters, waiting to ascend and sing. The balconies set the congregants face to face, no one more than 42 feet from the pulpit in any direction, so the sense of community is both magnified and celebrated. This is democratic worship, non-hierarchical.

The clear, high-set, clerestory windows connect worshippers with the sky, unlike most other churches, and the skylight allows sunlight in slivers that creep along the walls in playful patterns, evoking Leonard Cohen's "There's a crack in everything. That's how the light gets in." For now, though, they're hoping the cracks have all been sealed so the rain doesn't get in, like it used to.

The surprise in coming home isn't the joy congregants feel so much as recognizing how important this particular space is to their congregating.

"Oh, what a beautiful morning," the choir sings, select members soloing each Hammersteinian phrase. "All the sounds of the earth are like music," each voice blending seamlessly. "I've got a wonderful feeling everything's going my way." Individual differences and communal harmony, an important notion for this congregation.

"Send the good news, send the word," they sing. "We the people will be heard."

And later: "Go out and tell a story to your daughters and your sons. Let it echo far and wide. Make them hear you, make them hear you."

Worship here is serious, but not anesthetized. Senior Minister Alan Taylor welcomes attendees, long-timers and first-timers alike. "Bring all of who you are," he urges. "Whoever you are, wherever you are on your life journey, you are welcome here."

Rev. Emily Gage looks around and says, "I notice everybody's back in their regular seat." She invites the kids to sit on the soft carpet in front of the main-floor pews (original to Unity Temple, the woodwork restored to long-ago freshness) and tells them about the Unitarian tradition of Flower Communion. When she asks for volunteers, young hands (of which there are many) shoot up. They distribute floral sprigs to everyone in the congregation.

"Even if you didn't bring one this morning," Gage says, "you'll still leave with one. That's how we roll here."

This space has been renewed by two years of hard labor. The warm earth-tones are more vibrant, the walls subtly but beautifully textured, and the air between them cooled geo-thermally. But there's more going on than facility rehab, says Taylor during his sermon. "This building is not complete without our living, breathing congregation. That completes the design. Human connection powers our lives. ... This building is to be used. I claim full responsibility for the first spill. We are forgiven for our marks. It shows our use."

The congregation has changed, he noted, after two years. Those who died did not get to experience this homecoming.

"The journey to this day was longer than two years," Taylor observed. It made him think about the great cathedral of Chartres in France. "Those workers began something they knew they would not see. We too are building — on foundations we did not lay — a cathedral to the human spirit."

"Where love has lived, a house still holds its warmth," John O'Donohue wrote. "The beauty of a home is ultimately determined by the nature of its atmosphere, by the texture and spirit of those who dwell there."

Unity Temple is home again.

As of 2019, Unity Temple is also a World Heritage Site, one of roughly 30 in the United States and over a thousand worldwide, defined by UNESCO (United Nations Educational, Scientific and Cultural Organization) as "a natural or man-made site, area, or structure recognized as being of outstanding international importance and therefore as deserving special protection." Sites are nominated to, and designated by, the World Heritage Convention.

Marrying house and home (2016)

Home has been on my mind lately, homes being foundational to the Oak Park experience. Our village is a veritable living house museum, which culminates the third Saturday of each May with the Wright Plus housewalk, drawing people from all over the country and world, who no doubt ask themselves, "How did this place escape my notice until now?"

Our biggest industries are real estate and home improvement. The work of Wright and other Prairie School architects are the epicenter of our tourist trade. The 1968 Fair Housing Ordinance remains our greatest moral achievement as a village. Homeowners have invested enormous capital — and elbow grease — in upgrading the housing stock here over the last half-century.

On May 28, I attended the wedding of Tim and Kristen Kordesh, which took place on the broad, welcoming porch of the aforementioned Pleasant Home, the sky suddenly swept clean of clouds just as the ceremony began.

Afterward the entire wedding party started a long trek east, almost a mile, accompanied by a New Orleans-style jazz band playing "When the Saints Come Marching In" and "Will the Circle Be Unbroken?"

Our "second line" parade remained unbroken and the bride did, in fact, stop traffic — as did the rest of us — but all the honking sounded friendly. This welcome disturbance of the peace brought out plenty of curious neighbors, cellphone cameras ready, and social media that evening, no doubt, brimmed with short videos and photos of what must be the longest wedding recessional ever recorded here.

The final destination was the Kordesh family homestead, where an old-fashioned, at-home reception awaited us. I don't know why more freshly-wedded couples don't do this. I've never been a fan of the overdone, excessively-formulaic, banquet-hall experience.

A backyard reception would be poignant for the hosts, a culmination of the family's time spent turning the inert shell of a house into a home, the backyard setting adding an extra dimension to this celebration.

I didn't celebrate there for long, however, because my niece's high school graduation party was taking place in another backyard about a mile due south. Mary Therese is the third and final daughter of my brother and sister-in-law to graduate from Fenwick and launch South Bend-ward.

Such milestones are also poignant, and many a yard in this burg has been christened time and again, the ground consecrated by shared memories.

Then on May's final day, I was invited to the porch of Jim and Lynn Grogan's newly emptied abode on the 600 block of South Elmwood to toast their impending departure after 26 years building a life there, raising a family and launching them. And before the Grogans, Bud and Mary Bennett raised their large brood here.

Two home creators, hailing back to the early 1950s.

Surrounded by functional Gunderson four-squares, the Grogan house is, in my humble opinion and limited house experience, the Greatest Bungalow Ever Built, reflecting the under-appreciated artistry of architect Roy Hotchkiss. At any rate, it has to be the least claustrophobic bungalow ever built, evident as we walked through the structure, which, though vacant, nonetheless still housed a quarter-century of familial memories.

Those memories will live on because human beings have been blessed with a vivid spatial memory allowing each of us virtual re-admission to our family homes any time we wish. You can go there right now in your mind's eye and see every room in remarkable detail. Our memories may be slippery on other minutiae, but not on what really matters.

The Grogans had their pre-closing "walk-through" earlier that day, just as a microburst passed through town, knocking down trees a block on either side of them, but fortunately not on them (can you imagine?). The closing was scheduled for two days hence and Lynn was looking forward to her final day on the job after four decades of nursing and nurturing at Loyola Medical Center.

Rocking gently on the porch swing, I looked across the street at the house my parents vacated in 1999 and recalled what a moment that was, walking through those rooms for the last time. Now a young family lives there, I hear, the cycle starting anew.

A house is not a home, but it harbors one. In fact, it is the host of many homes, providing the fertile loam from which home springs. Just as a doorway is not the frame but the airy space we pass through, it's astonishing how much is contained within these inert walls.

As dusk thickened, it was time to go. Just then a car pulled up across the street, next door to my old house, and a young woman, perhaps newly graduated from OPRF or Fenwick or Trinity and beginning her last summer here as a full-time resident, got out and scurried into the warmly-lit enclosure, which in my era housed Don Madigan, a retired colonel, who was present on the U.S.S. Missouri for the signing of the treaty ending the war with Japan in 1945. She doesn't know that, of course, because she and her family are too busy cultivating their own home history, as is the family moving into "the Grogans' house."

The circle is unbroken, by and by.

Bye and Bye.

The real parade was on the parkways (2001)

If you want to experience the interconnectedness of community, our town offers numerous options: block parties, Farmers Market, outdoor theater in Austin Gardens, A Day in Our Village, the Fourth of July fireworks, movies at the Lake Theatre, youth baseball games in local parks, Sunday concerts at Scoville Park, Oaktoberfest, Wright Plus, Halloween trick-or-treating.

Any event or occasion that draws people you rarely see — or don't see as often as you might like — fosters a sense of community. Every town provides similar opportunities. The more you nurture connection, the stronger your community.

Now you can add the annual Fourth of July Parade, thanks to Rebekah Levin and a cohort of grassroots organizers who have resurrected an old tradition. No matter how long the new tradition lasts, it will be tough to match this year's inaugural. As July Fourths go, this was a weather wonder — low humidity, brilliant sunshine, deep blue sky, not too hot.

The organizers were smart to choose Ridgeland Avenue for the parade route. Most of us drive too quickly to appreciate this remarkable row of open-porched Victorians, but when you're riding slowly in the back of an open pickup truck during the parade, you can savor turn-of-the-last-century splendor.

Without the rush of two-way traffic, Ridgeland returns to its sleepier, small-town past. Ordinarily, this is not the kind of street where kids sit on curbs, dangling their feet in the gutters while adults set up lawn chairs on the parkway, but last Wednesday, a good chunk of the community could be found lining the street. Children wore red, white and blue and waved miniature flags. Adults, meanwhile, waved hands — in good-natured greeting. Some sat on front steps and sipped coffee. Friends and families congregated on open porches, everyone in full festivity mode.

Up ahead, a large double-decker bus filled with people wearing furry cartoon character costumes had to divert at South Boulevard and head a mile or so east to Central Avenue because that was the only overpass high enough to accommodate them. They must have been quite a sight cruising totally out of context through Chicago's West Side.

When you're in the parade, people lining the parkways become the parade as you slide past. That was really what I wanted to see — neighborliness, familiarity, the interdependence that a 225-year-old aspiring democracy is expected to induce. We celebrate our independence far more than our interdependence. And if the event was intended to showcase our residential diversity, it succeeded.

The only constructive criticism I heard was there ought to be something for people after the parade ends, maybe invite all the watchers to trail behind, marching up Ridgeland to Whittier School's playground for a giant "Community Breakfast," accompanied by Copland, Gershwin and Sousa tunes while the citizens mingle.

Maybe that's overly visionary, but I can think of one thing the organizers should definitely do next year.

Put on another parade.

Our three parades (2015)

On this, the most American of holidays in this, a most American community, we paraded our uniqueness. In the middle of a three-day weekend, middle of the year, straight up the middle of town, in the middle Midwest, in the midst of busy and not-so-busy lives, we grabbed our banners and marched in meandering fashion, Type As with Type Bs, point A to point B, showing off who we are in all of our multifaceted and multilayered glory.

People lined the curbs — and parkways and lawns and stairs and porches — houses decked with furls of fabric flags.

Ray Heise, retired longtime village attorney grabbed the PVC framework supporting our banner for gun responsibility and responsible gun regulation and we set off up Ridgeland Avenue from Adams to Chicago avenues.

Behind us marched the top brass of Oak Park's finest — Police Chief Rick Tanksley, deputy chiefs Anthony Ambrose and Frank Limon, and Commander LaDon Reynolds — which would have been a brilliant strategic maneuver on our part had we thought of asking them. But the chief asked us first.

If any officer on the force wonders whether this community appreciates their efforts — among the trickiest and most sensitive demanded of any suburban department — they would have been reassured by marching with us this Fourth of July, to sustained applause the length of the parade. Not perfunctory clapping, mind you. Enthusiastic acclaim.

Some approval was also directed toward our group and our partner organization, Moms Demand Action, arrayed behind us, combining to promote Universal Background Checks nationwide as a common-sense step toward reducing gun violence.

But none of the signage making our case was as effective as the statement made by Oak Park's top cops choosing to march with us in solidarity — sans gun in the chief's case.

For the record, the weather was about as good as July 4th gets: Summery and sunny, but mild enough for marchers and spectators alike.

And it held throughout the day into the evening when the second parade commenced, family and friends streaming north, south, east, west, walking off their BBQ bounty and their watermelon sangria, converging on the high school campus in the center of town from all points within — and beyond — our borders, to gaze wide-eyed upon the promised pyrotechnics.

Linden Avenue, to the west of the stadium and athletic fields, was lined with lawn chairs, blankets blanketed the tennis courts at the north end, the field south of Lake Street filled with non-competitors, while bleacher-tolerant backsides filled the stadium bleachers to not-quite-capacity — plenty of seats remaining even after the entry gates were shut down.

Then, as dusk darkened sufficiently to provide a proper background, rockets soared to satisfied ahs, accompanied by recorded serenades. We all came to look for America, as Paul Simon crooned, and found it in Ray Charles' soulful "Oh beautiful, for spacious skies." And finally, the spectacular newspaper-sponsored finale set those spacious skies afire, synched to Sousa's "Stars and Stripes Forever."

If only it could last forever.

Then the peak of summer having passed all too quickly (as it always does), parade number three began, winding its way through the pungent firework-powder haze. All manner of humanity and every strata of society funneled down closed-off streets in every direction, narrowing to sidewalks festooned with fireflies, which resembled some gently pulsing echo of the night's recently concluded razzle-dazzle, held close by the low canopy of trees.

This last was, perhaps, the most remarkable parade of the day — orderly, peaceful, the top brass clustered at ground zero in the middle of the East Avenue/Lake Street intersection, pretty much dead center of town, forming a casual command center to oversee the dispersal.

In the distant unseen surrounds, the chaos of individual firework frenzy let loose, reverberating for hours.

But for now, here, all was well.

After this annual big bang, July begins its languid unfurl, with August yet to follow.

So much of summer lies ahead.

But this was a good start.

'Everywhere you looked, there were rainbows' (2006)

There is, regrettably, still a cultural divide between gay and straight in this country — but you couldn't feel it at the Gay Games last week. The only thing you could feel in and around Oak Park and River Forest High School, where the games took place was, well, gaiety.

I used to object to raiding our collective glossary, appropriating the word "gay," and taking ownership of it. Granted, the word was expendable. People used it more frequently in the 1930s and '40s, judging by Hollywood films, but not much since.

It was the principle I objected to more than the word. And why "gay"? I'd never heard an adequate explanation.

But after observing the scene at the games last week, I think I'm beginning to understand.

There was undeniable gaiety surrounding this event. In all the discussions about same-sex marriage and sinfulness and homosexuality being an abomination in God's eyes, one overriding reality keeps rearing its lovely head: Gays and lesbians are funny, creative, smart, friendly, and invariably humane human beings.

They're a hard bunch to dislike — and, it turns out, they're also good athletes.

Anyone who dismisses gays, would have had their stereotypes sorely shaken if they'd watched any of the soccer competition this past week. These teams could hold their own with pretty much any group of amateur athletes. And they weren't messing around. At least one yellow card was thrown while I was watching.

I'm not sure why we're so locked into our traditional gender definitions and threatened by variations. On Wednesday afternoon, two notoriously testosterone-heavy subcultures intersected with the games with ease. The Oak Park police were on hand for security and seemed to be enjoying the competition and interaction as much as anyone. Meanwhile, OPRF football players made the rounds, padless but wearing their jerseys, attempting to sell discount cards as a fundraiser. I'm guessing they found a receptive audience.

On Sunday, when the temperature on the artificial turf was reportedly 140 degrees, the fire department kindly conducted a snorkel training exercise, setting up on the 100 block of North East Avenue and spraying the South Field, where teams had gathered to practice, with a cool mist. As one observer noted, "Everywhere you looked, there were rainbows."

On the south side of town at Barrie Park, meanwhile, one athlete said he felt uneasy, not knowing the neighborhood or what kind of reception they would find, until he spotted a sign in the window of a house across the street: "Who does God shun? No one! Welcome to the Gay Games."

We did good last week.

The Gay Games were good for Oak Park in many ways — good for business, good for making people more aware of who we are and what this village has to offer — but the games also felt like an island of sanity, an upbeat, energized oasis, away from a straight-and-narrow world too often gone mad. The athletes played hard, with pride, but didn't take it too seriously.

They were enthusiastic, joyous, merry, lively, cheerful, sportive, hilarious.

The very definition, in fact, of the word "gay."

A centennial worth celebrating (2001)

Oak Park began a centennial year of celebration on Saturday. That might surprise you since the first settlers, Joseph and Betty Kettlestrings, arrived here about 1833. Believe it or not, Kettlestrings are still living here today. David and Anne, last of the line, served as grand marshals of the Homecoming Parade on Lake Street this year.

But we're not celebrating settlement. We're celebrating our incorporation as a village — a process that culminated in 1901 and was finalized in 1902 — resulting in our de-annexation from Cicero Township and incorporation as an independent village.

Incorporation and de-annexation aren't sexy concepts, which may explain the lack of enthusiasm this centennial has generated thus far. Think of it this way: We're celebrating our declaration of independence from Cicero.

Yes, there's an element of snobbery. Snooty DOOPers (Dear Old Oak Parkers) wanted to disassociate from the ethnic riffraff of Cicero. Oak Park has always been a little full of itself. We consider ourselves a step above the run-of-the-mill. And in fact, Oak Park and Cicero have traveled very different paths since 1902. Oak Park, for instance, chose temperance, and Henry Austin cast out the demon rum while Cicero rewrote the book on bootlegging, thanks to Al Capone. Oak Park chose tolerance and racial diversity. Cicero ran Martin Luther King Jr. out of town.

But my mother grew up in Cicero, and a good portion of my extended family lived there. Both sets of grandparents moved to Oak Park in the 1940s. They were part of the Catholic invasion, card-carrying members of that era's ethnic riffraff.

My parents lived in Cicero for the first three years after they were married — in the basement apartment of a building owned by a relative because housing was scarce after World War II. They moved to Oak Park in 1952, a month before I was born.

That was a significant year in Oak Park. The "good government" movement — aka the Village Manager Association — evicted the Republican machine that prevailed in the late 1940s and early '50s here, and they convinced voters to approve the village manager form of government. The ethnic riffraff, by the way, made the difference in the campaign and the election. It was, in a sense, Oak Park's "second revolution" and came exactly 50 years after the first.

"Good government" turned into "fair government" in the 1960s, as Oak Park took deliberate steps to welcome the next wave of riffraff — those distinguished not by religion but by skin color.

In the 1980s and '90s, the village made room for yet another wave of riffraff, differentiated this time by sexual orientation.

Each influx provided an infusion of vitality. Now if only we could find parking for everyone.

But that vitality has made us strong — not to mention unique. No booze, no overnight parking, the VMA, Fair Housing, Integration, Home Rule, The Domestic Partnership Ordinance and Registry. Oak Park has consistently pursued the path less traveled. We're no longer "dry," but everything else is intact.

That's what this centennial is about — the determination to go our own way. It has become part of our identity. And the first big step occurred 100 years ago, when we parted ways with Cicero.

Two roads diverged, and we've been taking the one less traveled ever since.

And that's worth celebrating.

* * *

Sometimes it takes a centennial to make you appreciate where you live. That was certainly the case last Saturday night at the Mar Lac banquet hall where the Historical Society of Oak Park-River Forest threw a party celebrating Oak Park's 100th anniversary as an independent village.

There was Bill Zwecker of the Sun-Times chatting with Richard Christiansen of the Tribune; Village Trustee William J.J. Turner in a cowboy outfit; Stephanie Clemens and her troupe performing turn-of-the-century Doris Humphrey dances; Ginie Cassin in her Grace Hall

Hemingway feathery finery; Elsie Jacobsen in a spectacular, gold-embroidered Moroccan gown worn by Moroccan royalty; Barbara Ballinger, just back from following Hemingway's footsteps through Paris.

This was the kind of occasion where you could walk up to a Heisman Trophy winner from Notre Dame (Johnny Lattner) and discuss youth sports. The evening also featured one of the world's great trumpeters, Adolph Herseth of the Chicago Symphony Orchestra, leading the assembled in a chorus of "God Bless America"; a handwritten note from film star Mary Elizabeth Mastrantonio; and former state Senate President Phil Rock, who described local Oak Park politics as "a little squirrely."

Author Iris Krasnow talked about her father, Ted, who served as a village trustee during the tense and tumultuous term of 1969-1973, immediately following the passage of the Fair Housing Ordinance, which many Oak Parkers thought might be the end of the world — or at least the village. It wasn't. It was the beginning — of a whole new world.

Author Harriette Gillem Robinet, one of the first African American "settlers" in the 1960s, gave a quick history lesson on how the Open Communities Project brought us to that Fair Housing Ordinance.

Richard Christiansen spoke fondly of Adele Maze and the library branch on the south side of town that bears her name. He found it deeply comforting on a recent visit to see how little the Maze Branch had changed over the years.

Testimonials were heartfelt and reassuring. Most expressed gratitude that they grew up here or chose to live here. In retirement, Lattner and Herseth are quite content to remain in Oak Park. Herseth should probably get finder's fees for talking so many of his fellow Chicago Symphony musicians into moving here.

Zwecker, as emcee, was entertaining without growing tiresome. He even squeezed in a plug for an imminent meteor shower.

With all the speechifyin', the steaks were a little overdone, but you couldn't fault proprietor Lou Fabbri, who was on hand overseeing one of the last big bashes in his storied hall, which, in a previous incarnation, housed the storied Warrington Opera House. The sense of history here was palpable, aided visually by photo enlargements along the walls, courtesy of the Historical Society archives.

Thanksgiving, just a few days away, feels altogether different this year, following the 9/11 attacks. Celebrating our abundance could seem excessive, complacent, even a little smug, given the wider context of a world that doesn't have as much as this country does and resents us for it. Inequality, it's wise to be reminded, is unsustainable.

But Oak Park's abundance is different. Ours is an abundance of writers and artists, pragmatic idealists and eccentric characters, squirrely politics and civic volunteers and above all, history.

We are, first and foremost, storytellers because Oak Park has so many to tell. No other community is quite like this one. It makes us a little peculiar and we feel a little superior sometimes, but our story is a good one.

We haven't just survived a century as an incorporated municipality. We have evolved — into something worth talking about, something worth celebrating.

We keep trying to be better than we were. We're not just growing old.

We're growing up.

Mildred McDonald's secret to a long life (1995, 2016)

Not many people live to 103, but Mildred McDonald did. When she died last week, I wondered anew, "What is the secret to a long life?" And that took me back to December 1995 and a longstanding Christmas tradition:

Mildred McDonald's house always exudes warmth, but on this first Sunday in December, it is particularly warm inside. That's because today is Cookie Day, has been every year since 1965, and the oven has been working overtime since 10 a.m.

This 30th anniversary of the McDonald family cookie fest draws a particularly good turnout, with more than 20 people present, mostly women and children, from 3 years old on up, busily churning out batch after batch of sweet treats.

Efficiency and productivity, of course, are not the primary goals. That would be family togetherness and, judging by the energy level and general good cheer, it's a success. The McDonald family has expanded to include in-laws and friends, caught up in the thrill of the bake over the years, who are now regulars. The Willards came all the way from Kankakee.

Most of the husbands have been excused until dinner and drinks at 6 p.m., following this doughy marathon. The few on hand take refuge watching football in the living room, which doubles as a storage station for completed cookie batches — in tins, on trays, spread across the mantel, bookshelves and sundry other flat surfaces.

The kitchen and dining room, meanwhile, are a hotbed of frenzied activity. There isn't nearly enough room in the kitchen for the kind of production going on here, but it goes on anyway. This house would make the Keebler elves jealous.

The McDonald elves are busy decorating gingerbread in the dining room on a round table covered by newsprint, which in turn is covered with the carcasses of used Cake Mate tubes and every manner of sprinkle and confectionary adornment imaginable.

The kids are having a ball decorating myriad reindeer, Christmas trees, stars, etc. The rule is you take home whatever you decorate and each elf has an aluminum tray with his or her name taped to it.

Mildred is the dervish in the middle of this mayhem, introducing me to everyone and even putting me on the phone to say hello to her granddaughter Kelley, who has called from college, where she's a freshman. This is the first Cookie Day in her lifetime where she hasn't been present.

"It's funny," she says, "but I really miss it."

Cookie Day has evolved over the years. Back in 1965, Mildred's oldest daughter, Sue Vanek, complained to her mom that, with a new child and little room in her apartment kitchen, she couldn't bake Christmas cookies that year. Mildred invited her over and a tradition was forged. As each of Mildred's five children had kids, the assembly line grew, as did the cookie varieties. The family repertoire now numbers 15 recipes. More are added, but only if they garner rave reviews. Lemon snowballs look to be this year's hit.

Mildred provides the dough and decorations. Young Carey, who prefers baking gingerbread to decorating it, gives a detailed demonstration on how to roll it out and make handprints. "We like to eat the dough as we go along," he confides.

In the cramped kitchen, young adults sit around the narrow counter, greasing cookie sheets with Crisco, then rolling balls of dough for the latest batch. They finish the difficult, yet very popular "Spritz" (butter) cookies, then move on to thimble cookies (thumbprints filled with preserves or gumdrops). The chatter and banter roll on as relentlessly as the dough.

"Can somebody put on Christmas tunes?"

"Is this the right size?"

"Grandma, want to hear my joke?"

Colleen hands me a lovely gingerbread reindeer with my name on it, decorated with sprinkles. They get pretty creative with designs, culminating in last year's "Madonna" cookie, invented by Maureen Barry, using the caps of gel tubes for the entertainer's famous brassiere.

"We don't have any fun," Mildred deadpans. "I have to twist their arms to come."

Mildred's niece, Marilyn, excuses herself as she rushes by. "It's kind of like bedlam," she explains. Kind of?

"Mother's really the focal point," says Sue. "She's a grand lady in the old sense of the word. She knows how to do things and does 'em right." And this house, she adds, "has been a focal point since we moved here in 1950."

On my way out, Mildred stops dancing in the vestibule with Sue and little Michael long enough to hand me a large tin of cookies and an invitation to come back next year.

* * *

I never did go back, but over the years, I thought about Mildred and her family every time I went past the family homestead at the corner of Scoville and Van Buren.

How do you get to be 103? There are probably lots of reasons, but one is by living your way to it.

And Mildred McDonald knew how to live.

A story that binds us (2019)

"The greatest need is for collective rituals," wrote New York Times columnist David Brooks in 2019 before the pandemic struck. He didn't mean the religious kind. Not the personal kind either.

"A public civic compact, publicly sworn to, involving all," he wrote. "… It could be done on a spot that would become sacred, the beating heart of the community."

It would be an occasion to "tell a new version of the town's story," which is important because "a community is a group of people who share a common story."

Here's our story:

"They didn't give in to fear" should be inscribed on a monument somewhere in Oak Park — along with the names, a thousand strong, that appeared on an ad covering a two-full-page spread in the local newspapers — the Oak Leaves and the Village Economist — on April 16, 1964, just a few months after John F. Kennedy was assassinated, when things were a little, shall we say, unsettled in this country.

The ad was titled, "The Right of All People to Live Where They Choose," and everyone who attached their name to the document paid a dollar for the privilege, just enough to pay for the ad.

They were not, by any stretch, a bunch of wild-eyed radicals. They weren't even all Democrats. This was a largely Republican town in those days, and plenty of Republicans are on the list. A number of River Forest residents also signed on.

These ordinary citizens took an extraordinary public stand in favor of "open housing," which was not yet on the radar of most White residents in April of 1964.

Yet many signed up — 99 percent of them White — and in doing so, served notice to the world that this wasn't your ordinary suburb. They were willing to risk their property values for a principle: Fairness.

More than a thousand were willing to sign, many of them contacted through the local churches. Names from Ascension Parish, where I grew up, are well represented, including the pastor at the time, Msgr. John D. Fitzgerald, a distinguished, erudite gentleman whom no one would have mistaken for a rabble-rouser.

This was the kind of thing you had to think about before agreeing to do it. Nobody "just went along" because of peer pressure.

The text was written by community activist June Heinrich:

> *We, the undersigned residents of Oak Park and River Forest, believing in the essential oneness of humankind, and seeking to foster such unity in our communities, do hereby declare:*
>
> *That we want residence in our villages to be open to anyone interested in sharing our benefits and responsibilities, regardless of race, color, creed, or national origin.*
>
> *That we believe in equal opportunity for all in the fields of education, business, and the professions, in harmony with constitutional guarantees of equal rights to life, liberty, and the pursuit of happiness;*
>
> *That mutual understanding between people of diverse ethnic, racial, and religious backgrounds can best be attained by an attitude of reciprocal good will and increased association;*
>
> *That all citizens, in a spirit of justice, dignity, and kindness, should give serious consideration to the challenge that now faces all Americans in the achievement of brotherhood under God.*

The ad had quite an impact. It started the Open Housing Movement in Oak Park, which led, four years later, to the passage of a groundbreaking Fair Housing Ordinance, one of the first in the nation.

Once upon a time, in a village just outside Chicago, ordinary/extraordinary people stood up for a principle — the right of all people to live where they choose. Their names should be posted somewhere, an "honor roll" representing everything that's good and decent and right about us.

Here are a few of the names you might recognize:

Dr. Peter Baker, Barbara Ballinger, Al Belanger, Leo Blaber, Lee Brooke, Morris Buske, Bill and Virginia Cassin, John Gibson, Ruth

Hamilton, Adolph and Avis Herseth, Elsie Jacobsen, Heinz and Regina Kuehn, Rev. Timothy Lyne, James McClure, Kathryn Ross McDaniel, Joseph and Mary Massura, Donald Peaslee, Donald Peppard, Ray and Carolyn Poplett, Robert and Winifred Pozorski, Art Replogle, Vernette and Robert Schultz, Peg and Irv Studney, Art Thorpe, Nancy Waichler, Frank and Elizabeth Walsh, Isabel Wasson, Rev. Donald Wheat, Rev. Bernie White, Gregory White, and Dwight and Millie Follett.

Following all the names, the ad concluded with:

> *This is a paid advertisement sponsored by a temporary committee of citizens of Oak Pak and River Forest. The committee acknowledges and regrets that there are many residents who would have subscribed to this statement but who were not contacted due to the limitations of time. The committee received donations totaling $629; cost of the advertisements amounted to $620; supplies and postage came to $5, and there remains a surplus of $4. In the near future, the committee plans to sponsor meetings so that neighbors will meet and discuss the principles of social justice as they apply to housing. Temporary officers: A.J. Belanger, chairman; Miss G. Cravis, secretary; W.L. Brooke Jr., treasurer.*

Last fall, Regina Kuehn, one of the signers, dropped off a folder put together by Lee Brooke, which tells the story of the Citizens Committee for Human Rights and "The Ad," including a list of those who signed.

Perusing the names, I discovered the reason she sent me the folder. There, between Mrs. Josephine R. Tracy and Mr. & Mrs. Richard Tryba, I found Mr. & Mrs. Kenneth E. Trainor, my thoughtful, very Republican parents.

When I asked them about it, they downplayed their involvement. But standing up for your principles is always a big deal.

If you're proud of these towns, or simply enjoy living here, you're in their debt. Hemingway would have been impressed. Under pressure, they showed grace. They proved we are not the village of broad streets and narrow minds. They did the right thing. They took the road less traveled.

And you know what a difference that makes.

* * *

Our story isn't just that Oak Park passed a Fair Housing Ordinance in 1968 and lived happily ever after. The struggle to intentionally manage and maintain "stable diversity" (aka "integration") goes on — at the village government level and at the village resident level, and everywhere in between (especially in public education). The village put in place a raft of policies and partnered on others — from the Equity Assurance Program to the founding of the founding of the Oak Park Regional Housing Center, to real estate companies voluntarily agreeing not to post "For Sale" signs (to this day) and much more. It has been a comprehensive, cooperative effort.

And the journey continues. Oak Parkers are a self-critical group. "We aren't as great as we think," is often heard.

What they likely mean is "Oak Park isn't as great as we want it to be." We grouse about parking and taxes, but talk to any Oak Parker who has been here for 20 years or more, those who remain even after their kids are out of school, Black and White citizens who live next door to each other in every part of the village — from Austin Boulevard to Harlem Avenue, North Avenue to Roosevelt Road — and you're looking at people who have made diversity work like it has worked almost nowhere else in this country.

Most White Oak Parkers didn't cut and run. Most Black Oak Parkers didn't just move in. They became part of the community fabric.

And enforcing the Fair Housing Ordinance was the step that made this possible.

Oak Park's story, since 1963, has been about commitment to diversity. It's a good story — about overcoming fear, resisting White flight and resegregation — and it has broadened as we struggled to become more and more inclusive, embracing the LGBTQ community in the 1990s, and, more recently, declaring ourselves a "sanctuary community" for immigrants.

Now we're attempting to take diversity to the next level: equity. School districts 97 and 200 recently passed strong educational equity policies — declaring their determination to conquer the longstanding challenge of eliminating institutional racism from our schools and ensuring equal opportunity for all.

But passing a policy is not enough. As David Brooks put it, we need a collective ritual that reinforces our determination.

"It would be an occasion," he wrote, "for people to make promises to one another — specific ways they are going to use their gifts to solve the common challenge. Towns are built when people make promises to one another, hold one another accountable, and sacrifice together through repeated interaction toward a common end."

The new policies commit our local schools to taking specific steps to achieve educational equity, but what about the rest of the village? Shouldn't we, too, make a public commitment? What would that sound like? And where would it take place?

Every two years, following the municipal election, the new Village of Oak Park Board of Trustees votes to re-affirm Oak Park's commitment to diversity. The Diversity Statement was composed in 1973, revised in 1999, and again in 2019 by the Community Relations Commission, the most recent version putting greater emphasis on equity. The Diversity Statement is as close to a foundational document as we have, a creed stating our core village values.

Here is the Oak Park Equity, Diversity and Inclusion Statement, revised and adopted on Oct. 19, 2019:

> *The people of Oak Park choose this community, not just as a place to live, but as a way of life and as a place to seek shelter, refuge and acceptance. Oak Park commits itself to equity, diversity, and inclusion because these values make us a desirable and strong community for all people. Creating a mutually respectful, multi-cultural and equitable environment does not happen on its own; it must be intentional.*
>
> *We believe in equity. By embracing equity, with an explicit but*

not exclusive focus on racial equity, we work to break down systems of oppression, including racism, sexism, homophobia, xenophobia and other forms of bias and hate to achieve a society where race no longer determines one's outcomes, where everyone has what they need to thrive. This is both a process and a goal. We reject racial barriers that limit and divide us, and we reject bias toward any group of people.

We believe in diversity because our commonalities and differences are both assets. Oak Park is a dynamic community that welcomes, respects, and encourages the contributions of all people, in all our rich variety by race, color, ethnicity, ancestry, national origin, religion, age, sex, sexual orientation, gender identity or expression, marital and/or familial status, language, mental and/or physical impairment and/or disability, military status, economic class, immigration status, foster status, body size, criminal history, or any of the other characteristics that are often used to divide people.

We acknowledge intersectionality and the compounding effect of multiple forms of discrimination that many in our community experience. We affirm all people as members of the human family. Our goal is for people of widely differing backgrounds to do more than live next to one another. Through intentional interaction and fair treatment, we can respect our differences while fostering unity and developing a shared, intersectional vision for the future.

We believe in inclusion because we need to go beyond numerical diversity and strive for authentic representation, empowered participation, full access, and a true sense of belonging for all people. Oak Park recognizes that a free, open, and inclusive community is achieved through full and broad participation of all community members and the ongoing commitment to active and intentional engagement across lines of difference. We believe the best decisions are made when everyone is authentically represented in decision-making and power is shared collectively.

The Village of Oak Park commits itself to a future ensuring equity, diversity, and inclusion in all aspects of local governance and community life. We strive to make these values aspirational and operational, reflected in our everyday practices and priorities. This includes fair treatment, equal access, and full participation in all of the Village's institutions and programs, and the goal of racial equity in all Village operating policies. The Village of Oak Park must continue to support its fair housing philosophy that fosters integration and unity in our community. Our intention is that such principles will be a basis for policy and decision making in Oak Park. The President and Board of Trustees of the Village of Oak Park reaffirm their dedication and commitment to these precepts.

Voting on the Village Diversity Statement every two years, however, doesn't really qualify as a "public ritual" because very few village residents attend. We need a setting, preferably in the open air, that includes an annual reading of our creed, reaffirming our commitment to diversity and equity.

A civic compact, publicly sworn to, involving all, or as many as can attend.

The most likely setting would be A Day in Our Village each year on the first Sunday of June. Most of the essential village organizations are on hand to inform curious residents (and non-residents) of all that Oak Park has to offer.

At a prescribed time, high noon perhaps, the Village Diversity Statement could be read from the stage in Scoville Park, with the village president and trustees, along with members of the many organizations on hand — Oak Park Area Lesbian and Gay Association+ (OPALGA), African American Parents for Purposeful Leadership in Education (APPLE), the Community of Congregations, the Board of Realtors, and the Business and Civic Council, just to name a few — taking turns with the reading.

A musical soundtrack, accompanied by clips from Steve James' 2018 documentary series, *America to Me*, shown on a screen behind the stage as a lead-in, would get everyone's attention — because attention is essential.

Scoville Park is the right setting for this. Near the center of town, the park has long been known as "the village's front lawn," a wide lawn reflecting ever-widening minds.

If Brooks is right, telling our story once a year in the "beating heart of our community" would remind us of the aspirations that bind us to one another.

A community, he says, is a group of people who share a common story.

And our story is one worth telling.

6

Summer

Praising June (2021)

> *It was a quiet morning, the town covered over with darkness and at ease in bed. Summer gathered in the weather, the wind had the proper touch, the breathing of the world was long and warm and slow. You had only to rise, lean from your window, and know that this indeed was the first real time of freedom and living, this was the first morning of summer.*
>
> **Ray Bradbury**
> *Dandelion Wine*

The much-maligned season of summer has been with us since the Saturday before Memorial Day, when we finally bid 50 degrees a not-so-fond farewell. We can complain only about the heat now. I complain only about the cold because it dominates two-thirds of the year. Heat can be withering, but it will be gone too soon.

I complain about weather most of the year, but in summer I'm in praise mode. And it's all about warmth. In winter, I praise relative warmth (even the 40s get their due). In spring, I praise grudging warmth (the sun is trying, it really is, as it creeps north, inch by inch, measured along the ruler of the western horizon). Or, as my 7-year-old grandson Tyler said, when I noted that the sun was trying to break through, "The sun is always trying to break through." Good point — and a good way to look at life.

In autumn, I praise lingering warmth as the feckless sun plots the annual escape to its other lover, the Southern hemisphere.

In summer, though, warmth rules — and can be forgiven, in my opinion, if occasionally the heat index gets carried away. You never hear anyone say, "Gotta savor winter because you only get so many in a lifetime." People do say that about summer.

I love moderate summer mornings, bordering on cool, rousing the birds at 4 a.m. to their morning choir practice, sweetening the soft air with song in the grey pre-dawn. Summer offers a largesse of daylight hours — so jealously guarded until recently by winter's stingy, austere dominion. Early morning is now a viable option, inviting emergence from the cocoon of our bedding, giving us reason to rise, if only to sample and savor the awakening world, runners and walkers and their dogs, and workers setting about their daily commerce.

No price is exacted for getting out of bed on a summer morning, no chill tempts us back under covers for a few more comforting moments, forcing a daily battle of will vs. chill. In winter, getting out of bed is an act of moral courage. In summer, it is effortless.

Summer's early morning light steals into the room, coaxing sleepers awake well before the alarm clock sounds. Opening the blinds reveals low-angled sunlight, illuminating every crack and crevice, bathing the world in beauty. The more you see, the better you'll like it, the sun seems to say. Why let an hour lapse? If you can't get out, sit by an open window and watch the world flow past.

I love the evening warmth as well, but more than that, the extended light. In June, "night" is a relative term. The day's afterglow lingers past 9 p.m., extending boldly east along the northern horizon. In June, daylight lasts from 5 a.m. till 9 p.m., 16 hours at its peak. Balmy nights feel friendly, luxuriously perfumed by June flowers and blossoms. Walking at night is to conduct an olfactory tree inventory. The undifferentiated mass of leafy extravagance that we take for granted later, is easily identifiable during June blossoming: lindens, catalpas, black locusts, and horse chestnuts announce themselves by their scents.

With the mid-month arrival of fireflies, it's tempting to wish we could do without streetlights for several weeks.

Summer afternoons, admittedly, are an acquired taste, but the sun overhead whitewashes cumulus clouds and thunderheads, adrift in the blue vault. The midday heat can be withering, but that's why trees invented shade and why people invented front porches. The formerly frigid dead zones of winter are transformed into leafy oases that sway in the breeze and let in just enough dappled sunlight to make even sidewalks dance with fancy finery.

In summer, interior living spaces too often become air-conditioned fortresses, but when temps are tolerable, opening the windows that run the width of my living room draws the outdoors in, reminiscent of childhood summers spent reading on an enclosed porch, growing painfully up, socially awkward, turning inward — into books, but also outward into summer itself. Instead of fretting about how many books haven't been read, better to read the Book of Nature.

A summer afternoon's deep stillness is worth the walk — dodging the lawn care services that compete to out-decibel the cicadas with their infernal noisemakers. In the evening, the ethereal balm of crickets soon arrives to soothe assaulted ears.

Handling the afternoon heat requires cultivating a comfort level with the fine sheen of sweat, our breeze-activated cooling mechanism (far more effective than dogs' dangling tongues). When summer arrives, who can recall the last time a jacket or coat was necessary or what it feels like to be cold?

Summer is stingier with rain, more generous with sunshine. The grass browns, but the lawns are white with clover flowers, and native prairie plants with deep roots grow tall, where allowed. All feels full and right with the natural world.

After dreaming of this so often during the long 7-8 months of late autumn/midwinter/early spring, here in the upper Midwest, we are given four months of non-chilly, non-overcast, sun-basted weather to savor — five if we're lucky. Sans smartphones, unmediated by windshields and A/C, summer is a lovely space and time that should never be taken for granted.

Let the water sprinklers strafe your legs as you pass, contemplate caterpillars dangling over the sidewalk by a thread from the tree above. Learn the names of roadside wildflowers — purple chicory, Queen Anne's lace, black-eyed Susans, bee balm, purple coneflowers.

Sample summer's buffet. Inhale its bouquet.

Here. Now. Mid-June. Solstice.

It's summer. We get just so many in a lifetime.

See you on the porch.

Report from the resort (2022)

It happens every year. Summer brings our longest sustained stretch of sunny warmth, along with a recurring fantasy — that our urbanized suburb, located just outside a major metropolis, has been magically transformed into a summer resort town.

While viewing Shakespeare under the stars in Austin Gardens, with aircraft ripping through the atmosphere overhead or ambulance sirens screaming emergencies at the local elder facility, and the steady screech of cicadas doing their best to burst the bubble, it's not always the easiest fantasy to entertain.

Yet sipping coffee and nibbling an apple tartelette outside Lea's French Street Food on Marion Street is a fine way to start a morning — as is sitting on a bench in Mills Park or Austin Gardens, watching dogs frolic while owners schmooze, or attending bird-song recitals and basking in a breezeway before the thermometer climbs and drives us indoors.

Imbibing or abiding, the day starts earlier in summer and is worth leaving our confines behind. It's summertime and the goin' out is easy.

The rest of the year feels like a race with the present, trying to keep a step ahead. In summer, it's wiser to surrender to the here and now and, like a beachcomber, collect moments cast up on summer's shore:

Sitting on a friend's porch, eating rhubarb pie, served warm; spooning a Black Cow at a table outside Petersen's ice cream parlor on a hot Sunday afternoon; the subtle scent of catalpa blossoms and the heavy perfume of lindens, blended and suspended in the thick night air; mulberries crushed on the sidewalk, staining the concrete purple; the chilly A/C blast passing open shop doors; wildflowers taking over highway roadsides; swimmers flip-flopping home from the Ridgeland Common or Rehm Park pools, sarong-ed by towels; morning and afternoon klatches outside scattered coffee shops; actors spraying their spittle in the stage-light glow of a Shakespearean evening; crickets trilling and dogs sounding alerts as pedestrians pass on a walk down streets densely overhung by trees, accompanied by the scattershot brilliance of fireflies in the darkening dusk;

standing on a rooftop deck, dwarfed by an ocean of air, the departed sun reflecting off coral reefs and shining sandbars of clouds, as swallows dart to and fro skimming mosquitos.

This is living, a skill we master too late — a moment-by-moment proposition that seems diametrically at odds with "making a living."

In summer, weekends stretch before the resort residents like a limitless chain of possibility. October seems a long way off as Saturday morning shoppers load up on stalks of brilliant gladiolas, ripe tomatoes and sweet corn at Farmers Market. Front-yard gardens are fully arrayed with hydrangeas and adored by passersby.

Cycling is back in vogue, thanks to the pandemic. Pilgrims from all over the world parade past Frank Lloyd Wright homes and a bounty of other Prairie-style masterpieces. Sidewalk sales lure curious customers to Oak Park Avenue and Lake Street. T-ball games are contested, after a fashion, on fields of parental dreams each June. The Lake Theatre offers sanctuary from the sultriness of July and August — and the promise of two hours of armchair travel.

Work and other forms of busyness inveigh against the resort illusion, but vacation is ultimately a state of mind. Dining in the quaint cobblestone gangway next to Il Vicolo Ristorante, on Oak Park Avenue, makes it easy to mistake familiar surroundings for a European getaway. Nursing a glass of wine with friends on the corner out front of Anfora Wine Merchants across from Poor Phil's, at Marion and Pleasant, adds to the air of cosmopolitan civility. Some evenings it seems as if the entire resort is dining al fresco. And every August, the MicroBrew Review brings out the craft beer crowd to Down Town Oak Park.

Sunday night concerts in Scoville Park, meanwhile, are almost as entertaining to listen to as the frolicking kids are to watch.

As resorts go, Oak Park (and River Forest) are fine places to spend the summer months. You can hear live music most nights outside FitzGerald's on the Berwyn side of Roosevelt Road. Thursday Night Out offers a progressive dinner on Marion Street, sampling cuisine from local restaurants, while musicians entertain. On weekends, art galleries beckon on Harrison Street, down by the expressway.

Summer is the time to be outside, when a park feels as familiar as a living room, and offers more room for living. Curling up with a good book in one of our three branch libraries is an excellent way to while the time, but the reading is just as good on a park bench, a chair in the shade — or even a hammock strung between two trees, as some seem inclined to recline.

Martha's Vineyard may have more celebrities, Aspen has the mountains, and Chicago boasts beaches along a Great Lake, but we have far more trees per square foot, and shade is a lovely consequence of our decidedly deciduous leafery.

For a few golden weeks each summer, this community holds its own as a resort.

At any rate, as famous native son E. Hemingway famously said in *The Sun Also Rises*, isn't it lovely to think so?

Ripening (2015)

Last week, I treated myself to the modern equivalent of a double feature at the Lake Theatre, Downtown Oak Park's neon centerpiece, eight decades old and counting. Two movies in two nights, an end-of-summer indulgence.

On the first night I walked up Marion Street, already abuzz at 6:45 with Thursday Night Out, downtown's weekly dine-around block party.

Jazz singer Petra Van Nuis was midway through a Bossa Nova version of "When You Wish Upon a Star," the Jiminy Cricket classic that makes the bold assertion: "If you heart is in your dream, no request is too extreme" — the theme song of every romantic and an appropriate prelude to viewing Hollywood's dreams, framed on the "silver screen."

Audiences never seem to get enough of Sherlock Holmes, who in his latest outing, *Mr. Holmes*, shows the mastermind confronting his humanity and finding his heart at last. Ian McKellen, who has now played two of our favorite wizards, Gandalf and Sherlock, has never been better.

Emerging from this secular Church of the Creative and Imaginative Mind — and feeling a bit more human myself, which is the point of these forays into the cave where reality's shadows are projected, Plato-like, upon the wall — I followed the brown brick road back down Marion and found the evening's second act, a reggae band, surrounded by appreciative listeners, some swaying slowly in that last-dance-of-the-evening way as the witching hour neared. Bewitching is a better word for the unfolding scene. Overnight, the trees seem to have grown tall enough to tamp down the streetlights, the streetscape ambiance devolving from glare to glow.

Those who remained were not there to chow down and gab. They had entered the moment where music is the food and lovingly plays on. Looking back on the scene when I reached the end of the block, I couldn't help feeling that our town is growing up.

No, not growing.

Ripening.

Continuing on past the dinner conversations outside Poor Phil's — named for Philander Barclay, a good, if sad, story for another time — I headed east on Pleasant Street with a nearly full moon poised like a ripe peach over Mills Park and Pleasant Home.

A comforting chorus of crickets bathed everything in soothing sonic microbursts, a reminder that we're never really alone on summery late-night strolls toward home.

We live our lives, it seems, in threes. Our days are divided into mornings, afternoons and evenings. Stories have beginnings, middles and ends. Weekends consist of Friday night, Saturday and Sunday. Three strikes, you're out. The Christian deity is said to comprise Father, Son and Holy Spirit. Human beings, apparently, have a thing for threes.

True, there are four seasons in a year, and the Irish divide life into four seasons ("20 years of being born, 20 years of growing, 20 years of living and 20 years of dying"). But generally we don't rectangulate, we triangulate.

One is forever splitting into two. Binary seeks unity. One plus One = Tension. With three, we seem to regain our balance.

Summer forms its own triumvirate. June is summer's Friday night, our release from the FallWinterSpring grindstone. The good weather hasn't settled in yet. We're just beginning to slow down, but haven't quite come down from nine months of busyness. Technically, summer doesn't even begin till three weeks into June.

July is summer's Saturday. June eased us into the slowdown mindset. By July, the turbulent, up-and-down yo-yo of spring is forgotten. August provides a buffer against the busy season to come. Like Saturday, July is anchored in the eternal now, the month when past and future infringe the least. If you can't take a deep breath in July, you never will.

August is summer's Sunday, probably the least popular month of our annual "weekend." Sunday night "depression" begins its slow in-creep. The stone is ready to grind again. The future hovers, crowding us, reminding us we have gears other than "R" — for reverse (or recreation).

But August is also a time of untethering, for ambling instead of walking, and watching the wind untangle itself from the tall treetops in our parks, for surrendering the severity of judgment and relaxing the death grip of control over our corner of the known universe.

The word "august" means "inspiring reverence or admiration, majestic, venerable, eminent." Instead, we refer to this month, the under-appreciated third leg of our summer tripod, as "the dog days," named for the constellation Canis Major, which contains Sirius, the "dog star." Not exactly majestic or eminent.

August is a good time to remind ourselves that we aren't powerless before the passage of time. We still have the power to delight, communicate, amuse, inspire, construct, facilitate, enlighten, persuade, explain, motivate, encourage, persevere, create, console, feed, entertain, generate, engage, clarify, mediate, counsel, attract, interpret, question, comprehend, start, finish, connect, appreciate, simplify, relieve, relive, redeem, predict, heal, reform, renew, collaborate, observe, organize, romance, and summarize.

Or summerize.

Not all of these powers are fully developed in each of us, of course, but in August, we only need to live comfortably within our skin, to give hurry the month off, to make peace with our circumstances and briefly taste something that transcends every one of our attached strings.

Freedom.

The following night I returned to The Lake, this time to spend a couple of hours in the virtual presence of the amazing David Foster Wallace, writer extraordinaire, as played by actor Jason Segel, recalled by writer David Lipsky in *The End of the Tour*.

Another mastermind with a heart, another humanizing experience, followed by another end-of-summer tour through the neighborhood and another scene: this one at Pleasant Home, the mansion with a fascinating history, where over 100 viewers packed the expansive porch and front steps of architect George Maher's Prairie-style mansion for the last silent movie of the summer, just in time to catch Charlie Chaplin's peripatetic Tramp, balanced precariously on a tight wire in *The Circus*. Having lost his safety cord, distracted by mischievous monkeys and working without a net, the Tramp's antics generated belly-laughs, crowned by the soaring giggles of children, accompanied by an improvised soundtrack, performed live on the home's piano.

A 21st-century, intergenerational audience taking delight in an early-20th-century film under the overhang of an early-20th-century porch. Ripening indeed.

When a full moon hangs over Pleasant Home and the crickets' string section is fully tuned, as the dense overhang of trees creates a lovers' lane and porch lights warm the way, Pleasant Street, for all its twists and turns, looks like the kind of setting the movies are always trying, and failing, to recreate.

Awash in the cricket sound bath (though paying much more attention to each other), high school students, suffused with victory, ambled home following the first football game of a new season under newly installed Friday night lights, something they couldn't have imagined just a few years ago.

A gentle reminder that autumn is almost upon us.

The season of ripening.

7

Characters with Character

We are not predominantly a community of "olders," as a friend calls them. Nor are we largely a population under 30. Nor are we mostly 20-somethings, or young professionals, or established professionals, or new parents or mid-lifers, or White or Black or Brown or other people of color.

We're all of the above.

Demographically diverse.

We are wealthy in people with character — plus plenty of characters, including Mike Clark, aka the "Mayor of Oak Park," who seems to be everywhere — sometimes, it seems, simultaneously (making one wonder if he's been cloned), and whose standard greeting is "Oh no, not you again!" spoken at a decibel level that can be heard for an entire block.

Long ago there was the "balloon man," actually the father and son duo of Angelo and Carmen Pistilli, in successive stints, selling their colorful, helium-filled clusters, a reliable presence at the corner of Oak Park and Chicago avenues on Sundays for decades. A plaque, courtesy of the local historical society, recognizes the role they played in the lives of countless children.

Another of our local characters, John Stanger, who has written the "DOOPer's Memories" column in the paper for so many years that he qualifies as a notable part of our historical record, knew the balloon man (number 2) as "Gentle Joe" who manned the corner from the late 1940s until the mid-'80s. "Whenever it rained," Stanger recalled, "he would stand on our porch [across Oak Park Avenue] until the rain stopped. He was a very gracious man, but he was a man of few words. One Sunday I saw him save a young lad from certain death. The little guy wasn't paying attention, and he stepped onto Chicago Avenue right into westbound traffic. Mr. Joe released his balloons, jumped into the street and pulled the boy to safety. The neighborhood guys were playing softball on the corner lot, and one of us let out a yell for the boy to get back on the curb, but the boy didn't hear the warning. Thank heavens Joe was at the right spot at the right time."

Or the "scissors grinder," who walked up and down alleys with his bell-ringing pushcart, signaling residents to grab their implements and run out to the alley for sharpening.

And more recently the panhandler who reads our paper faithfully and calls out to me by name when our paths cross.

It takes all kinds, they say.

Here are a few of the characters (with character) who make up the mosaic of us:

In the wake of courage, grace (2012)

As we go about our daily lives, we are surrounded by quiet profiles in courage. I was reminded of this one Sunday morning when I ran into Kristin Gehring and her parents, Betty and Phil, at Courageous Bakery and Café, where they meet with a few friends before going to church at First United Church, two blocks west on Lake Street.

Kristin's brother's wife died several years back, so the Gehrings moved up here from their longtime home in Valparaiso, Indiana — where Phil enjoyed a long, distinguished career teaching music at the university — to help their son raise three girls (all adopted from Ukraine, all with challenges). As you might imagine, this new chapter in their lives has had its ups and downs, some of them significant.

The Gehrings say many blessings come bundled with the challenges, and no doubt that's true, but it still takes courage to start over late in life facing a difficult situation.

Last week, the local paper ran Judy Southwick's obituary. She and her husband Bill lost their daughter to a sudden, unexplained illness 10 years ago while she was on a business trip to China. Judy and Bill were willing to tell that painful story. Going public like that takes courage. Enduring the grief takes even more. The next time I saw Judy, she was coordinating the Ekklesia speakers series at St. Giles Parish. She had cancer, but stayed active and involved. That requires plenty of courage, too. And Bill — imagine what it takes to survive losing your daughter, then your wife in the course of a decade.

Carol Lydecker showed remarkable courage by throwing a farewell party at FitzGerald's a couple of Wednesdays ago. Carol has stage 4 cancer. She stopped chemo, so it's only a matter of time. A talented stage performer and choreographer, she and her husband, Bill Dwyer, wanted to be surrounded by love, laughter and song one more time, which they got, and then some, during a very entertaining evening in which joy temporarily overshadowed the sadness. Her spirit undiminished, Carol summoned the strength to deliver a touching farewell speech. Who was giving the gift and who was receiving it became gloriously unclear as the evening went on.

Carol and Bill, Betty and Phil, and Judy and Bill all exemplify courage, but something else, too: Grace.

Ernest Hemingway famously defined courage as "grace under pressure."

Learning how to function in spite of fear is a good baseline definition of courage. We all live with fear. We function in spite of it, though some do it more "gracefully" than others. Many of our fears are vague or exaggerated and, fortunately, most do not materialize. Waking in the wee hours, I am no stranger to anxieties creeping up my mental stairwell, trying to take charge of my consciousness and ruining sleep.

At those moments, imagination turns into fear's accomplice, spinning worst-case scenarios in vivid detail and enumerating a long list of people and things to fret about. In the light of day, fortunately, much of the apprehension fades. And taking action to address our fears is a wonderful antidote.

For some, nightmares become all too real — the Iraq war veteran I saw at Oaktoberfest last weekend, young and in his prime, missing an arm; the unemployed older workers I know, too young to retire but, shamefully in this age-ist society, too "old" to hire, based largely on bias; the unemployed young worker looking for the chance to get established.

Examples abound. After visiting the Gehrings that Sunday morning, I ran into a friend who retired earlier this year and six months later, his wife, the love of his life and a woman of great vitality, died of cancer.

If courage is functioning in the face of our fears, grace is what follows in the wake of facing them. It builds as we weather each storm.

It's hard to know if it's cause or effect, but grace is that imperturbable place inside that nothing seems able to unsettle, the steady voice within, when you're frozen and holding back, that says you can't claim to love someone unless you're actually, actively loving them.

In our fear, we have trouble believing the best because we're too busy dreading the worst. We don't trust the light because we're so afraid of encroaching darkness.

Grace is resilience. It keeps life from being just a dreary procession from one crisis to another, grinding us down. It enables us to rise to each occasion, to transcend.

Quiet profiles in courage can be found all around. We live in a time that demands courage because every era demands it. But if we face our fears, we can look forward, with some confidence, to grace, that most mysterious of qualities, to help us pull through.

Where it comes from is a mystery.

But it arrives in the wake of courage.

A birthday bash for Shawn Weakliss (2018)

If I told you the community threw a surprise 44th birthday party at Brown Cow Ice Cream Parlor on Madison Street in Forest Park for a ticket-taker from the Lake Theatre in Oak Park who lives in Maywood, you might say, "Come again?"

If nothing else, it proves that, in the age of social media, you have to be careful about what you say.

Shawn Weakliss has something to say to pretty much every movie-goer when they hand their ticket to him. He calls the young women "Supermodel," their mothers "Supermom," and male companions "Bodyguard."

"He has a good word for everyone," said BJ Richards, who found herself waiting in the theater lobby on Mother's Day while her daughter, Dandara, parked the car. During the ensuing small talk, Shawn mentioned his upcoming birthday (May 15). No, he wasn't planning anything special. In fact, he couldn't remember ever having a birthday party. People would "roast" him or "prank" him, but never an actual party.

Richards, who has run BJ's Kids daycare center, first in Oak Park, now in Forest Park for 23 years — 40 years altogether — is the nurturing type. So she decided he needed a surprise party and put the word out on Facebook, not at all sure they could pull off a party this year, maybe next year. The response, she said, was overwhelming.

"I expected 20 people," Richards said, "and would have been happy with 20. It was a school night and work night, dinner time and rainy. It was also short notice. Yet people came."

Over 100 packed Brown Cow's back room, surrounded by balloon clusters, Happy Birthday signs, and kids licking ice cream cones, the scene illuminated by glowing smartphones. A couple of false-alarm "shhhhs!" circulated when it looked like the guest of honor might have arrived. Someone called out, "Do we have an ETA?" BJ called back, "I sure don't!"

"There he is!" whispers spread, as Shawn finally made his way toward us, and then a resounding roar: "Surprise!"

Nodding his head and smirking, Shawn waded into the crowd as if he knew all along. Later I asked if he was surprised.

"Shocked!" he said, as if he were shocked about feeling shocked. But he worked the room like a member of the family, which, for many, he is.

Anthony Clark, unofficial emcee of the Tri-Village area (Oak Park, Forest Park, River Forest) because he shows up everywhere, took over. "We all love you, Shawn. You're special to us."

Clark handed him a $200 gift certificate to One Stop Comics. I don't know the going rate, but that sounds like a lot of comic books. An ice cream cake awaited him at the back of the room, adorned with many candles — which he snuffed in one extended blow, to great applause and a chorus of "Happy Birthday" and "He's a Jolly Good Fellow."

And jolly he was.

BJ was relieved. "I've been a nervous wreck all day," she said. For her efforts, she received many thanks from Facebook friends. "I don't know a third of these people," she said looking at her phone.

"You put something out and the world comes," she marveled.

The art students of Haj Mohammed, owner of Magical Minds Studio in Oak Park, made a giant card for Shawn that read, "Thank you for always greeting everyone with a smile (It is contagious). We hope this day is as awesome as you are."

Connie Brown, Brown Cow's proprietor, said she moved to Forest Park 18 years ago, about the time Shawn started at The Lake. "He's the only one who's taken our tickets," she said — which means she only goes to the movies on Friday and Sunday, the two nights Shawn works, hence his nickname: "Mr. Weekend."

Community engagement is nothing new for the Browns, who have already had a significant impact in Forest Park.

Appropriately, her business is located in an old movie theater, which opened on Madison Street in 1912. Brown and her husband opened their ice cream emporium in the early 2000s.

Doug Clayton, technically Shawn's boss, is also an admirer. "He's an icon," Clayton said, "a familiar face. They see him first and he's warm and welcoming. He always rides his bike to work — rain, sleet, snow, it doesn't matter. He's a good guy."

Shawn was suspicious when Clayton, now a manager at The Lake but originally hired the same week as Shawn 18 years ago, said he wanted to treat him to Brown Cow — on a Monday night.

"I figured he was going to prank me," Shawn said, "or a mercy date set-up."

This is a story about a community where a local movie-house ticket-taker can turn into a celebrity. It's about a local theater company that hires a kid from Maywood with lots of personality and doesn't try to stifle it. It's about a local movie theater that people from numerous communities patronize, inspiring enough good memories to bring them out on a rainy Monday night to honor someone they only interact with for a few seconds — but over and over again, spanning an entire childhood. And it's about living in a digital era where a do-gooder's impulse is magnified and capable of summoning over 100 people to give one good guy from Maywood a birthday he'll never forget.

Ultimately, though, it's a story about being, and staying, connected.

"Shawn told us he felt the love of the community," BJ said.

One boundary-less, big-hearted community.

Shawn was reportedly laid off during the pandemic when the Lake Theatre was closed. He has since moved on to other jobs, much to the disappointment of local movie fans.

Glen Toppen: That guy across the street (2001, 2010)

Glenn Toppen died in 2010 at the age of 62 of congestive heart failure. A lifer, he attended Lincoln School here in Oak Park, graduating from OPRF High School in 1966.

After working as a Realtor in Oak Park until 1983, he moved into marketing with Neighborhood Housing Services (NHS) of Chicago, a nonprofit organization providing low-interest loans to low-income families. He also served on various boards focusing on homelessness and financial education for those in poverty. He volunteered regularly with PADS and Habitat for Humanity.

The kind of guy we're blessed with in abundance. The guy across the street or down the block. The guy who shares his tools or his knowledge. The guy you get to know at block parties.

But Glenn Toppen did something at one of those block parties that made him stand out.

Block parties developed in Oak Park as part of the integration effort — a tool used to create close-knit neighborhoods as the neighbors became more diverse. A lot of people will tell you block parties saved Oak Park.

In May of 2001, one of them saved Cynthia Sanders' life.

Cynthia turned 22 on July 20, 2001. A week earlier, she received her best birthday present ever — a new lease on life — thanks to a donated kidney.

A year before, she was a student at DePaul University pursuing a degree in marketing when her life plans jumped the rails. Renal failure, the long-delayed ripple of a severe case of strep throat suffered as a child, forced her into a regular routine of dialysis, which effectively put her dreams on hold.

Her name was placed on a five-year waiting list for a kidney transplant, making her dependent on the kindness of some stranger who died. Not everyone on the list gets the organ they need, and when it comes to kidneys, the chances of a transplant succeeding are much greater if the kidney comes from a living donor.

Which is what Cynthia's mom, Christel, was telling a couple of neighbors at the annual block party. That's one of the benefits of block parties. It gives residents a chance to catch up with one another's lives.

One of the neighbors listening to Christel Sanders that day was Diane Toppen, who lives across the street. Later, she told her husband Glenn about Cynthia's predicament, and mentioned her blood type: O+.

"That's my blood type," Glenn said, which started him thinking. But blood type is only one of the factors that need to match. Remarkably, all the factors aligned and on July 13, the transfer took place.

So far so good, said Christel, who wants as many people as possible to know about Glenn Toppen's magnificent gift.

"He is a hero. He is an angel. He is everything," she said.

Glenn is also doing well, she reported. He started a new job this fall and she's seen him working on his house.

The transplant certainly changed Cynthia's life. She attended Triton College, taking science classes. Not coincidentally, she has a part-time job at the Kidney Foundation.

Walter and Christel Sanders came to this country from Germany. They moved to Oak Park 27 years ago. Cynthia is their only child. If they had picked a town where people didn't have block parties, didn't get to know one another, the story might have turned out differently.

"For us it's still unbelievable," said Christel. "I'd like to do something for him."

Well, she and the other neighbors on the 1100 block of Home did do something for Glenn Toppen. They threw another block party, in September, and made Glenn the guest of honor, awarding him a trophy, Christel says, "to thank him for his gracious gift."

Not surprisingly, when Glenn died, his body was donated to science. Maybe his other kidney saved someone else's life.

Cynthia Sanders, who now has a master's in public administration and is special assistant to the head of UIC's Department of Pharmacology — and who still lives across the street — delivered one of the readings at his funeral.

"No one realizes how important a kidney is until it stops working," Christel said.

And no one realizes how important a heart is until it opens.

Donnell White: From sidelines to spotlight (2008)

Haven't talked to Donnell White in a while, not since he became a teacher in 2002 — the year our sons graduated from OPRF High School.

That's how it works around here when you raise a family. From kindergarten through high school, you're on "the parent circuit." You get to know a lot of people because you share school events and sports sidelines for 13 years, and then the kids go their separate ways, to college and beyond, and you hardly see them or their parents again, except maybe at Farmers Market or the Lake Theatre or at church or in a local restaurant.

Once upon a time, and a very good time it was, Donnell White and I shared the sidelines. Our sons played T-ball together in the early 1990s, Keith and Dylan, both promising athletes, and we hovered and worried and lived and died by their prowess. Keith was a quiet, shy kid, but a silky-smooth athlete who glided around the bases. My son was all intensity and unrealized promise.

Donnell was going through what I was going through, suffering the way I was suffering, so we had something in common. He was easy to talk to, with a sense of humor, not full of himself.

He really cared about his kids and was a natural instructor.

That was confirmed this past week when officials showed up in his classroom at Michele Clark Middle School in Chicago's Austin neighborhood to surprise him and his math students with the news that he'd been named a winner of the Golden Apple Award for excellence in teaching. A prestigious honor, only 10 awards are given each year.

It's a sweet story — a West Side kid who goes to work for the post office, moves to Oak Park to raise his family, upwardly mobile but never forgets his roots, and eventually goes back the West Side to teach, where he reaches kids, the kind of kids he once was.

Donnell was growing up when Oak Park was opening up. African Americans began moving here, and moving up the socio-economic ladder, like the other ethnic groups that started out in the city and moved out as they moved up — Irish Americans, Italian Americans, Polish Americans, African Americans. Many stayed here and put down roots.

Oak Park is perfectly suited and situated to serve a critical function in this country's evolution — increasing the Black middle class. There's so much potential here, so much possible synergy between Oak Park and the West Side.

Donnell White is a perfect example of how it works when it works.

He's also a good example of the involved, caring, responsible Black father of whom, too many claim, there aren't enough. Well, you'll find plenty in Oak Park.

Our town doesn't deserve the credit. This village simply created the kind of environment where it happens naturally when all the other factors working against Black males in this society are removed (or significantly reduced).

In the introduction to the 1994 Answer Book, our annual community guide, which features a photo of Donnell instructing his daughter, Kelly, on how to hit, I wrote that the photo "represents one of the strengths of our villages — caring parents who take the time to help their kids keep their eyes on the ball."

Fourteen years later, Donnell White is still doing it.

But he's not on the sidelines anymore.

He's in the spotlight.

Kevin Reid: Building community, one hug at a time (2011)

If you saw a 48-year-old man standing on the corner of a busy intersection giving out hugs, what would you do?

Kevin Reid decided to find out. He positioned himself by the Horse Show Fountain at the entrance to Scoville Park, Oak Park Avenue and Lake Street, virtual center of town, for two hours on a recent Sunday morning and held up a hand-written sign: "Free Hugs."

It was May 1, May Day, so anything goes, right? I was sitting in the window of the coffee shop across the street, looking out at the park, and there he was.

Some people are huggers, some aren't. But hugging total strangers on a Sunday morning at a busy corner is outside the comfort zone for most of us. And that was Reid's goal:

Widening our comfort zone.

Frankly, he looked like he needed a hug, so I went over and gave him one. I was the first. Things snowballed from there.

"It was really an incredible experience," Reid said the following day when I called, noting that drivers were honking and waving. Cars stopped at the light, and people got out for a quick squeeze. A boy, roughly middle-school age, kept circling on his bike, then finally came up to get hugged. A teenage boy walked by, very shy, but eventually accepted one.

"As he was walking away," Reid recalls, "he turned around and called out, 'You really made my day!'"

Not everyone was sold on the idea, of course. One guy passed and muttered, "Creepy." A middle-age woman asked, "Don't you get enough hugs from people you know?"

The answer came from the numerous hug-ees who testified, in effect, "You can never get enough hugs."

They have a point. Hugging a stranger is liberating. Permission to hug changes things. So many of our one-on-one interactions these days are digital, virtual, a step removed. Hugging a stranger is immediate, real.

Reid said it was simple. Just hold the sign, smile, "and let people come to you."

An Australian started the "free hugs" movement in 2004, Reid said. He calls himself Juan Mann (as in, "One Man"). You can find out more at FreeHugsCampaign.org.

Reid is a musician and guitar teacher who recently returned to the area following a four-year hiatus in L.A., Sedona and Nashville. He describes Nashville as "a culture of friendliness. Nobody walks by without smiling or speaking."

He got tired of walking past Oak Parkers without being acknowledged.

"It's a cool thing, breaking down barriers, creating a sense of community."

Two of his young students, Lia Flannery and Isabel Smith, came along and got into the spirit of the moment. Lia's mom, Millie, shot video, which is undoubtedly on social media by now.

"Kids were running and leaping into our arms," Reid said. "We gave out over 100 hugs, including several group hugs."

A lot of people asked why he was doing this.

"It's very much an extension of my world view," said the man who recorded "We Are One, A World Anthem" with his brothers and a host of other musicians.

"I like to be a positive influence in my environment. This creates a bunch of ripples. People left with huge smiles." One young man from India put it best when he told Reid, "It's kind of a love-thy-neighbor thing."

A community is built one interaction at a time. People meet at church, school events, youth sports sidelines, the Lake Theatre, Farmers Market, block parties. Giving free hugs is just one of many community-building techniques. My good friend, Bob Sullivan, has made it his life's mission to strike up conversations with strangers on the CTA or while standing in line at the post office.

But never underestimate the importance of touch. Too many people in our community have lived for years without being touched at all.

Think about that.

Reid insists he's not an extrovert. "This was definitely out of my comfort zone," he said. "I was not eager to get out there." But several more of his students have expressed interest, so he's planning to get out there again in June. A Day in Our Village might be a good opportunity.

As they were leaving the park on May 1, a guy up on the hill by the war memorial came running after them, calling, "Hey, hey, can I get a hug?"

"Let's connect," Reid says. "Let's rival Nashville. Instead of just ignoring one another, let Oak Park be known as one of the friendliest communities.

"Let's not just be known for our architecture."

Jim Malone and other micro-heroes (2009)

Most Sundays I take my mother to church because she doesn't drive anymore, and it's a good way to spend time with her. Because I'm not a fan of the overly-hierarchical Catholic institution, I'm not sure I would attend church without her.

And then I run into Jim Malone.

Jim has been an usher at 9 o'clock Sunday Mass for roughly 50 years. He's in his 80s, but his sense of humor keeps him young. Or his inner youth makes him funny. Not sure how that works.

Jim doesn't just greet people. He hands out personally decorated church bulletins ("The Dome," named after Ascension Church's most distinctive architectural feature). The Dome is outlined, underlined and overlined in colored markers (pastel pink and purple during the Easter season, red and royal blue last Sunday for Pentecost) and decorated with stickers (smiley faces, hearts, suns and flowers). It takes him about six hours to decorate 50, and this labor of love represents his artistic contribution to the proceedings — a little flourish to make Sunday special.

You could say it's his ministry.

Inside, he adds his own text: On May 10, he wrote, "Today is Mother's Day, a day to honor mothers living, and remembering those deceased. Those who have mothers living, I envy you. You can see her once in a while and give her a call. I sure wish I could call mine."

When he sees my mom, he leans in and says, "We're old enough to kiss each other. We don't care if people talk. Let 'em talk. A little scandal's a good thing once in a while." Then he plants one on her cheek.

When I ask, "How are you, Jim?" he replies, "I'm going to make it." He doesn't say what "it" is or where, but at the very least he's going to make it through Sunday Mass. Jim Malone's face is never far from a smile.

He's a ray of sunshine. He makes your day. Pick your cliché. I have all kinds of issues with the Church, but if you judge an institution by the people who attend it, you'd have to conclude the Catholic Church — or at least this particular parish — is a pretty good place to be.

I have a theory about "micro-heroism," the capacity for a small measure of greatness in every man and woman. Most of us are too modest to consider ourselves heroes, but maybe we can acknowledge one another's micro-heroism. That's easier for modest, middle-class, Midwestern, aw-shucksters. We all know a few micro-heroes, maybe more than a few. I would nominate all parents of kids with disabilities. They would likely reject the hero label, but maybe they'll accept micro-hero.

A choral director at Bradley University in Peoria named John Jost, for instance, has led a group of music professionals down to Haiti every summer for the past 30 years to teach at a summer music institute outside Port au Prince.

If you read *Mountains Beyond Mountains*, a terrific book by Tracy Kidder about Dr. Paul Farmer's heroic public health efforts there, you know Haiti is the poorest country in the western hemisphere (the title comes from the Haitian proverb, "Beyond mountains, there are mountains," which tells you all you need to know about the challenges they face). The country is politically unstable, so some summers it's just too dangerous to take others along, but Jost never stays home. He also suffers from Parkinson's disease. I know about him because an Oak Park friend has accompanied him twice.

Maybe "micro" isn't adequate to describe his heroism, but he definitely makes the list. So does Marty Swisher, my friend.

On a recent morning, walking on the 300 block of Wesley, I passed an elderly man sprucing up the garden in his front yard. I'm guessing he's lived there for decades and all this time has worked diligently to keep his house and grounds looking good, a testament to perseverance and endurance. That, to me, is a form of micro-heroism, and Oak Park is better for his efforts. I admire anyone who upholds a personal standard of quality to the very end of life.

"I'll make it," Jim Malone likes to say. Maybe he means to the very end of life — maybe he means to whatever comes next.

Jim gets my nomination as a micro-hero.

Here's to the micro-heroes all around us.

The Robinets and the power of showing up (2022)

I believe that any people's story is every people's story and that from stories, we can all learn something to enrich our lives.

Harriette Gillem Robinet
If You Please, President Lincoln

When you enter the Main Branch of the Oak Park Public Library, just inside the library proper, the quote above is the first thing encountered, inlaid on the floor before you. Good words. But then Harriette and McLouis Robinet have a good word for everyone.

That word is "home."

The Robinet family was recently honored by the Historical Society of Oak Park-River Forest with their annual Heart of Our Villages Award. The Historical Society could not have chosen better — or closer to the heart of who we are as a community.

Before the Robinets made Oak Park home in 1965, they were part of the Great Migration of African Americans, away from the awful repression of the Jim Crow South to the highly segregated and too often unwelcoming North. Harriette grew up in the Washington D.C. area. Her maternal grandfather was a slave on Robert E. Lee's plantation. Mac grew up in a small town in Louisiana, a place where Black families couldn't paint their houses or buy a new car because it would make them look too uppity and put the family in danger. "I grew up," Mac says, "where making trouble was the last thing you wanted to do."

Harriette and Mac both had a scientific bent and met at Xavier University in Louisiana where they were teaching. They fell in love. Harriette got a job in microbiology in Washington. Mac landed a teaching position at the University of Illinois Chicago. Later he worked at Argonne National Laboratory for almost 40 years. They married in 1960 and started a family in 1964 with the birth of Stephen. Their next four children were adopted, Philip, Rita, Jonathan and Marsha. Then Linda was born, completing their family. The growing family needed more room than the tiny, zero-bedroom UIC staff apartment where they lived in the early '60s.

Friends suggested they look for a home in Oak Park. But Oak Park didn't want them. At any rate the local real estate industry didn't want them here. Happily, that has since changed for people of color but at that time, house-hunting in Oak Park was practically impossible.

To expose the industry's racially motivated practices, the Robinets joined Project Open Community, which documented the unequal treatment accorded to Black couples and White couples. When a Black couple asked about homes to purchase, nothing was available. When a White couple followed and asked about the same properties, they suddenly became available. Blacks in 1965 needed a White "straw buyer" to purchase a home for them, an unavoidable subterfuge to work around unjust restrictions.

For Mac and Harriette, that straw buyer turned out to be Don and Joyce Beisswenger who had purchased a house on the 200 block of South Elmwood, then offered to sell it to the Robinets. There was one catch, Don said. "The police say you have to move in mid-day, mid-week, and you have to move in this week."

That's how the Robinet family joined the first wave of Oak Park integrators in the 1960s, along with the Registers (Don and the late Dolores) and the Reids (the late Henry and the late Sherlynn).

The Robinets, fortunately, were received with mostly open arms ... and free appliances. Mac says they moved in with little more than a card table and a frying pan. Then one neighbor gave them a washing machine. Another donated a refrigerator. They were even gifted with a piano.

The neighbor next door, however, couldn't handle the change. "Why would you want to live someplace where you're not welcome? Now I have to leave," she told them. She was gone in a month.

Harriette chronicled those early years in an article for Redbook Magazine, part of their "Young Mothers" series. It was published in February 1968 and titled, "I'm a Mother, Not a Pioneer."

Turns out Harriette was both, as became evident a couple of months later when Martin Luther King Jr. was assassinated in Memphis.

Home alone with three kids, the only Black family on the block, one of the first and few in the village, her husband working 7 miles away at UIC, Harriette couldn't help feeling vulnerable as the world around her was about to burst into flames. One can only imagine what it was like for newly arrived Black families.

Here's what it was like: Harriette wanted to do something instead of just feeling helpless, so she brought out their star-spangled banner and put it up outside. A few hours later when she glanced out the window, almost every house on the block was flying the flag.

Harriette used the Redbook article as a springboard. She had left the workplace to stay home with the kids, and she obviously had a knack for writing and research. Between 1976 and 2003, she penned (longhand)

12 books, the first two featuring a child with disabilities as the central character. *Ride the Red Cycle* was inspired by their son Jonathan who has cerebral palsy and now lives in the Ryan Farrelly Home in Oak Park. According to their daughter Linda, Mac was the inspiration for the father in that book, who built a number of quad-cycles and hand-cycles for his son to get about. The other books were works of historical fiction, beginning with *Children of the Fire* about the Great Chicago Fire of 1871.

Harriette's books won numerous awards, but the greater honor is that her daughter still uses them to teach her students at Beye Elementary School. For the last 17 of her 21 years in District 97, Linda has taught fourth grade — in the same classroom where she was a fourth-grader.

Of her books, Harriette says (on her website), "Unless we know our history, we have no perspective on life today. How can we know where we're going, or appreciate where we are today, if we don't know where we're coming from?"

Of her parents' example, Linda says: "They have the most powerful love I have ever witnessed. Their love has always been strongly rooted in the Roman Catholic faith. Being Christian, for them, is not about being perfect but about being vulnerable, weak, and human and being called to help, to be in service to each other first; to care for others and the planet — and that all people are God's children.

"I became a teacher because of my parents. They were constantly teaching all of my brothers and sisters. They are still teaching me to this day about grace and humility and enduring love and, always, the pursuit of learning."

Grace and humility for sure. Mac likes to downplay the significance of their contributions to this village.

"We didn't really do anything," he says. "We just showed up."

Well, an old adage holds that 80% of success in life is just showing up, but when you're African American from the Jim Crow South, just showing up is an act of courage.

As for the other 20%, we're really glad the Robinets showed up in time to join the local Citizens Committee for Human Rights and help lead Open Housing marches, starting in 1966 — from Stevenson Park, west on Lake Street to Downtown Oak Park, to picket and protest against those unethical real estate practices. We're glad they lobbied the village board to pass the groundbreaking Fair Housing Ordinance in May of 1968. We're glad they raised six kids here, who have contributed in their own ways — two teachers, a social worker, an eBay entrepreneur, and an IT specialist at Gottlieb Hospital and longtime employee at the local library. We're glad Harriette and Mac walked to daily Mass at St. Edmund, hand in hand, and were such active parishioners there. We're glad they got involved in the Oak Park Climate Action Network and also started the Repair Café nine years ago so we can keep our old appliances functioning, everything from breast pumps to chainsaws, and keep them out of landfills.

And we're glad they made some trouble — the good kind, as John Lewis would say. When they moved in, their cranky neighbor next door said, "Oak Park will never be the same."

We're particularly glad about that.

When they first moved in, Mac said, "Oak Park seemed like another planet" compared to every other place they had been. He also said, "This was the first place where we felt part of the community."

Fifty-four years after the Robinets helped make Oak Park a better place, they're still here in the same house. And they're still here partly because of that April day in 1968 when their neighbors demonstrated in clear terms that Oak Parkers were capable of rising above their biases and fears to become one people.

From many flags, one people.

Or as Harriette put it when she first told me about that day, "That's when I knew I was home."

Those who know their history tend to love their town. And if you love your town, you naturally try to make it a better place.

Thanks, Harriette and Mac, for coming home.

Isabel Wilkerson: 'We are the same people' (2010)

I was leaving the South to fling myself into the unknown. ... I was taking a part of the South to transplant in alien soil, to see if it could grow differently, if it could drink of new and cool rains, bend in strange winds, respond to the warmth of other suns and, perhaps, to bloom.

Richard Wright
Black Boy

Talking with Isabel Wilkerson last week about the Black diaspora put a lot in perspective. Wilkerson, a Pulitzer Prize-winning N.Y. Times bureau chief, who was an Oak Park resident in 1994 when she won the Pulitzer, is the author of *The Warmth of Other Suns – The Epic Story of America's Great Migration*.

Sometime during World War I, fed up with the Jim Crow laws that made them all-but-slaves in the wake of Reconstruction, African Americans started leaving the South, turning their backs on intolerable injustice and violence, heading North, figuring anything had to be better than their previous lives. The migration lasted over 50 years and relocated some six million, who ended up in northern, eastern and western cities. Today, more African Americans live in Chicago than in the entire state of Mississippi.

Most African Americans in this area are only a few generations removed from Alabama, Mississippi, Louisiana and other Southern states. They came here looking for better lives.

They didn't always find them.

But the story of injustice isn't what I've been thinking about. I'm more interested in how the Great Migration transformed this country and forced it to come to terms with race and the legacy of slavery.

If slavery is this nation's original sin, then racism has punished both sides of that divide. Overcoming racism remains this country's unfinished business. Until World War I, 90 percent of African Americans were stuck in the South, treated like inmates. The subsequent migration was essentially our nation's largest prison break. Black Americans could no longer be ignored.

In the process, three streams of migrants (East, Midwest and West) set off a cultural big bang that transformed our sports, music, literature, theater and much more. It's a remarkable story, a very American story. In some ways it is our most inspiring story. In other ways, it's our least inspiring story. The experiences of Black migrants were similar to those of immigrants from other countries who were moving into our cities at the same time. But in critical ways it was very different.

That migratory convergence, predictably, caused social tension and explains the virulent racism many of us grew up witnessing in Chicago and other U.S. cities. The newcomers competed with one another for a foothold on the ladder to social acceptance and economic viability. Their "otherness" made them fear one another, and African Americans had the distinct additional disadvantage of irrational prejudice against their skin color.

But as Wilkerson noted when I talked to her, "They were the same people." They had much more in common than anyone realized at the time. They were all migrants or descended from migrants. They knew what it was like to pull up stakes and start over in a strange land. It's a tragedy, Wilkerson says, that social and economic barriers prevented them from getting to know one another.

Some of this has changed, thanks to the Herculean efforts of the Black minority and a too-slowly-evolving White majority. And Oak Park has played a small, but positive role in that story.

We are the same people.

I have my own Great Migration story to tell. Beatrice Little, the woman who takes care of my mother these days, and who has been connected to our family for a half-century, moved to Chicago from Panola, Ala., as a very young girl in 1929 (Panola comes from the Choctaw word for "cotton"). Bea has no memories of her mother, Aurelia, who died giving birth when Bea was very young. What's more, the family had no photographic record, so Bea has never seen a picture of her own mother,

her only clue being that older family members tell her that Bea's daughter, Sharon, closely resembles her.

Bea's story gave me a glimpse of what some Americans went through to find a better life.

It taught me that we are the same people.

African Americans are justly proud of their progress toward equality. All Americans should be proud of their efforts. It is the most American story ever told. All of us, no matter how removed, have the migrant experience in our family lore. Some families have been established in this country much longer than others, but all have at least some acquaintance with what it took to get here and what it took to move up the ladder.

We are the same people. We live under the same sun. Someday, we will all bloom in the warmth of mutual acceptance.

We share the same goal: understanding one another better, being better neighbors, becoming one people.

And blossoming under the same sun.

> *At the front of the signing line was this very diminutive, grandmotherly figure. Her arms were filled with books that she had bought; she wanted me to sign them. But her eyes were red. She said, "I just cannot talk about this book. If I start talking about the book, I'm going to cry for sure because this book is my story. I'm an immigrant from Greece, and this is my story." She said she was going to have the rest of her family read it. That was, within my heart, my hope — that [this book] could cross boundaries.*
> **Isabel Wilkerson**
> *Interview for the NPR show, "On Being"*

Anan Abu-Taleb: Safe space vs. brave space (2019)

Should Oak Park be a "safe space"? Or should it be a "brave space"? After several weeks of tempestuous conflict at village board meetings, one can't resist channeling L.A. street philosopher Rodney King, who famously asked, "Can't we all just get along?"

Well, we can't "just" get along. That seems too complicated at this point in Homo Sapiens' evolution. At the moment we need to learn to get along when we passionately disagree.

But is that even possible? Mayor Anan Abu-Taleb, who assumed the role of peacemaker at last week's village board meeting, seems to think so, and since he grew up in Palestine, in Gaza, he may be uniquely qualified to practice peacemaking. To that end, he read part of a poem about creating "brave space," a place for uncomfortably honest dialogue.

Mayor Anan runs marathons. He writes essays of surprising depth and substance in the Viewpoints section of the local newspaper. He even quotes poetry. Anan will surprise you.

And he must be a fan of *On Being*, the spiritually uplifting interview show on National Public Radio. The poem Anan referenced about "brave space" was featured during Krista Tippett's interview with Rev. Jennifer Bailey and Lennon Flowers, who co-founded The People's Supper, bringing together those who passionately disagree in order to share a meal — over 1,500 meals, in fact, since 2017.

Not all of us are ready to be "bridge people," they pointed out, but we can still ask people to "be brave." Their mantra at The People's Supper is: "Relationships move at the speed of trust, and social change moves at the speed of relationships."

"There has been no movement for justice or equity in this country that didn't start with relationship," Bailey said.

Interaction, in other words, is the yeast. Why did same-sex marriage become the law of the land seemingly overnight? The foundation was laid painstakingly over long years by dedicated advocates, but the final push was provided by relationships between ordinary people — queer and straight — who got to know one another, which widened their respective comfort zones and elevated their caring level. They became family and friends, no longer "other." Familiarity, it turns out, breeds not contempt, but trust.

However, relationship-building isn't easy, especially now. In response to Rev. Martin Luther King's question, "Where do we go from here, chaos or community?" Bailey wrote, "I choose community. The community I long for will not be found in shallow platitudes promoting reconciliation. It will require the courage of everyday heroes to dig deep and find within themselves the wherewithal to lean into one another and repair the breach of relationships that the [2016] election has exposed."

What is required is stepping into the fray and making ourselves vulnerable. Too often, said Flowers, "I think we've outsourced the role of being human to experts and professionals."

Bailey added, "If we are going to grow into being fully human, to grow into the promise of America, to be in process, then we have to be teachable. We have to be willing to engage one another and be wrong sometimes."

In other words, accepting "An Invitation to Brave Space," the poem by Micky ScottBey Jones that Anan quoted from, which begins every one of The People's Suppers:

Together we will create brave space
Because there is no such thing as a 'safe space.'
We exist in the real world
We all carry scars and we have all caused wounds.
In this space
We seek to turn down the volume of the outside world,
We amplify voices that fight to be heard elsewhere,
We call each other to more truth and love.

We have the right to start somewhere and continue to grow.
We have the responsibility to examine what we think we know.
We will not be perfect.
This space will not be perfect.
It will not always be what we wish it to be
But it will be our brave space together,
And we will work on it, side by side.

Ironically, the recent village board squabble that raised questions about whether trustees could get along was about revising the Village Diversity Statement, which long ago aspired to make Oak Park a safe space for all residents. Those who pushed for the revision wanted to take the next step and make Oak Park (and all village institutions) a brave space, working hard together to achieve "equity," breaking down "systems of oppression." A couple of trustees thought the language went too far. Civility broke down.

I wouldn't have phrased it the way Trustee Susan Buchanan did, but I agree with her that males — white males in particular — would benefit from talking less and listening a whole lot more.

The poem above says there's no such thing as safe space, not if it rules out truth-telling, so we must create a brave space where we call each other both to more truth *and* more love. That space will always be imperfect because we are imperfect.

Any village board is susceptible to toxic reactivity. There will always be personality conflicts. This board, I think, would benefit from 15 minutes of mindfulness meditation before every meeting.

Mindfulness makes us more aware of our tendency to react impulsively, reflexively, and excessively. It adds an important tool to our kit: an inner voice that allows us to step back and say — without berating ourselves — "There I go again. What's that all about?" It's amazing how much it helps.

Board members might want to try it.

And once in a while, one-on-one, they might also want to share a meal.

8

Settings

Our town has a strong sense of place. Our lives "take place" in specific settings. We aspire to transcend our "houses" by imbuing them with the qualities that turn them into "homes." We don't live in a "housetown" but a hometown, which implies a sense of authentic community.

Nostalgia comes from the Greek word, *nostos*, which means a feeling for home, especially when one is distant from it. We miss our homes and hometowns long after we leave. If the feeling is strong enough, we diagnose it as being "homesick."

Scoville Park

Many of us, during the lockdown phase of the pandemic, rediscovered the nourishing dimensions that define "home." We were reminded that home is more than mere walls, more than a base of operations, more than a headquarters. "Home" is why the term "homemade" is so much more appealing than the restaurant term "housemade," which lands with a thud.

Oak Park's largest "mansion" is known as "Pleasant Home." In addition to being located at the intersection of Pleasant Street and Home Avenue, the words "Pleasant Home" are engraved above the great hearth in the entry foyer. Hearth itself is a lovely term, containing the word "heart." The fire that burns in the hearth, also burns within us.

If you describe the town you live in as your "hometown," it likely means you have in mind a list of places, favorite settings.

Here are a few of mine:

Lake Theatre: The reel thing (2002, 2021)

The best line of the evening during the 2021 Oscars ceremony came from the winner of the Best Documentary Feature film, *My Octopus Teacher*, who said, "A man forming a relationship with an octopus sort of makes you wonder what else might be possible."

What indeed.

Good films make us wonder, which is just one of the reasons to celebrate the recent Lake Theatre reopening following the pandemic. As it was following the September 11 attacks, the pandemic has been a time for going back to basics and "The Lake" is the real thing — or the reel thing anyway, a purveyor of virtual reality.

Movies are a major cog in our mythmaking machinery, and the myth of America is what we hold onto, especially in difficult times. Movie houses, therefore, have long played a central role in presenting the central stories we tell ourselves, which create the consensual myths of who we are — or, more importantly, who we would like to be, which is why our national myth is forever evolving.

All of which was the focus of a film showing at The Lake back in 2002 titled, *The Majestic*, about a movie house and the central role it plays in reawakening a small town to who they are. But first the film explores how, as a nation, we frequently fall short of who we want to be — which was particularly pertinent during McCarthyism, but also in every era since.

One of the majestic moments in the film comes when the theater's rehabbed marquee first lights up the night. With the magic of movie editing, it is impressive, but The Lake's marquee is a match, its large deep-blue L-A-K-E successively blinking downward to the red, white and blue neon wraparound, accented by white bulbs "chasing" sequentially — a marvelous sight, especially in the deep freeze of January and February, when darkness grips the northern hemisphere and threatens to obliterate even the memory of other seasons.

Except on the screens inside. One of the payoffs of movie-going is instant transport, not only to exotic locales but other seasons — where the sun shines and the grass grows green. For a couple of hours, we experience, at least vicariously, other climes, a momentary, but necessary, liberation from the heavy anchor of reality. It is also a chance to live other lives briefly, risk everything, survive implausible thrill rides of absurd vulnerability, solve perplexing mysteries with breathtaking brilliance, putting ourselves vicariously in the kind of jeopardy to which we would never dream of exposing ourselves in actual life.

Films push our emotional hot buttons and stroke our pleasure centers, unleashing adrenaline rushes, making us laugh, then landing us back on terra firma without a perceptible jostle. More pronounced escapes from reality can be hazardous to one's health. Two or three hours in the fertile imaginary dark, with or without popcorn, is just about right for most of us.

Then we gush back onto the streets of reality beneath that brilliant marquee to say good night or head to a local eatery for post-film discussion.

Going to The Lake is a communal experience — an antidote to the isolation imposed by living in a severe climate, a place to briefly reconnect in the lobby or the aisle or the concession stand. And in the fierce freeze of winter, when Oscar-nominated hopefuls find their way to neighborhood screens, the pickings are plentiful.

About four decades back, like just about every other old movie house that hoped to survive, The Lake subdivided (and expanded its footprint) to create seven theaters instead of one.

In theater #2, though, you can still get a sense of the size of the original movie "palace" this was once upon a time. It takes 529 tickets to sell out theater #2, which comprises the main aisle and screen of the original theater, a vast expanse, or so it seemed to us as kids, where we could happily lose ourselves in an afternoon's double feature, accompanied by cartoons, sweetened by concessionary candy.

The walls closed in as changing economic pressures forced The Lake to fragment its singular viewing space, but if you walk far enough forward, the newer walls end and the front of the old theater broadens out to its original dimensions, with bare-breasted nymphs in alcoves flanking the screen. This is where I usually sit, surrounded by teens and pre-teens who like to make their movie-going an energized, communal experience.

It's enjoyable being swept along by another generation's hormonal surges. Sometimes adults forget to have fun at the movies, but the kids up front at The Lake haven't. And once in a while, even the adults sitting next to them during one of these two-hour roller-coaster rides manage to un-stifle their innate sense of delight.

Getting out of our confined houses is healthy. The lighted marquee battling the darkness is hopeful. Films provide a temporary release from the ordinary. It all works and shouldn't be underestimated.

A movie house can do a lot for a town, as it does in *The Majestic*. The Lake has done that and more for Oak Park. It anchored the economic renaissance following the downtown downturns of the '70s and '80s and continues to entertain and bring people together. It's a place where kids and parents can be in one place at the same time — not always, but often, watching the same film — and have a good time. No small feat.

Not many towns have a Lake Theatre. When you're looking for something real to hold onto, go back to basics.

This one is positively majestic.

Maze Library: A storybook place to dream (2021)

Maze Branch Library was a place you could go to be launched into the wider world, which is where the future lived. Growing up in Oak Park, there was church and school, the ballfields, candy stores, and Maze Branch. All the institutions a kid needed in south Oak Park in the late 1950s, early '60s.

Maze was where I went to dream.

Biographies covered the south wall of the kids' section, raised several steps up from the main floor, split-level style. John Tunis sports novels were found against the west wall. Maze is where I opened my first World Book Encyclopedia. School assignments forced my first encounters with the Readers Guide to Periodical Literature, that era's cumbersome equivalent of Google, a treasure trove of sources, not all of them located at Maze, leading me occasionally to the modernity of the Main Library on the north side of town.

But I rarely wanted more than Maze had to offer. The three-block walk from my house was odyssey enough back then.

Coziness and low-tech charm still define the space. Maze is exquisitely quaint. Anyone trying to lure a friend to live in Oak Park should take them to the Lake Theatre, Austin Gardens, Scoville Park, the Conservatory, Unity Temple, the Wright Home & Studio, and the Hemingway Birth Home to whet their appetite and pique their interest. Save Maze for last — to seal the deal.

As we get older and come to terms with the transitory nature of life's impermanence, it is comforting to have at least one shrine to innocence preserved. For some, that's Wrigley Field, home of the Cubs, on the North Side of Chicago. For me it's the triple draw of Maze Branch: an incubator of dreams, a cocoon, and a launching pad. Not a labyrinth but a name: Adele Maze, one of those fortunate few who had a single, all-consuming focus in life — a branch librarian for decades, ruling it with a firm but benevolent hand until she expired, right there at the front desk, in 1957.

The building, designed by Prairie-School architect E.E. Roberts and his son, E.C. Roberts, opened in 1936 (same year as the Lake Theatre), and expanded during renovation a couple of decades back at a cost of more than $2 million, is still a gem.

Patronized by loyalists who come as much for the ambiance as the resources, this is a place designed to make kids fall in love with books — and with libraries. It's cozy enough to feel at home but connected enough to provide a portal to the world writ large. A kid only had to read to sample that world and begin to imagine his place in it. Books are better at that than television or movies. A book — and the world it creates — can absorb you for days, even weeks, at a time.

Childhood is largely about biding time, impatiently waiting to grow up. One of my imaginings involved writing something someday that might enchant a child as much as I was charmed, sitting in a comfortable nook, reading and dreaming out the window as seasons slowly passed.

There I found Hugh Lofting's Dr. Dolittle books, *Onion John*, and the Bounty Trilogy (*Mutiny on the Bounty, Men Against the Sea* and *Pitcairn's Island*) to name just a portion of the bounty that awaited.

Mostly I read biographies of famous men and women — actors, athletes, soldiers, explorers, doctors, presidents, writers and teachers. I hauled them home and camped all summer long on our screened-in front porch, exploring life scenarios that invariably led to the fulfillment of dreams. I figured no matter what life might throw at me, I could handle it as long as I had books to read. I would never be bored. And boredom was what I dreaded most.

Maze is probably the finest example of "gingerbread architecture." It's like entering a scene from *Snow White and the Seven Dwarfs*, a fairyland of woodwork. Overhead, the ornate triangular cross-beams overflow half-way down the walls, ending in carved scrolls, with flowers in relief. The original built-in white oak bookshelves still line the walls. The adult reading area features a gas fireplace flanked by two leather reading chairs and a mantle, above which hangs a painting by Carl Krafft, a highly regarded artist from Oak Park, who was the founding president of the Oak Park Art League.

Outside, the red-brick-and-limestone façade is warmly lit at night, with a welcoming entry, now reached by a cleverly-disguised ramp, making it accessible to wheelchairs — without having to remove the original cement front steps.

Something about the quiet industry inside a library soothes minds and souls. It's like a church without solemnity, combined with a living room minus the bustle and noise.

In autumn, window panes are adorned with many-colored construction-paper cut-out leaves, followed by snowflakes in winter, then Valentine's Day hearts, St. Patrick's Day shamrocks, and pastel eggs or flowers for Easter, signaling the longed-for arrival of spring.

At once insular and connected, this library provides an oasis, a comfort zone, brimming with stirring tales of adventure that take us beyond our comfort zones. I wish I had a list of every book I ever checked out of Maze and read during my youth. Better yet, I wish I could touch the books themselves, smell the pages, and flip through the memories.

From time to time, we probably all feel a longing to revisit childhood. Whenever I need to be reminded of how magical life felt back then, I'm drawn back to Maze. It wasn't "magic" at all, of course — just the small miracle of being alive and the enchantment of dreaming how life might unfold. Life is "storybook" by nature. This place merely confirms it. When I walk the streets of this town and look at the lovely old homes, street after street, I often feel as if I've stumbled upon the setting of a classic children's novel where something wonderful and memorable is about to take place.

Stenciled on one of the walls here is a testament by Adele Maze from 1954:

"All of these activities were fun for both youngsters and grown-ups and were instrumental in making all realize that the library was a friendly, happy place as well as a storehouse of books and knowledge."

Maze is a touchstone. I keep coming back because, occasionally, I need to revisit dreams once dreamed and the happy spaces that blessed my childhood.

Outside on the south patio is a brick with my name on it, inscribed: "A childhood well spent here."

Austin Gardens and the art of doing nothing (2001, 2003)

Austin Gardens is many things, but that might not be your first impression.

The forested section happens to be a fragile preserve filled with wildflowers, lovingly planted some 50 years ago by three community activists, Elizabeth Walsh, Charlotte Peterson, and Julia Spears who carted jugs of water in baby carriages to keep the flowers nourished early on.

Recently, I joined a "wildflower tour" in that portion of the park, led by Charlie Ruedebusch (pronounced "read a bush," an apt name for a gardening guru). A volunteer group calling themselves Save Austin Gardens for Everyone (SAGE) did considerable work last fall, clearing saplings, brush and invasive plants that crowded out the wildflowers each spring. This year revealed the results.

Wildflowers are small and unless you pay attention and know what you're looking for, you'll miss the trout lilies, Dutchman's breeches, toothwort, spring beauty, false Solomon's seal, and mayapples. Even the more visible Virginia bluebells, wild phlox and wild geraniums seem to escape the attention of dog walkers who let their beloved canines poop and pee, then tear up stands of red trillium with the useless, instinctive scraping of their back paws.

The forested section may look like a conveniently overgrown public toilet to some, but it means much more to the rest of us.

The park was originally the homestead of Henry Warren Austin Sr., closer of the village's last saloon, well before Prohibition, and developer of the Austin neighborhood in Chicago. His son, Henry Jr., founded Oak Park Trust and Savings, our first bank. He and his wife, Edna, bequeathed what is now Austin Gardens to the park district in 1947 with an endowment — and the stipulation that the property be kept in its natural state. The Historical Society of Oak Park-River Forest recently put a marker with an old photo of the Austin home near the newly constructed environmental center in the park.

Entering Austin Gardens last week, I passed a couple of kids, sister and brother probably, maybe 10 and 7 years old respectively. The boy carried a kite. The girl asked two questions, without pausing:

"Why are you wearing those pants? Why do people come to this park to do nothing?"

I admire well-phrased questions. She didn't ask, "How come people don't do anything in this park?" That would imply inertly wasting time.

If most visitors are like me, they come to Austin Gardens specifically to "do nothing," likely because most of us are doing too much before we get here and after we leave. Austin Gardens is a park where the pastoral supersedes, but doesn't preclude, the recreational. There just aren't enough places to do nothing these days, which is why many of us end up here.

"Nothing," of course, is a relative and misleading term. A lot goes on in Austin Gardens while people are "doing nothing." Some are busily putting their day, or even their lives, in order or perspective. Some are remembering: people, places and things that won't let them go. Some feed the squirrels, pigeons and sparrows. Some feed themselves, eating lunch in a serene setting that soothes the soul even as they satisfy the stomach. For some, the afternoon's productivity (their required "something") hinges largely on doing this nothing.

Some come here to self-medicate — smoking cigarettes to maintain their addiction's requisite nicotine level or sipping coffee to ward off a mid-afternoon biorhythmic droop.

Teens hang out after school — a fidgety, frequently hyperactive form of doing nothing. Lovers touch, talk and nestle.

Squirrels chase each other up and down trees or search for long-lost food stashes.

In the center of the open meadow, a bare patch indicates where poor (but skilled) players strut and fret their hours upon the stage erected here every summer for Festival Theatre's outdoor performances.

Plaques set in the ground by various trees mark the place where loved ones spend precious moments doing nothing other than paying respects to a departed relative or friend.

Bodies sprawl on blankets soaking up sunshine. Dogs lead their leashed owners around the paved circle path or chase the aforementioned squirrels when allowed to.

I watch for migrating birds, take inventory of the wildflowers, think (and sometimes fret) about all the people I love and carry on imaginary dialogues with some of them, scribble (in a back-pocket notebook) surfaced thoughts I want to remember, run through the ongoing "to do" list and the more extensive "wish I could do" list, imagine more interesting lives I could lead and take note of how interesting my current life is, look forward to whatever I have to look forward to and remember things worth remembering, and at times try very hard not to think about any of this but simply let my senses pull me out of my head and into the world to pay attention to how much more than nothing is happening every moment.

I don't know if that answer would satisfy the impatient little girl's question.

And I haven't a clue why her little brother was wearing those pants.

The next day, I spotted their kite dangling in the branches of a tree in the center of the park, so now they know at least one of the reasons people do nothing in Austin Gardens.

Festival Theatre: A star-crossed night (1993)

In some parks you play ball or barbecue or run your dog or play hacky-sack. And then there are parks like Austin Gardens, where, for six weeks each summer, Shakespeare's players strut and fret their hours upon a temporary stage. Think of it as Stratford on Forest Avenue.

Normally, this is a place of repose — part woods, part meadow, circled by a paved walkway. There's also a gravel path through the wildflowers (in spring) among the trees on the north end. This is about the last place you'd expect to find impassioned soliloquies, desperate swordfights, and star-crossed lovers, but that's what's in store on this muggy evening for the 100 or so spectators who have staked their turf with lawn chairs and blankets, forming an expansive semi-circle that fans out from the wooden stage.

Four tall erector-set towers roughly define the parameters of the seating area. A cluster of lights perch on top, aimed at the stage below. A cat's cradle of wires connects the towers, and ground cables wind like snakes through the grass.

This summer's scheduled Shakespeare al fresco is *Romeo and Juliet*, courtesy of Festival Theatre, which has been doing this for decades, but that fearful consequence hangs in the stars, which won't be visible until dusk thickens into night. At the moment, wine and cheese and full-blown picnics are currently the centerpiece. Salami, crackers, and fluted glasses form lovely still-life arrangements atop wicker baskets, short-legged tables, and plastic coolers.

Petunias in window boxes decorate the skeletal stage, which will shortly serve as a villa, garden and Verona's town square. "I'll bet I know where Juliet stands," observes one sharp-eyed patron d'art, pointing to a balconesque construct to the right. A man wearing a blue Festival Theatre T-shirt interrupts consumption and conversation, *in medias res*, to beseech the audience to fill out their surveys, necessary for future grants.

They need to know how often we attend the theater, how much money we make, and how much time and how many dollars we've spent in Oak Park as part of our "theater experience." Don't forget babysitting charges. You can see where all this is heading, but given the vagaries of funding, one can forgive an arts organization its sense of urgency about hustling for support.

As dusk deepens, the thicket of trees behind the stage seems to close ranks and creep forward like Dunsinane Wood (but that's another story). Renaissance music flows from the speakers on either side of the stage. The heavy, drapery-like costumes can't be comfortable on a summery night like this.

In the front row, two young gentlemen (not from Verona) invite two young ladies to combine blankets with them. Perhaps more stars will cross this night than the doomed duo onstage.

Lights bathe the set, accented by sporadic fireflies and heat lightning to the north, providing an appropriate backdrop to the charged atmosphere of ancient grudge and bloody mutiny that is the business of our next three hours.

The actors speak their speeches trippingly from the tongue (yet another story). Along the western edge of the park, the lit windows of a condo building remain open, perhaps to catch this midsummer night's livestream.

Overhead, an occasional phantom aircraft crosses the Big Dipper like some evil omen. As if on cue, the fortunes of our two heroes take a decided turn for the worse. There never was a tale of more woe, but the crowd doesn't seem bummed. Their applause, though swallowed by the surrounding ambiance of the great suburban outdoors, is appreciative, in spite of the decidedly unhappy ending.

Nonetheless, it's a civilized way to spend an evening in the village's most civilized park, and the audience lingers afterward on the green meadow, nailing down vacation plans, finishing drinks, packing coolers, and, finally, strolling off into the star-crossed night.

Barrie Park: Rising from the coal tar (2005)

I didn't get to Barrie Park's unveiling until dusk. The sunset's afterglow painted the cirrus red high overhead, which seemed appropriate. It's been a long time since this park and neighborhood had a rosy outlook.

The first and most dramatic impression of the new, and much cleaner, Barrie Park is openness. Lombard Avenue in particular, which for so long enjoyed the protective canopy of one of Oak Park's surviving elm groves, has lost its cover. A few trees have been replanted on the parkway, but not enough, and the growing will take years.

One of the first people I ran into was David Gullo, who served as the park board's pit bull during the often-contentious negotiations with the utilities, which, to no one's surprise, were reluctant to put their heart and soul (and coffers) into this massive remediation.

Gullo isn't ready to let go yet. He noted that one of the easily-overlooked provisions of the agreement is that the utilities are required to replace a certain number of "tree-girth" inches around the park. Gullo figures ComEd and Nicor owe us at least 30 more trees.

He is one of the many who deserve some sort of municipal medal for their role in this 7-year saga. Another is Marion Biagi, who lives next to the park and became a fierce advocate for the park neighbors. She proudly led me on a tour of her side and back yards, which were remediated and re-landscaped (and the house foundation reinforced) by the utilities because she wouldn't take no for an answer. She deserves every bit of what she got and then some, but she wasn't satisfied because not all of her neighbors had received their due. Many had to move away from their homes for six years.

Marion and Bill Biagi moved here in 1963 — just a few years after Barrie became a park — and raised a large family. They're empty-nesters now and thinking of moving sooner than later. I wonder if the family they sell to, or any subsequent owner, will know what a gift they have been bequeathed.

Such are the civic heroes who get too little recognition.

This, however, is not a day for accounting but for celebration. The openness of this village green feels right, feels clean. Kids are rolling happily down the steep sledding hill. A group of older youth are tossing a football around. On the temporary stage, a musician is trying to whip up some late-in-the-day enthusiasm from an obviously mellow crowd. A screen has been hung for the showing of the movie *Hook*, based, of course, on the most famous work of fiction by James Barrie, whom the park is named after.

Parents supervise youngsters in the new tot lot on the southeast corner, where once upon a time, back in the early 1990s, my son faced his first pitched baseball in an organized game. As I recall, he singled.

My memories go back even further, to the mid-1960s when I played flag football with full equipment in a park district league under lights that no longer exist. Bud Corry, the longtime park staffer and later board member, told me when they were digging the standards for those lights, they often hit coal tar.

In the late 1950s, Oak Park created Barrie Park out of an environmental hell-hole, the site of a former gasification plant where they actually melted coal in order to harvest the gas. The by-product left behind was coal tar. Now the land is clean — remediated down some 20-25 feet, replacing 350,000 tons of soil at a cost of $100 million.

It only took a half-century to complete Barrie Park. The slough of despond is now coal tar-free.

This civic triumph will soon be all but forgotten, and most of the kids who play here will never know what transpired, but the rest of us should never take it for granted. An ecological cesspool was, if not sanitized, then at least neutralized. A God-forsaken parcel of industrial filth has been transformed into a lovely village green.

It took a long time — too long — but looking around at the kids enjoying this recreational rectangle, it now seems worth the ordeal.

Kids bid summer adieu (2001)

Last Friday was a beaut — low humidity, low 80s, not a cloud in the sky, unless you count a few feathery cirrus set like fish fossils in the ocean of blue above. In other words, a beautiful day for a ballgame. The Cubs were playing the Cards at Wrigley Field, but that's organized ball. Organized ball barely has a pulse anymore.

The real thing was taking place at Euclid Park on the south end of Oak Park near Roosevelt Road. It's one of my favorite parks, surrounded by side streets and single-family homes, fitting neatly into the neighborhood, utterly unpretentious. It features a playground, a few neglected tennis courts, tree-topped berms and a ballfield.

I stopped by to eat lunch on a bench and discovered a lob ball game in progress. Norman Rockwellian poetry in motion. There's nothing like the easy grace of preteens playing lob ball. I didn't think kids did this anymore, the way we used to in the early '60s before heading to the penny candy store to trade baseball cards and pop our Bazooka bubblegum.

On this day it was four-on-four, pitcher's hands out and right field foul. With the exception of the aluminum bat glinting in the sun and the metallic ping when it made contact, little has changed. An old mitt served as third base, a ruck sack for second. First base looked like a shoe. After every third out, players tossed their mitts to the other team as they jogged in to bat.

One player was shirtless. Another played in an open Hawaiian shirt. A third wore a long, untucked Bulls jersey with Michael Jordan's 23 draped across his butt.

Rules were constantly clarified. "No leadoffs," barked the left-fielder to the runner on second. "You have to go back," advised the defense when a runner tried to take an extra base.

Sometimes the rulings were humbly accepted, sometimes contested. It took a while before an "I quit" was finally uttered — an empty threat and time-honored negotiating ploy. Indeed, the players displayed remarkable equanimity in the face of frustrations that might put a more serious athlete over the edge.

"E-7!" taunted a batter as he rounded the bases. "I didn't touch it," the left-fielder insisted as he headed over the berm that served as a buffer for the tennis courts.

"18-15, our lead," the runner gloated crossing the plate, which appeared to be more theoretical than real.

Like Carl Hubbell of yore mowing down Murderers' Row, the pitcher heaved the ball lazily and with a pronounced arc in the direction of the batter, who either whiffed or belted it. When he whiffed, the outfielders feigned wind resistance and testified they could "feel it all the way out here."

Long drives led to desperate measures. "I had to pull it out of the fence," claimed the left-fielder, "ground-rule double." Sometimes it worked; sometimes the plea was ignored.

"Who made last out?" they asked, jogging in for their next at-bats. The other team can't remember either. Doesn't matter. This is casual, nonchalant, the way baseball was meant to be played — not the overtaught, overwrought, overgrown neurotics who spit compulsively in their overstocked major league dugouts.

Here, no one seemed overly invested, except the pudgy kid in the purple cap in center. He thinks the line drive over second base landed on the right field side and argued the point as he searched in vain for the ball on the far side of a berm.

"Hey, dumbass, the ball's right there," called one of his teammates. Peer review in the heat of a game can be brutal.

Baseball can't compete with girls, of course, and the game quickly dissolved when they showed up. Second base reverted to a (very dusty) backpack. The group split off in two directions. At 2 p.m., there was still plenty of afternoon left.

Suddenly the park was empty — except for the dragonflies, a sunbather, kids on the playground swings, sunshine on the scorched grass and crabapple trees, and the bread scent wafting past from nearby Turano Bakery.

In other words, nothing left but the rest of summer.

9

Tourism

What draws visitors to Oak Park? One day as I passed the Hemingway Museum, two women were leaving. As they came down the steps, one said to the other, "Hemingway in Oak Park … who knew?" She discovered the connection while noodling around online, and now here were bona fide tourists. Maybe they spent dollars to boost the local economy. Maybe not. The public transit station is just two blocks south. It's a straight shot out from the city and a straight shot back to the Loop.

But if they didn't know about Hemingway in Oak Park, how many other prospective visitors are equally in the dark? The Hemingway Museum was worth a visit, but the Hemingway Foundation closed it because they didn't have the resources to do everything they wanted to. The Hemingway Birth Home is now doubling as the Hemingway Birth Home Museum and much that was in the museum can now be found on the third floor of the public library. But closing the original venue is a loss.

Frank Lloyd Wright, meanwhile, brings many more people to Oak Park — and neighboring River Forest — to see the largest concentration of Wright-designed homes anywhere in the world.

Wright and Hemingway are the Big Two, but what about Tarzan's creator, Edgar Rice Burroughs?

Tarzan and Oak Park? Who knew?

Oak Park may not be Tarzana, California, but Burroughs' first Tarzan book, and many others, were written while he was raising his young family here, before making his move to California.

Ray Kroc, of McDonald's fame, grew up here. You'd think McDonald's might want to play that up. Not yet. And the inventor of the Twinkie, James DeWar (pronounced Do-er), lived here, though TwinkieFest might be a tougher sell.

Oak Park has many claims to fame, including Percy Julian, whose chemistry patents transformed life for ordinary Americans by making the breakthrough that made steroids inexpensive and mass-produce-able. An African American, he was named Chicagoan of the Year in 1950. Can you imagine what it took for one of the most segregated cities in America to do such a thing in 1950?

Someday, maybe Oak Park will take full advantage of all our connections to celebrity. In the meantime, the following is a non-exhaustive list (listing all would be exhausting) of those who found fame and had an Oak Park connection (born here, grew up here, or lived here for a time) from the book *Legendary Locals of Oak Park*, by local legend Doug Deuchler:

- Grace Wilbur Trout, champion of women's right to vote, president of the Illinois Equal Suffrage Association.
- Charles MacArthur, journalist, co-writer (with Ben Hecht) of *The Front Page*, screenwriter (also with Hecht), married to actor Helen Hayes, brother of John D. MacArthur (of genius grant fame).
- Anne Baxter, Oscar-winning actress, granddaughter of Frank Lloyd Wright, actively supported restoration of the Wright Home & Studio in Oak Park.
- Adolph "Bud" Herseth, principal trumpet of the Chicago Symphony Orchestra for 53 years.
- Charles Simic, Pulitzer Prize-winning poet (1990), U.S. Poet Laureate (2007-08).

- Carol Warner Shields, Pulitzer Prize-winning novelist for *The Stone Diaries* (1993).

Tavi Gevinson

- Tavi Gevinson, fashion wunderkind, author of the *Style Rookie* fashion blog, actor.
- Rev. Andrew Greeley, priest, sociologist, and prolific author.
- Walter Burley Griffin, architect who worked with Frank Lloyd Wright in Oak Park, designed (with co-worker and wife Marion Mahoney) the capital of Australia, Canberra.
- Authors Jane Hamilton, Alex Kotlowitz, and Elizabeth Berg.
- Chris Ware, graphic novelist, illustrator, known for his New Yorker covers, often depicting scenes in Oak Park.

Chris Ware

- Steve James, filmmaker, known for his documentary *Hoop Dreams*

and his 2018 docu-series about Oak Park and River Forest High School, *America to Me*.
- Marjorie Judith Vincent, Miss America, 1991, her family emigrating from Haiti to Oak Park when she was 3.
- Peter Sagal, host of National Public Radio's popular quiz show, *Wait, Wait, Don't Tell Me*.
- Sam Giancana, Mafia godfather who ordered many mob executions and was eventually murdered in his Oak Park home in 1975.
- Joe Tinker, Hall of Fame shortstop, part of the famous double-play combination "Tinker to Evers to Chance," lived here while playing for the 1907-1908 World Series champion Cubs.
- David Axelrod, campaign strategist and advisor to presidents Bill Clinton and Barack Obama, media commentator.
- Dorothy Thompson, earned the moniker "first lady of American journalism" in the 1920s, first journalist expelled from Germany by the Nazis, married to novelist Sinclair Lewis.

Johnny Lattner

- Johnny Lattner, played for Fenwick High School, won the 1953 Heisman Trophy and the 1952 and '53 Maxwell Trophy, playing for Notre Dame.
- George Trafton, played for OPRF High School, center for the Chicago Bears in the 1920s and early '30s. Member of the NFL Hall of Fame.
- Donald Duncan, the "Yo-Yo King," mass-produced the spinning wonder for the Duncan Toy Company and turned them into a national fad. Also credited with inventing the parking meter.

- Richard Sears, "mail-order king," turned Sears, Roebuck & Co. and the Sears catalog into national institutions.
- Frank Ross and Frank Skiff, brothers-in-law and business partners, founded the Jewel Tea Company grocery store chain in 1899.

Betty White

- Actors and show business personalities Betty White (Golden Girls), Bob Newhart (*The Bob Newhart Show*), Cecily Strong (*Saturday Night Live*), Mary Elizabeth Mastrantonio (*The Color of Money*), Tom Lennon (*A Night at the Museum*), Johnny Galecki (*The Big Bang Theory*), Dan Castellaneta (voice of Homer Simpson), Kathy Griffin (comedian), John Mahoney (*Frasier*), Ludacris (rapper, actor, original name Christopher Bridges), John Sturges (director, *The Magnificent Seven*), John Avildsen (director, *Rocky*), Judy Tenuta (comedian), Rich Koz (Svengoolie).

John Mahoney

- Joseph Kerwin, Fenwick grad, medical doctor, astronaut.

- Carl Rogers, clinical psychologist/ therapist, author of *On Becoming a Person*.

The following is a highly abbreviated tour of our town's hall of cultural giants:

A museum, 200 years in the telling (2017)

It's a storytelling place, says Frank Lipo, during a 2½-hour tour of the new Oak Park River Forest Museum. This restored-and-refashioned former firehouse at Lombard and Lake is well worth a visit. Even the floor is both old and new. They flipped all the floorboards, sanded and finished them, and it looks brand new — yet also old. The idea came from one of the contractors, who emigrated from Poland. That's what they do with older buildings back home, he said. Brilliant ... and makes a good story.

Lipo has hundreds of stories. He's a fast talker but not a word is wasted. He could have gone on for another 2½ hours and I would have gladly listened. Listening to him, someone said, is like "drinking from a fire hose." Imagine trying to take notes. So many stories to tell. So many.

Jan Dressel, who's been part of the Historical Society story for decades, also has a tale to tell — about Elsie Jacobsen's coffeepot. The late, great Elsie, chair of the village's Beautification Committee and so much more (there's a story), followed the motto, "Live well, do good work, and inspire others." She inspired Jan to join the society's board early on and at her first meeting, the board had a lengthy discussion on whether buying a Mr. Coffee machine was a good use of their limited funds.

"This group needs to expand its vision," Dressel thought. Fifty years later, after raising nearly a million dollars from private sources (there's a story), she sweeps her arm, encompassing the entire up-to-date facility, which celebrates its grand opening this Saturday and says, "Some coffeepot."

Lipo has a tale to tell about the beautifully carved, heavy oak table in the center of the second floor, which once anchored the social hall during Grand Army of the Republic meetings (another story). Next to the table is an intricately carved wooden arm chair. The origins of each, for a time, were a mystery.

Virginia (Ginie) Cassin, the first female village clerk, salvaged the table from the old village hall, at Euclid and Lake, and had it transported to the new village hall, now located at Madison and Lombard, in the mid-1970s, where it was used as a decoration until the village donated it to the new History Museum. The chair came to the museum separately, but no one knew its back story — until Lipo came across an old photo of early Oak Park settler James Scoville at the Scoville Institute, which served as the village's public library for the better part of a century, until it was torn down in 1962 (definitely a story).

In the photo, Scoville is standing between this very same oak table and chair. The table's journey from Institute to Old Village Hall to New Village Hall to this museum in the former Cicero Township firehouse building is a pretty good story about Oak Park's commitment to continuity.

The Historical Society's journey to this Saturday's grand opening, meanwhile, reflects that same perseverance. In 1968, Elsie Jacobsen and her committee received a letter from the state of Illinois, as did most other municipalities, asking them to join the statewide celebration of Illinois' sesquicentennial and suggesting they form a local history organization, leading up to the nation's bicentennial in 1976.

Ever game for a challenge, Elsie, who had just come into possession of a treasure trove of photographic negatives left behind by turn-of-the century camera buff Philander Barclay (a sad but important story), established the Historical Society of Oak Park-River Forest (in spite of the aforementioned coffeepot crisis).

In 1970, the society was granted an upstairs room in Pleasant Home and assembled a small museum that enabled the Park District of Oak Park, which owned the home — sold by the family following the death, in 1939, of Herbert Mills, aka the "Slot Machine King" (now there's a story) — to levy a museum tax that funded the home's ongoing restoration.

The Historical Society kept expanding into other rooms until 1992, when they negotiated a deal to take over the second and third floors entirely. They also hired Lipo as their first full-time executive director, who, although he didn't know it at the time, would make this his life's work (another story).

The deal came with a proviso: The society had to begin searching for a permanent home (with no firm deadline set). Numerous promising options were explored: the original Drechsler Funeral Home building on Lake Street, the former Curtis Casket Co. (later a dance studio) next to Pieritz Bros. on South Boulevard near Ridgeland, one of the Wright "Bootleg" houses (there's a story) on Chicago Avenue, a former garage on the first block of Chicago Avenue near Austin Boulevard, the former River Forest Women's Club, the Marshall Field building at Lake and Harlem, and the former swimming pool in the basement of the 19th Century Club on Forest Avenue. The economic downturn in 2008-2009 dampened fundraising prospects, and the historical society realized they couldn't generate enough donations to both purchase a building and renovate it. So they set their sights on village-owned buildings and hoped for a deal.

Their first walk-through at the former Cicero firehouse, with Village Manager Carl Swenson and Village President Barbara Furlong, took place in 2001. In 2007, after construction of the new Public Works building, Frank called new Village Manager Tom Barwin and asked if the old firehouse might be available. Good timing. Barwin was receptive to a low-cost lease but said the society would have to raise all the funds for restoration.

They successfully pursued landmark status to protect the structure from demolition, then began fundraising in earnest. The deal with the village, formalized in 2009, called for a 30-year lease, with an option to renew for another 20 years, at the grand sum of a dollar a year (and since occupancy, a monthly payment has been earmarked for later capital improvements. The village also granted a four-year window to raise the funds, with a four-year extension, both of which were needed.

The society landed two state grants, totaling $200,000, which the state was slow in appropriating, but those grants encouraged private donors to contribute. The turning point came, Lipo said, when Jeanette Fields (there's a story) donated $100,000 because she had used the society's research room at Pleasant Home (for the architecture columns she wrote for the local paper) and wanted them to upgrade that part of the operation.

Lipo is happy with the location of the new museum. Since they started developing plans to renovate the building, he noted, Pete's Fresh Market, the School of Rock, the rehabbed Ridgeland Common complex, and the Gymnastics Center have all opened along Lake Street between Ridgeland and Austin. He sees the new museum as part of the general upswing.

Lake Street itself is integral to Oak Park history — an old Indian trail that eventually became the route of the first railroad west from Chicago, contributing to Oak Park's population boom (stories upon stories). And the firehouse is the oldest village-owned building in continuous use since Oak Park incorporated, following its secession from Cicero Township in 1902 (stories galore).

Lipo describes it as "a 21st-century museum in a 19th-century firehouse."

"The grand opening is on Philander Barclay's birthday," he added, "so that's good karma."

At long last they have their storytelling place — also a time machine, a back-to-the-future DeLorean, a portal to our past with links to our future (past being prologue).

Visitors to the new museum will find the original Georgia pine beadboard walls and ceilings, LED lighting in old-fashioned replica fixtures,

A/C provided by three geothermal wells, and, of course, the Tarzan exhibit.

You don't know about Oak Park's connection to Tarzan? Now there's a story.

"Good things take time," said Lipo, looking around. "This was worth waiting for."

Spoken like a true historian.

Percy Julian: Standing in no one's shadow (1999)

Centennial celebrations are reserved for individuals who make extraordinary contributions to their society. And just as we have been graced by two blue moons this year, Oak Park enjoys the unusual distinction of celebrating not one, but two significant centennials this year. Everyone knows about that guy named Ernie. Not as many are familiar with Percy.

That would be Percy Lavon Julian, Oak Park resident for the last 25 years of his life and one of the most accomplished scientists of the 20th century — a feat made even more remarkable by the fact that he was African American.

"Percy Julian is at least as famous in scientific circles as Hemingway is in literary circles," says Norb Teclaw, co-chair with former village trustee William Fillmore of the Julian Centennial Banquet on April 11, 1999, the 100th anniversary of Julian's birth in Montgomery, Alabama.

Julian served as director of research at Glidden Paint Co. on Chicago's West Side, 1936-54, a time period during which many of his discoveries occurred. Julian used soy beans to produce — cheaply and in mass quantities — artificial hormones, or "sterols," which had applications that led to birth control pills, cortisone, and fire extinguishing foam used on U.S. Navy vessels during World War II, which saved many lives.

In the 1950s, he started his own lab, Julian Laboratories in Franklin Park (and Mexico City). Using the root of a wild Mexican yam, he produced a treatment for glaucoma, developed a process for converting cholesterol to a substance used in the manufacture of vitamin D, and created a soy protein extract used in coating and sizing paper. He worked long hours and was eventually credited with well over 100 patents.

Julian, in fact, was already a celebrated scientist when he purchased a home in Oak Park in 1950, the year he was voted "Chicago's Man of the Year" in a Sun-Times poll, but his reception here was rocky. Even before the family could move into the house at 515 N. East Ave., it was firebombed, and it happened again after they moved in. But Julian had overcome bigger obstacles in his life and he became one of the village's most admired citizens.

Three schools have been named after him (including Percy Julian Middle School in Oak Park) and along with numerous honorary doctorates, buildings on several university campuses bear his name as well. The U.S. Postal Service honored him with a stamp in 1993.

In other words, a figure worthy of a centennial celebration.

Fortunately, a number of local citizens came together last September and formed a Centennial Committee to plan the event. The committee includes Sherlynn Reid, director of Community Relations for the village of Oak Park; Daphne Lecesne, OPRF faculty member and Julian parent; Bette Wilson, director of District 97's Multicultural Education Department; Bill McGlynn, director of Julian's CAST theater/arts program; OPRF High School Dean Kevin Washington; journalist Stan West; Jeri Stenson, head of Maywood's West Town Cultural Museum; Frank Lipo, director of the Historical Society of Oak Park-River Forest; Peggy Sinko, Historical Society volunteer; and Jennings Miller, who will videotape the proceedings.

The celebration begins with an open house at the school named for him, which includes displays of a number of student projects, poetry readings, a performance by the jazz band, dance demonstrations, readings by winners of the essay contest the high school sponsored, awards in the inventor and art logo competitions, and the hanging of a mural.

The Julian CAST program produced an original work titled, "Different Voices," based on Julian's writings and speeches, and the students will perform it again this Sunday in the OPRF High School library.

Stan West will moderate a discussion on Julian's life with a panel that includes such distinguished guests as Dr. Arnold Hirsch, chief chemist at Julian Laboratories; Dr. William Clusin, an Oak Park native who teaches at the Stanford University School of Medicine (who was inspired by Julian to get involved in the civil rights struggle); and Julian's daughter, Faith, who still lives in the family home in Oak Park.

The dinner at the Mar-Lac Banquet Hall features music by jazz saxophonist Audley L. Reid (Julian worked his way through college playing saxophone and piano), and testimonials from Hirsh, Congressman Danny Davis, and journalist Vernon Jarrett. Money raised will fund a bronze bust of Dr. Julian (now located outside the Oak Park Public Library).

The Historical Society exhibit of Julian memorabilia will be on display in the showcases at the high school this week (and later at the society's Oak Park River Forest Museum), and Teclaw says a display used in an earlier Julian commemoration in Anaheim, California, sponsored by the American Chemical Society, will be on hand for viewing at the banquet.

Teclaw taught physics at the high school for 30 years and remembers when Julian visited the school in the 1970s. Teclaw got involved in organizing the banquet this past January after reading a letter in the paper from Julian's personal secretary. The co-chairs commissioned 14 banners, which the village volunteered to hang throughout the village.

"I feel like I'm walking around in his skin," Teclaw says, describing Julian as much more than an accomplished scientist. "He had a focus and he walked that road. He was a taskmaster. He knew the potential of people and he brought that out." Julian Laboratories, he noted, was like "a working U.N."

Julian was always driven by his scientific work, he said, "but he also had a strong community bent" and will be remembered for his humanitarian efforts as well.

"He needs to become a hero for our youth," Teclaw added. "That's what I'm hoping for.

"He doesn't stand in anybody's shadow."

Burroughs' birthday Dum-Dum (2010)

September 1 would have been Edgar Rice Burroughs' 135th birthday — if he had lived forever. Thanks to the Burroughs Bibliophiles, he may do just that — at least in memory.

Name doesn't ring a bell? Burroughs was one of the bestselling authors of the 20th century. Still nothing? How about John Carter, Mars adventurer? OK, here's the giveaway: Me Tarzan, You Jane.

To celebrate his birthday, the Bibliophiles, some 75 strong — counting special guests — descended on the village where Burroughs once lived and wrote, to celebrate one of the most fertile imaginations in pulp fiction history.

ERB aficionados call these get-togethers "Dum-Dums," a reference to the "great gatherings of apes" from the Tarzan books (the English version is called ECOF, Edgar Rice Burroughs Chain of Friendship). The last Oak Park Dum-Dum was held in 2005 at First Baptist Church of Oak Park.

This year's gathering was distinctive because, for the first time, it featured Burroughs' descendants as well as Jim Sullos, president of Edgar Rice Burroughs Inc., the firm in Tarzana, California, that handles marketing, licensing and copyright oversight.

Sullos has been president for only two years, but he was the firm's outside accountant for the previous four decades. Burroughs, he says, incorporated in 1923, the first American author to do so. For someone who had no particular success in business prior to 1911, when he started writing, ERB turned into a very canny businessman. He bought 550 acres from the publisher of the L.A. Times and named his ranch Tarzana after his most famous fictional character. For the next three decades, he subdivided and sold off parcels, adding to the family fortune. ERB Inc. is still family owned.

Linda Burroughs, widow of Burroughs' grandson, Danton (named for another of his granddad's fictional characters), also made the trip, along with her two 20-something daughters, Dejah (named for the

Princess of Mars) and Llana Jane (named for a Mars character, plus you know who).

Danton Burroughs was an avid collector of ERB memorabilia, as well as jukeboxes and slot machines, making their home a veritable, and very cramped, museum. A 2008 fire destroyed a portion of the collection, and Danton never really recovered from the shock. He died of a heart attack several months later.

"He was like a big kid," says Sue-On Hillman, who, with her husband Bill, maintains ERBzine.com, a website that has pretty much everything you ever wanted to know about "the master of fantasy adventure."

"Danton was tireless," says Linda Burroughs. "He made it exciting," and that excitement rubbed off on his daughters. Dejah has read all of the books in which her namesake character is featured. The girls say people ask about their unusual names, but most aren't familiar with the Mars series.

That may change, however, since Disney is planning to release its first John Carter film in June 2012, coinciding with the 100th anniversary of his first published work, *Under the Moons of Mars*, which appeared in installments in All-Story Magazine in 1912. Sullos says a commemorative stamp may be issued, and there's talk of a star on Hollywood Boulevard to honor the occasion.

Approximately 50 Tarzan films have graced the silver screen, including *Tarzan of the Apes*, starring the very first celluloid Tarzan, Elmo Lincoln, in 1918. That film is of particular interest to Al Bohl and his daughter Allison, who are in the process of making a documentary about it called, "Tarzan: Lord of the Louisiana Jungle." Bohl says it was the first Hollywood film made on location, and they chose Morgan City, Louisiana, because they needed a jungle setting, a large cast of African Americans and a train station. Morgan City had all three.

Bohl became interested because he'd heard that the monkeys used in the film were all left behind when the crew went back to Hollywood. Local lore has it that the monkeys' descendants still live in the bayous.

So do they?

"You'll have to see our film to find out," Bohl says.

This visit included a tour of the four houses ERB lived in while residing in Oak Park and a reception at Pleasant Home, where the Historical Society of Oak Park-River Forest gave a tour of its Burroughs exhibit, most of which is on more-or-less permanent loan from Jerry Spannraft, who likely has the world's largest ERB collection. Spannraft, 72, an Oak Park and River Forest High School grad (class of 1955) has been a Bibliophile since 1963 and a Burroughs fan since 1951 when he went to a friend's house after an afternoon playing ball. His friend let him borrow a Tarzan book and he fell in love. Spannraft hosted a Dum-Dum dinner at his house on Thursday night.

The local chapter of the Bibliophiles, the Muckers (named for yet another series in ERB's prodigious output), hosted the four-day gathering, anchored at the Best Western in Hillside. Special guests included George McWhorter, curator of the Edgar Rice Burroughs Memorial Collection, located at Ekstrom Library, University of Louisville; Stephen Korshak, author of a book about J. Allen St. John, who painted the covers of a number of Burroughs' books; and Tom Floyd, illustrator of graphic novels.

The Muckers were formerly known as the "Normal Beans," a reference to Burroughs' early pen name. Sullos says ERB chose Normal Bean because his stories were so outlandish and fantastic, he feared his publisher would think he was crazy. But his editor thought it was a typo and changed it to Norman Bean, so Burroughs gave up and went with his own moniker.

It was hot and humid on the front porch at Pleasant Home the Friday before last as Bibliophiles and guests noshed on sandwiches at tables covered with leopard-skin tablecloths.

Tarzan, and Burroughs, would have felt right at home.

Stephanie Clemens' dance with Doris Humphrey (2008)

How her hometown, a century later, became aware of Doris Humphrey is a story in itself. A contemporary of Frank Lloyd Wright and Ernest Hemingway — and, like Hemingway, an Oak Park native — she was as influential in modern dance as they were in architecture and literature.

Born on Oct. 17, 1895, Humphrey opened a dance school in Oak Park at the age of 18 to help support her struggling family. In 1917, the year Hemingway graduated from OPRF High School, Humphrey attended a summer program in Los Angeles offered by modern dance pioneers Ruth St. Denis and Ted Shawn, who recruited her for their Denishawn dance company.

In 1928, she formed her own dance troupe, the Humphrey-Weidman Group (with dance partner Charles Weidman), which lasted until 1944. She later directed the Jose Limon Dance Company, then taught in the Juilliard School Dance Department. In the process, she became renowned as much for her groundbreaking choreography as her dancing.

Doris Humphrey died on Dec. 29, 1958, the year before Wright and two years before Hemingway.

But it's doubtful Oak Park would know much about, arguably, its most famous native daughter, if not for Stephanie Clemens, who was growing up in California at the time Humphrey was coming to the end of her long, distinguished career.

Clemens' father was a portrait painter who had some pretty famous clients — Frank Sinatra, Ava Gardner, John and Ethel Barrymore, Katharine Hepburn and Audrey Hepburn. He taught at the Otis Art Institute in Los Angeles.

As it happens, dancers from the Denishawn dance troupe also served as models at the institute. She was frequently taken to the Ruth St. Denis Studio, which was located near her father's studio in Hollywood. They would watch her, and Stephanie in turn got an education in dance by watching their rehearsals.

"I grew up with dancers in nautch skirts, saris and ankle bells," she recalls.

And Clemens happened to be a student at the Juilliard School in '58 when Humphrey died. She remembers attending a memorial performance of Humphrey's masterpiece, *Passacaglia and Fugue*, danced in her honor.

First performed in 1938, Humphrey was conscious of the rise of fascism in Europe when she explained to a critic, "I picked Bach because he has these very qualities of variety held in unity, of grandeur of the human spirit, of grace for fallen man. ... Now is the time for me to tell of the nobility the human spirit is capable of, stress the grace that is in us, give the young dancers a chance to move harmoniously with each other." The music, she said, seems to ask the question, "How can a man be saved and be content in a world of infinite despair?" The dance, she said, was inspired by "the need for love, tolerance and nobility in a world given more and more to the denial of these things."

When Clemens moved to Oak Park in 1969, it wasn't because of Doris Humphrey. Her husband, Jim Tenuta, was hired to teach at the University of Illinois Chicago. Clemens didn't even know Humphrey came from Oak Park when she started her dance school.

"I started teaching in my living room in 1971 — rolled up the rug," she recalls.

Her enterprise grew and she took over the remaining portion of the old Bishop Quarter Military Academy at East and Lake (including the gym that now serves as their performance space), which became the home of the Academy of Movement and Music.

As her pupils got older, Clemens founded MOMENTA, a professional dance troupe for her alums and advanced students. In 1988, her husband, a co-founder of the troupe, suggested they put on a "Doris Humphrey Festival."

"He knew she had been born here, and he saw all the publicity surrounding Wright and Hemingway," Clemens recalls.

She wasn't sure they were equipped for such an undertaking, but she made a connection with Eleanor King and Ernestine Stodelle, who had danced with, or for, Humphrey and helped Clemens recreate the choreography largely from their own memories.

In the ensuing years, MOMENTA and Clemens have not only performed Humphrey's dances, they've also put together six "coaching" videos on five of her major works, plus one on Humphrey's dance techniques, with a seventh in the works.

With the aid of Humphrey's son, Charles Humphrey Woodford, they have accumulated a collection of photos and original, mint-condition Denishawn dance programs from the 1920s. More photos were added earlier this year, purchased from the estate of Jack Cole.

Gradually they have built a respectable archive, overseen by the Doris Humphrey Society, which Clemens created for that purpose, but they don't have the proper facilities for storing that extensive legacy.

Chicago's Newberry Library, on the other hand, boasts probably the best dance collection in the country, Clemens says, in a climate-controlled setting. They offer the added benefit of allowing the Doris Humphrey Society to maintain ownership of all the materials.

As soon as they can get all the photos digitized, Clemens says, materials will be available online at www.newberrry.org/collections/dance-abstracts.html.

"It feels good," says Clemens. "When you're passionate about your mission, it feels good when you've carried it out."

She also danced it out, enjoying a long career as a dancer herself — who often takes part in the biannual March and November dance concerts. Her dance to Frank Sinatra's "Once Upon A Time" was memorable.

> *Once upon a time the world was sweeter than we knew*
> *Everything was ours, how happy we were then*

But somehow once upon a time never comes again.

Maybe, but her dance enterprise continues to look ahead and break new ground. MOMENTA has, in recent years, begun to add a specialization in dancers with disabilities.

Kris Lenzo, an Oak Park resident and wheelchair athlete, who lost his legs in an accident in his youth, has joined the performing troupe, and Clemens is taking advantage of a growing body of choreographic work devoted to the disabled. Lenzo will perform in the upcoming November program.

Richard Bailey, a local resident who suffers from Parkinson's tremors, will perform as well. Bailey takes dance classes with MOMENTA alum Sarah Cullen Fuller.

"When he is moving to music," Clemens says, "all the shaking in his hands stops."

MOMENTA's efforts have not gone unnoticed. Dance St. Louis, which will hold Spring to Dance Festival 2009, has asked Lenzo and MOMENTA veteran Sandra Kaufmann (who also heads the dance department at Loyola University) to recreate the dance "Ashes."

When they started performing Humphrey's works in 1988, Clemens recalls, "I was concerned that our young company could not do her works justice, so we started with some of the smaller, earlier works." This past spring, for their 20th anniversary, Clemens finally felt they had the experience and resources to tackle Humphrey's masterwork, *Passacaglia and Fugue.*

"Doing *Passacaglia* is a measure of how much MOMENTA has grown in 20 years," says Clemens.

> *Since my dance is concerned with immediate human values, my basic technique lies in the natural movements of the body. One cannot express contemporary life without humanizing movement, as distinguished from dehumanization of the ballet. The modern dancer must come down from the points to the bare foot in order to establish his human relation to gravity and reality.*

I wish my dance to reflect some experience of my own in relationship to the outside world: to be based on reality illumined by imagination; to be organic rather than synthetic; to call forth a definite reaction from my audience; and to make its contribution toward the drama of life.

Doris Humphrey

Wright Plus rain (2017)

The "Plus" in the annual Wright Plus housewalk is the unexpected bonus of non-Wright homes, which varies from year to year. This year there was an additional "plus," Wright Plus Rain — steady showers, punctuated by downpours, a little thundery rumbling, but no lightning to chase away the architecture buffs and the army of volunteers, some 500 strong.

Wetness prevention added an extra wrinkle to the usual logistical challenges of this annual event. Dripping umbrellas were surrendered at the front door and clustered in the backyard for pickup on the way out. Clear plastic ponchos were provided to those caught protection-less. The dedicated corps of volunteers thought of everything. Some of the 'splainers were world class, but a few seemed more concerned about moving us through without leaving puddles and touching the furniture.

Some said it was the first rainy Wright Plus ever. Others claimed it was the third in 42 years. Either way it was unusual for this normally weather-charmed third Saturday of May event. But the clouds dried up around noon and, besides, Oak Park looks good even in the rain, or at least this portion does, arguably the prettiest stretch in the village, a concentrated collection of greatest-hit homes between Chicago Avenue and Elizabeth Court, Forest Avenue to Kenilworth, otherwise known as the Frank Lloyd Wright/Prairie School Historic District.

This year's walk included nine homes in all (10 if you were a member or held a fast pass). We managed to see eight, beginning at 9 a.m. sharp with the Laura Gale and Mayo houses on Elizabeth Court, then moving up the east side of Kenilworth, to and through the homes (once upon a time) of Harrison Young, John Schmidt, and Charles Matthews. We broke for lunch at Winberie's, then resumed on Forest Avenue with the Heurtley (longest line), Hills-DeCaro and Charles Purcell houses. By then it was 4:30 and we were spent.

People come from all over the world for this walk and likely wonder, "How is it I've never heard of this town? Is it all this lovely?" Well, not quite, but rich or poor — and we cover the full range of socio-economic strata — almost all the homes front their streets. There are no security posts to pass. Some front yards are fenced but few block vision. The more "private" the fence, the more local passersby shake their heads in disapproval. We are a democratic people, an integrated community, and we don't like it when people isolate and insulate. It is nice, in fact, to see that a number of our "museum quality" homes have kids living in them, their toys neatly stacked in bins as we passed bedroom or playroom doors. I like to think they're not always so neatly stored.

Every third Saturday in May, private homeowners are willing to make their showcase homes accessible to the public, another sign of our interwoven community.

Moving along, we encountered longtime volunteers like Frank Pond, Pat Cannon (one of the originals who helped save the Home & Studio in the early '70s), Yvonne Smith (who researched the Laura Gale House), and Doug Freerksen (of Von Dreele-Freerksen, which has worked on no less than 28 Wright homes, including the Heurtley House renovation).

Even my old neighbor Jack Koberstine, who has lived in a Gunderson home on the 600 block of South Elmwood for almost 60 years and is now within shouting distance of 90, is here giving a room spiel. All have been volunteers for 30 years or more and remain devoted to this remarkable heritage enterprise.

The past comes alive as we pass through: imagining what it must have been like on rainy mornings as former owners looked out these windows and went about their lives. Our sense of community includes the echoes of those who came before.

There are homes in Oak Park that extend back almost to the birth of Frank Lloyd Wright (1867), whose sesquicentennial we mark this June 8. The firehouse-red Schmidt House on the tour this year, for instance, dates back to 1872. It was probably built to house the rapid influx of Chicagoans who fled the Great Fire the previous year.

That's a lot of lives, and a lot of living.

One docent last Saturday pointed out the level of detail that Wright applied to reinforce his trademark, Prairie-style horizontality: using a lighter mortar along the uninterrupted length of the Roman brick, but between the vertical ends, a darker mortar matches the color of the bricks. The style complements, and compliments, the flat prairies on which these homes were built, in contrast to the hierarchical verticality of European architecture. For Wright, the horizontal was more egalitarian, more democratic, and therefore truly American.

Being the bricks of this community, we know the mortar that binds us is the essential element. As Irish author John O'Donohue puts it in his book, *Beauty*:

"This is one of the deepest poverties in our times. That whole web of 'betweenness' seems to be unraveling. It is rarely acknowledged anymore, but that does not mean it has ceased to exist. The 'web of betweenness' is still there but in order to become a presence again, it needs to be invoked. As in the rain forest, a dazzling diversity of life-forms complement and sustain each other; there is secret oxygen with which we unknowingly sustain one another. True community is not produced; it is invoked and awakened. True community is an ideal where the full identities of awakened and realized individuals challenge and complement each other. In this sense, both individuality and originality enrich self and others."

That pretty well sums up the "plus" in my Wright Plus experience this year, here in the rain forest of Oak Park.

Hemingway's tragic heroism (2021)

A fuller story has finally been told. The fullest to date anyway. Ken Burns and Lynn Novick looked at Ernest Hemingway from both sides now in the three-part series, *Hemingway*, which aired on PBS last week.

While he was alive, the story was of a larger-than-life, high-living, celebrity author. After his death, it turned into a story of overblown reputation and toxic masculinity. Because he wrote in simple, declarative sentences, people assumed he was a simple, declarative man. The simplicity of his prose was mistaken for shallow and his work misjudged as overrated.

This series, at last, captures his complexity.

Because he caroused and passionately pursued pleasure, he couldn't possibly be a disciplined writer and serious artist, could he? But he was — up early and writing every morning. The work kept him alive.

"The great thing," he said, "is to last and get your work done."

Many of those who venture back to his work — and learn more about him — change their mind about Hemingway. There is an appealing clarity to his writing. You can see the brook trout in the stream. It's like reading in sunlight. All the edges are distinct.

Hemingway left Oak Park and rose to great heights, and his fall from grace (under pressure) wasn't pretty. It was in many ways his destiny, but his choices accelerated it. His strengths, as a person and a writer, were outsized. His flaws were enormous and, ultimately, decisive.

Part 3 of the series raises the Hemingway story to the level of classical tragedy, but parts 1 and 2 are necessary to experience the full effect.

Awareness of the inevitability of death is the thread running through both his writing and his life. There are no happy endings in Hemingway stories. He comes closest in *A Moveable Feast*, a love letter to Paris written in an elegiac tone, looking back on youth near the end of life. It was his last great book, composed during his rapidly advancing decline. Amazing that he could write anything at all at that point.

His fascination with bullfighting in Spain, and big-game hunting in Africa, which, understandably, turns many readers off, can only be understood in terms of his obsession with death.

What was it about bullfighting that fascinated him enough to write a book-length treatment titled, *Death in the Afternoon*? Bullfighting, if it makes sense at all, only makes sense as a primal, quasi-religious ritual that incorporates considerable artistry — a ballet of life and death performed by the matador (with help from picadors, who lance the bull, gradually weakening him). Hemingway admired the matadors, but I suspect he identified with the bull — a powerful force of nature, disabled and brought low by a system (and body) rigged against him.

An apt metaphor for someone so enormously gifted and enormously cursed, undone by the daggers of his demons: genetic mental illness, long years of alcoholic self-medication, PTSD from close involvement in three wars, and numerous concussions causing brain damage, including two plane crashes in two days in Africa near the end of his life, both of which he somehow survived.

Hemingway's only surviving son, Patrick, compared his father as he neared the end to Shakespeare's King Lear, howling on the heath. According to Greek — and Shakespearean — tragedy, a person of high station in life is undone and brought low by his own actions. That is Hemingway's life story. Tragedy traditionally plays out against the backdrop of the chorus, a stand-in for the audience, which is not a passive voyeur so much as an active witness to, and commenting on, the hero's demise. The experience is intended to elicit an elevated form of pity, seasoned by sympathy. When it works, we leave the theater sensitized, more in touch with our humanity.

But we fail the test of tragedy if we leave the story feeling dismissive: "He had it coming," as the young revenger in Clint Eastwood's film, *The Unforgiven*, says in an attempt to justify killing a man for the first time. "We all have it coming," Eastwood replies, sounding like a character in one of Hemingway's stories. Yes, Hemingway brought it on himself. But if that makes us dismissive, we bring it on ourselves as well.

The end of Hemingway's story was in many ways pre-ordained, but even in the disintegration and degradation of his last few years, he managed to rise above it with the aforementioned *Moveable Feast* as well as *The Old Man and the Sea* — the myth of his life stripped to its bare essentials. He hooked the big fish, but the sharks feasted on it before he got it home. Though easily parodied because of its hyper-simplicity, it tells an important truth when the old fisherman, speaking for the author, says in the end, "I went out too far."

By 1961, Hemingway could no longer write, due partly to electro-shock therapy. Only one form of agency remained and he placed a gun barrel against his forehead and pulled the trigger. The bull became his own matador.

In a Zoom discussion, one of a series of conversations held by Burns and Novick with guest authors and scholars in the weeks leading up to the series, author Joyce Carol Oates had this to say to Hemingway's critics:

"I think we are expecting something of him that he was not able to provide. ... His father had committed suicide. He was deeply insecure. He made out of the material of his life a very beautiful and lasting monument to just getting through it. He lived to be about 62 and then he killed himself. But he might have died much younger. ... There is something heroic in these people enduring as long as they did — especially Hemingway, who was haunted by the possibility of dying by suicide all through his life."

Hemingway himself once said, "I have always [felt] it was more important, or as important, to be a good man as to be a great writer. I may turn out to be neither but would like to be both."

He wasn't always a good person, but he was a very good writer, and he was eminently human. He captured in the "lasting monument" of his work the good, the bad, the ugly and the beautiful.

When it comes to Hemingway, too many Oak Parkers turn a blind eye to the treasure that his growing up here represents. As this series shows, it is worth our while to get re-acquainted.

It would be easy to reduce Ernest Hemingway to a cautionary tale, but if, in our role as members of the chorus, we remain unmoved by the story of his life and the stories he wrote during his life, then we miss his heroism — as well as the heroism of other tragic figures like Oedipus and Lear.

And we miss the lesson tragedy teaches: that honestly, even radically, facing the truth — about living and dying, both sides now, no illusions — is what makes us truly human.

The old man and the sangria (1999)

It was late. Scoville Park had never looked worse. Prostrate bodies everywhere. The Centennial Fiesta de Hemingway had turned into Siesta de Hemingway. Everyone had too much sangria.

Including me, come to think of it. In fact, things were looking pretty fuzzy by the time the old man sat down on the bench next to me. He looked tired, beat. He looked like he had just lost a Hemingway Look-Alike Contest.

"Hey, old man," I said in my friendliest manner, "what's wrong? You look like hell."

"I just lost the Hemingway Look-Alike Contest," he said.

Hard to believe, I told him. He was a dead ringer (so to speak).

Turns out he lost on the desert island tiebreaker question: "Which modernist author would you most like to be stranded on a desert island with?"

"I answered, 'Gertrude Stein.' They laughed so hard I lost my temper. I used a word with more than two syllables, so they disqualified me. Life just isn't fair."

Clearly the old man was more than a look-alike. He was impersonating Hemingway's very soul. I decided to play along.

"What would the great DiMaggio say?" I heard him mutter sadly to no one in particular.

"A nation turns its lonely eyes to you," I replied. "Sorry, that song came out after you died." He looked at me with so much conviction, I felt I'd better change the subject.

"What do you think of the old town? It's been a while since you were here."

"All so different," he said, shaking his shaggy comb-over. "When did they put up that war memorial?"

"I believe it was 1925. It's called 'Peace Triumphant.' You had already moved on. Your name is on it, though."

"I don't get it," he said. "The lawns seem so much narrower and the minds much too broad. Since when is a prophet honored in his own land?"

"This isn't your father's All-America City," I offered helpfully.

He scratched his beard and muttered, "Somewhere along the line the century passed me by."

"Don't despair," I said cheerfully. "They've made a lot of progress on chronic depression. A little physical therapy, a little Prozac, and you'd be back at your typewriter pounding away in no time. Of course, you might want to invest in a laptop. Very useful. You could even take it on safari."

"No good," he said. "Computers tempt writers to say more than they need to. They get carried away."

"I've been meaning to ask," I interjected, "why such short, clipped sentences?"

"The main thing wrong with the world," he replied, "then and now, is phoniness. Too many write too much and don't say enough. I went after what's real. I wouldn't put a word down until it spoke to me first. Isn't that what art and artists are supposed to be about, the search for what's real?"

"You mean authenticity?"

"Too many syllables."

"Did you find what was real?"

"A lot of people claim I turned into a phony, a victim of my own image-making. But not my writing. There's no fat in it."

"Have you found anything real back here in Oak Park?"

"They tell me the town showed grace under pressure in the decades after I died. Wish I could have seen that."

"What do you think of your 100th birthday bash?"

"They like me," he said, shaking his craggy head. "They really like me."

As he limped off into the night, I felt for him.

I called out, "But the sun also rises."

Then I heard him from a distance.

"Isn't it pretty to think so?"

10

Autumn

Turning inward (2017)

He had never before been quite so acutely aware of the particular quality and function of November, its ripeness and its sadness. The year proceeds not in a straight line through the seasons, but in a circle that brings the world and man back to the dimness and mystery in which both began, and out of which a new seed-time and a new generation are about to begin. Old men, thought Cadfael, believe in that new beginning, but experience only the ending. It may be that God is reminding me that I am approaching my November. Well, why regret it? November has beauty, has seen the harvest into the barns, even laid by next year's seed. No need to fret about not being allowed to stay and sow it; someone else will do that. So go contentedly into the earth with the moist, gentle, skeletal leaves, worn to cobweb fragility, like the skins of very old men, that bruise and stain at the mere brushing of the breeze, and flower into brown blotches as the leaves into rotting gold. The colors of late autumn are the colors of the sunset: the farewell of the year and the farewell of the day. And of the life of man? Well, if it ends in a flourish of gold, that is no bad ending.

Ellis Peters
Brother Cadfael's Penance

    A two-block stretch of Oak Park Avenue is closed for the annual Halloween Parade on this last Saturday of October. Parents and costumed kids march north to Lake Street under the train viaduct, bags in hand. When they reach Lake, the marchers double back to do a little trick-or-treating with the street's merchants.

    "This is strawberry pineapple," says one proprietor, bending over a future customer and inspecting a sucker wrapper. "I don't think we have coconut."

    One twosome, a princess and a witch (classic fairy-tale dichotomy) break into a rendition of "Jingle Bells," supplying their own words. Mom says, "Oh no, we're not doing *that* yet."

Tiny superheroes, pharaohs and Chinese emperors keep company with young parents and aging grandparents. One woman holds a dragon by one hand and a fireman by the other — firebreather and firefighter, a perfect combo.

We're heading into the year's home stretch, and the weather makes that indisputably clear — blustery and raw, temperature hanging by its fingertips to the 40s, ragged-edged cloud banks roiling overhead, searching for patches of blue to blot out where the overcast has briefly thinned.

But the gamers on the ground are undeterred. Star Wars storm troopers and bishops and wizards and whatnot. And those are the parents. The kids are furred and whiskered and Harry Pottered and Luke Skywalkered. One girl is a taco. Another is either a warlock or a Supreme Court justice. It's hard sometimes to tell the difference.

Continuing on, changes in the leafy canopy become more evident. Brighter colors are finally dominating, though not so brilliant as in years past, at least not yet. Perhaps that is global warming's doing (or undoing).

But on this day, over at Elmwood and Lake, the weather isn't conducive to a comfortable savoring of the last Farmers Market of this year.

"We'll get donuts," one father explains to his impatient, stroller-bound son. They'd better hurry. The line is long and customers are ordering dozens like there's no tomorrow — because there isn't.

"Hey, buddy," he says, "do you want to stop and see Grandpa?" Oh to live in a town where you can wheel your kid to a market that sells freshly-made donuts and where Grandpa lives along the glide-path home.

A 20-something waiting patiently in line explains the donut thing to an older man who's new to all this: "My mom brought me every Saturday when I was growing up. It was a tradition. I don't live here anymore, but I was in town for a few days and felt nostalgic, so I had to come over."

At one of the booths, a vendor advises two senior citizens who stare in disbelief at three gargantuan pumpkins the size of large boulders.

"All you have to do," the seller says, "is put it in a big burlap sack, then each of you grab a corner and drag it."

A few hardy souls huddle with coffee and donuts at the tables, but the musicians have called it a season. The circle has been broken. Vendors, however, have braved the elements and the waning harvest and are here to see the growing season to its late-October denouement.

Friends who meet here all summer cluster for a photo on this final go-round.

Pilgrim Congregational Church, which has hosted and person-powered this community-building exercise for more than a generation, is selling the year's final donuts and coffee under the tent, where a rotating roster of good causes and organizations raised funds each week during the summer and fall to the benefit of sweet-teeth and the detriment of waistlines.

The vendors' wares, meanwhile, have narrowed, mostly to apples and root vegetables, pumpkins and squash and peppers and Brussels sprouts on long stalks.

Cold hands count out the change and bag the produce.

"Barry's Berries," repeats one patient vendor to a customer who isn't catching the pun. "B-A-R-R-Y-S ... B-E-R-R-I-E-S."

Customers and sellers exchange fond farewells.

"See you next year."

The guy at the bread tent adds, "If God's willing and the creek don't rise." And if the bread does rise.

Bears fans banter with the Packers fan in the corner who sells Indian corn and dared to wear his team's logo on his sweatshirt. "It's the only team worth rooting for," he says with a mischievous grin. Based on their respective records, Bears boosters are in no position to rebut.

The sky begins to spritz and the vendor notes that in the wee hours this morning as he drove past O'Hare, he spotted a few flakes. It won't be long before that's the precipitation norm.

At the tables along Lake Street, a political partisan waves a hand-out at passersby. "We need to get rid of this regime," he says. "Trump's got his finger on the nukes." At a separate table nearby, the Democratic Party of Oak Park offers signature petitions on clipboards for an array of candidates trying to get on the ballot.

As I put cream in my coffee, a friend sidles up and says, "The jet stream has buckled, and we're on the wrong side of it." A woman to my right says, "It's perfect weather for a finale." For finality anyway.

The warm Saturdays of summer are already a fading memory. Since late May, this has been a place where you pick up flowers and fixings and farm stock. It's also where you pick up where you left off with the lives of people you may not have seen all winter. Farmers Market crowns the "outside" portion of the year here in the upper Midwest. Farmers raise their crops and we raise our kids, some of whom are running back and forth on the soccer field across the street. We trade pleasantries and tips and updates and how-are-yous and revel in the abundance and relax in the cool of the first mornings of our weekends.

But November is now fast upon us and with it the turning inward that begins, appropriately, on the Day of the Dead. The farmers let their fields fall fallow and find other ways to occupy their time. Soon the sandhill cranes will fly over, heading south for a warmer winter than we can offer.

I purchase a few last edible-looking tomatoes and a couple of deep red peppers and call it a season.

"Have a good winter," says the seller, chipper to the very end.

A good winter.

There's a concept.

Trick-or-treating, adult style (2000)

Halloween evening, I went out for an atmosphere soak during peak trick-or-treat time — walking the neighborhood from Euclid to Elmwood avenues, South Boulevard to Washington Boulevard — big old houses, thickly arbored parkways, and loads of kids, not all from that neighborhood, I'm guessing.

Doesn't matter. Halloween isn't territorial. It's about gracious giving, even if the gifts are bad for your teeth (the real trick in trick-or-treating).

We've been blessed the last four years with balmy weather on Halloween, but this year was best. Must have been 70 degrees, judging by how many residents sat on their porches and front steps. The majority of houses were warmly lit inside, with most of the porch lights turned on as well. The housing stock boasts ample front porches and spacious picture windows.

Normally when you walk down a block, there's a clear demarcation between outside and inside, private and public, but on this night, in this neighborhood, that barrier completely disappeared.

The air, temperate and bug-free, allowed front doors to be thrown wide open. So many open doors, it seemed at first to break some unwritten rule, but once the incongruity faded, it felt so ... welcoming, neighborly, as if privacy needs took a backseat to the more urgent imperative of communal connection.

On a night like this, it's possible to glimpse what life might be like in some future utopia of harmonious interdependence — if only humanity could find the courage to take that next giant leap for humankind.

For now, though, it's enough to be the village of "open doors and porch lights." Let this be the logical next step in our long commitment to open housing. The holiday delirium feels downright visionary. Just as we have A Day in Our Village, this is A Night in Our Village. Call it our annual Porchlight Festival. One night each year, we should encourage residents to turn on every light in their house and throw open their doors.

Overhead, the branches of largely leafless trees twist gracefully against the twilight. The fingernail moon sails westward like a single-masted ship in the afterglow of the setting sun, pursuing its master with slavish devotion.

Kids scurry from house to house, the hems of their costumes brushing the pavement, shoes scuffling through the parched and curling leaves.

Jack o' Lanterns and assorted other luminaria gleam from nearly every stairstep and window with savage contortions or friendly grins. A giant cobweb, strung between two houses, rises two stories. Burial mounds of leaf mash line the curbs. Ceramic pumpkins are fused into totem poles of frightful visages.

On one front lawn, a fire pit blazes while residents recline in white wicker furniture, sipping wine and doling out sweets to costumed passersby.

Adults are nearly as numerous as kids — commuters returning from work, parents accompanying little ones, directing them, reminding them to say "trick or treat" and express gratitude for the latter. Thanksgiving can't hold a candle to Halloween; on this night, kids say "thank-you" far more often.

Like most communities, most of the year, we are afflicted by an epidemic of "porch neglect." But this is the evening to take advantage of the best room outside the house. Back decks are for those who crave privacy. Front porches are the stitching in our social weave.

For all its frightfulness and grotesque gory ghoulery, Halloween teaches kids a lesson in neighborly benevolence. Heretofore anonymous strangers become willing accomplices in a vast conspiracy to create idyllic moments that will cure for many years till needed for medicinal application to life's sores, just like the memories that were created for us.

Parents play a bigger role in trick-or-treating than in those long-gone days. Though borne of fear, there is an unintended bonus: getting reacquainted with once-upon-a-time magic allows us to steep in dreamy nostalgia about the past and hopeful idealism about the future.

As you get older, the treats become intangible, filling personal pillowcases with sweetmeat memories and neighborly good will.

None of which causes tooth decay.

As the leaves leave ... (2017)

The year begins leafless and ends leafless. But in between, oh my.

The last leaves are falling in droves, but it was quite a party while it lasted. The altered array of sometimes dazzling hues draws attention, as if to say, "Look at us now. You will miss us when we're gone." Green gave way to gold reluctantly this year, orange and red leaving their imprint on the eyes before the landscape goes brown and grey and silver and white. Leafletting the sidewalks, unceremoniously dumped following a recent hard freeze, plastered in piles on the ground, warning us of what's ahead.

I miss them already and never took them for granted, but look forward to the next generation, issued by these soldier-straight chlorophyll factories, next year's buds already fixed in place.

The leafless limbs of winter resemble exposed nerve endings — raw, unprotected, painfully vulnerable — but a different kind of beauty can be found in the gracefully curving limbs, tapering to capillary branches against a grey, late autumn sky. Skeletal shapes, minus their festive overcoats, take their own lovely form.

Trees defy winter's impressive impersonation of death, impervious to the frosted icing and whatever other affronts the arctic winds cast their way. They teach us, year in and out, to hold fast, in our deepest despair, to the belief that a small miracle awaits come spring, these trunks a reminder that the Old English word for truth is *treowth*, inspired by the true-ness of their sky-reaching growth.

Dinosaurs of the plant world, they seem inert but remain very much alive, even as they mimic the silence of God.

Come spring, against all odds, green tips will pierce the protective shells of buds; blossoms will burst, turning nectar-seeking bees into agents of cross-fertilizing consummation; seeds will be shed, elms dropping motherlodes of uncooked oatmeal, maples whirly-coptering in search of fecund landings, cottonwoods re-enacting snowfall in their late-May release. A new generation will briefly astonish, as the canopy thickens, obscuring the sky, inhaling carbon, exhaling oxygen, our mirror opposites, as if placed here to save us from ourselves.

Come summer, the dense foliage overhangs, enfolds us and nearly overwhelms, bordering on the tropical, creating the illusion of permanence. We take it for granted except for the shade, which holds off the too-close-for-comfort Northern Hemisphere sun, soothing us even as, like Wilbur's sieve, it lets through a ray here, a dapple there.

Tree roots heave up heavy slabs of sidewalk, trunks grow right through chain-link fences. Blossoms perfume the air, bear fruit, drop acorns and black walnuts to fatten the squirrels, offer insects their textured bark for burrowing — even those with exotic names like emerald ash-borer which will kill them — and they harbor hidden nests for generations of birds and wasps.

They cool our houses, anchor our soil, reach skyward to filter the air and dig waterward, deep underground. They serve as memorials to our dearly departed, plaques at their feet. They model for us how to live — strong and fixed at their base, bendable and flexible in their limbs, sinking roots, providing hospitable refuge, bearing fruit, casting seeds to the wind on the off chance some will germinate.

The ultimate optimists.

Some are older than our ancestors and inspire those of us who question whether truth even exists anymore. It does, they say. Look at us, look all around. And we do, sitting on benches made from their cellulose. We surround ourselves with harvested wood in our homes and public buildings, and we invite fir trees inside during the winter holidays to fill our homes with the scent of the North Woods.

Of all their gifts, though, the greatest is beauty.

We are wealthy in trees — roughly 18,000 in the village right-of-way, according to the village forester, plus another 2,500 or so in our parks, according to the park district. No one knows how many more can be found on private property. Our "urban forest" counts old-growth oaks and survivor elms, besieged ash, umbrella maples, sweetgums, tulip trees, magnolias, horse chestnuts and buckeyes, redbuds and dogwoods, catalpas, lindens, crabapple, hawthorns and hackberries, alders and cedars, black locusts and honey locusts, shagbark hickories, river birches, boxelders, sycamores, beeches whose bark resembles elephant skin, and ornamental pears whose leaves are the last to turn and drop — even ginkgos in spite of their stinkberries (though noble in all other respects). Their names fall from the tongue as easily as bird songs strike the ear.

So many varieties, yet they never go to sleep in winter as Norway maples and wake up in the spring as yellow poplars. They know who they are. Trees have mastered the seasons — the flamboyant changeability of spring and fall, the reliable steadfastness of summer and winter.

And here they are again on the cusp of winter. The last leaves falling. The boughs having purged themselves, releasing what isn't permanent and preparing to go dormant. Meanwhile, we busy ourselves with raking and blowing and disposing of this year's crop, so much so that we forget the one task that remains.

Saying a proper goodbye.

And thanks.

11

Scenery

Objects of meaning and merit, animate and inanimate, artistic and otherwise — our non-human assets, if you will — say plenty about us.

The play *Our Town* is famous for its lack of stage scenery — sitting atop ladders to simulate upper-story windows, actors sitting in chairs to simulate graves in the cemetery.

In our town Oak Park, architecture is one of our most prominent "props," thanks to the presence of Frank Lloyd Wright and the other Prairie-School architects who practiced here in the 20th century.

Trees are another, possibly our greatest, asset. Foresightful foresters kept our "urban forest" intact, healthy and lush — in spite of the onslaught of beetles and borers and other invasive infestations. As a result, we routinely earned a "Tree City USA" designation for decades.

Inanimate objects often animate us, and some rise to the level of objets d'art. Lawn signs proclaim our beliefs and convictions, and the simplest ones pose the most challenging of reminders ("Help each other"). Even sidewalk squares can proclaim our love for someone decades later. Bells ring out with joy or alarm — or simply remind us that time is passing and we should make the most of it.

Here is an inventory of our more prominent props:

The American dream of belonging (2017, 2020)

On Memorial Day, patriotism was in evidence all over Oak Park and River Forest. Not just the traditional display — star-spangled banners, jutting out at a 45-degree angle from many a house. This year a new kind of patriotism joined the mix: lawn signs have sprouted since the Electoral College "virtually" elected a baggage-heavy president who lost the popular vote.

On Elizabeth Court, for instance, a sign testifies, "In this house we believe: Black Lives Matter, Women's Rights are Human Rights, No Human is Illegal, Science is Real, Love is Love, No Matter Your Faith or Ability, Kindness is Everything."

Such testimonials are part of the new resistance movement, which, judging by the quantity, has myriad members in our community.

On the 700 block of Wisconsin, I find "Hate Has No Home Here" signs, blue on one side, red on the other, written in numerous languages. At the bottom of the sign is a heart with an American flag imbedded. Eight of these signs line the east side of the block; nine on the west side echo the sentiment.

On the 600 block of Clinton, a "Hate Has No Home Here" sign features four oak leaves with a green stripe above and blue stripe below, a modified version of the Chicago flag, stating, "We Believe Integration Matters! We Support the Oak Park Regional Housing Center" underneath.

Another reads, "Love Your Neighbor: Your Differently Abled, Black, White, Brown, Immigrant, LGBTQ, Religiously Diverse, Fully Human Neighbor." Nearby is a sign that says simply, "On the Side of Love," a Unitarian/Universalist-inspired slogan.

On the 300 block of South Grove, a sign in white letters on a pink background proclaims, "I Stand with Planned Parenthood." Another, in three languages (English, Spanish and Arabic) and three colors, states uncategorically, "No Matter Where You Are From, We're Glad You're Our Neighbor."

And on the 100 block of Home Avenue, a variation of the Elizabeth Court sign is popular: "Here We Believe: Love is Love, No Human is Illegal, Black Lives Matter, Science is Real, Women's Rights are Human Rights, Water is Life, Kindness is Everything." (Visit herewebelieve.org, if you want to learn more.)

This, too, is patriotic, stating plainly and firmly what community members stand for, inspired by what this country claims to stand for. It's healthy for kids to grow up around people who have the courage of their convictions and whose stated beliefs are welcoming, inclusive and affirming — what the real America is all about, a patriotism that honors the courage to live in an open society.

A new patriotism is emerging. Lawn signs are just one manifestation. Awakened awareness and increased activism are also heartening. We are rediscovering what it means to be proud of what America stands for, and our determination to make the nation great again.

But as we struggle to make that happen, let's not overlook the other sign spotted on the 800 block of Clinton this Memorial Day, which proclaims, "Porch Rules: Feel the Breeze, Listen to the Birds, Converse, Have a Drink, Relax and Unwind."

In other words, don't forget that the best way to resist the insanity of our times is to remain sane yourself.

* * *

But not everyone sees this as an act of patriotism.

Last week, I received an email from an old friend. Our friendship, which goes all the way back to high school, has been tested occasionally by the fact that we vigorously disagree on matters political. But we respect each other's sincerity, which is essential. He grew up and lives in Chicago but has connections here in Oak Park. He consented to sharing his email in the interest of promoting dialogue.

> *I was waiting for my wife who is seeing a doctor at Rush Oak Park Hospital today (can't be with her because of COVID concerns). While killing time I took a little walk down Wisconsin and Wenonah and all the other little side streets in the neighborhood. I*

thought of you and how you too like to walk through the streets of your hometown. That's why I'm writing this email — to tell you what I saw.

I wanted to experience that small-town America feel that Oak Park creates and about which you sometimes write — that "village feel" for which the community is known: the porches dotted with wicker chairs, the wide lawns, kids playing, and cicadas screeching their late-summer song.

I saw something different though. Yes, there were wide yards and some kids playing. But there was also a plethora of lecturing message signs with what has come to represent the standard progressive warnings: 'Black Lives Matter'; 'Hate Has No Home Here'; 'We believe in ...'

The number of signs was actually very impressive — sure enough, Oak Park is now a certified progressive village if one judges by the placards Oak Parkers plant next to their traditional four-squares and bungalows. I even saw many rainbow flags — fitted into old stanchions on their porch pillars — telling everyone the folks inside are gay or at least devoted in one way or another to LGBTQ rights.

Ironically, these are the same flag holders which an earlier generation of Oak Parkers employed to express a different message — love of country, pride in the nation, respect, perhaps even a sense of belonging and togetherness as Americans. Displaying the Stars & Stripes was to marvel at the audacious dream America could be for every citizen.

Now, amid the hectoring signs of special interest, preaching an ironic gospel of exclusion pretending to be inclusion, there were no American flags in any yard I saw. Not one. So perhaps the dream of America, the land of the free and the home of the brave, has died, leaving in its place a desolate, cranky and bickering collection of deaf people interested in nothing other than their "just" cause of the moment.

I turned back to the hospital. The cicadas stopped for a moment.

> The sunny day began to set, sending those slanted August afternoon rays bouncing off the yard signs. I mused over just how much "progress" Oak Park has really made, and wondered how it "all got this crazy," to borrow the Eagle's line.

Thanks, for your challenge. No truly progressive community should ever feel their progress has been "enough," whether it's Black Lives Matter or Conservative Opinions Matter.

So we'll start there. Your opinion matters. But I will note that if you walked all the streets of Oak Park, you would find plenty of American flags flying proudly from their porch stanchions. I counted five in a row on one block recently, and it's not even July.

You stated well what the flag represents: love of country, pride in nation, respect, a sense of belonging and togetherness as Americans, marveling at the audacious dream America could be for every citizen. I would add "liberty, justice and equality for all" to that list.

But America has not yet achieved that audacious dream, and progressives will not rest until we do. That's the progress we hunger for. And we become downright "cranky" as you put it, when we find ourselves moving in the opposite direction.

One of the ways we channel our dissatisfaction is putting up lawn signs proclaiming, "Here we believe. ..." It's a start. We believe Black Lives Matter, No Human is Illegal, Love is Love, Women's Rights are Human Rights, Science is Real, Injustice Anywhere is a Threat to Justice Everywhere, and Kindness is Everything, as one sign I recently saw proclaimed.

You describe these signs as "lecturing" and "hectoring" and "standard progressive warnings." I don't see "Black Lives Matter" as a warning. I see it as an overdue statement of solidarity with African Americans who have suffered from inequality for too long.

These signs are expressions of our patriotism, which can be distilled to five words: "Everyone is welcome. Everyone belongs."

Conservatives tell me that when they see "Hate Has No Home Here," they feel unwelcome, even accused. Mostly, that message is directed at this president and his White Nationalist supporters, but it's important for progressives to hear your concern about the broadness of our brush.

Are Oak Park's lawn signs "preaching an ironic gospel of exclusion pretending to be inclusion"? It's a question worth asking. Stating what you believe is important, but meaningless unless you live it. There has always been too great a gap in this country between aspiration and action. The truest patriots, like Abraham Lincoln, Martin Luther King Jr., and John Lewis call on us to live up to our creed.

The greatest patriots are usually also prophets.

The only thing in your email I truly take issue with is the notion that the "dream of America" might be dying. The dream doesn't die. It beckons us ever onward to be better citizens and to create a better country.

How did it all get this crazy? I think conservatives need to ask how they have contributed to the current craziness. And progressives need to do the same. That's the first step toward genuine dialogue.

We have a road map. Abraham Lincoln identified True North for us: "With malice toward none, with charity for all ..." We must learn to speak from the better angels of our nature to the better angels of the other's nature. That's the only way to create Dr. King's "beloved community," where everybody belongs.

Which, let's face it, is the real American Dream.

Thanks for taking a step in that direction.

And if the cicadas ever shut up, maybe we'll be able to hear one another at last.

Adding a story to a tall building (2017)

By the time you read this, our village trustees will have made their decision on the Albion proposal to build an 18-story building at the corner of Lake Street and Forest Avenue.

I propose adding a story. Not to the building. To the discussion.

It's a long story, but a good one, a story about stages of development at that corner, which goes all the way back to the first Anglo settlers of Oak Park, which was then known as Oak Ridge. Joseph and Betty Kettlestrings arrived in the early 1830s, about the time the Blackhawk War drove the native Potawatomi people out of Illinois. Not one of this nation's finest hours.

Suddenly there was a lot of real estate for the acquiring and the Kettlestrings bought most of what is now west central Oak Park, then, little by little, sold it off. But they didn't sell all of it. According to Gertrude Fox Hoagland's 1937 book, *Historical Survey of Oak Park, Illinois*, "When Joseph Kettlestrings returned to Oak Park early in 1854, he donated land at the [northwest] corner of Lake and Forest, on which a one-story, frame structure was built (1855) for a school and meeting house." It was the village's first school, with less than 20 students under the watchful tutelage of Principal A.D. Thomas.

In 1859, Oak Ridge School was built kitty corner (you can still see the cornerstone in the ground on Lake Street), which later became known as Central School, then Lowell School, in a much larger building. That structure, in turn, was torn down in the 1970s to make way for a controversial high-rise development, which never got further than its infamous name, "Stankus Hole," for the crater that sat there like a deserted quarry for many years. Eventually, 100 Forest Place, our first true high-rise, rose from those depths in the 1980s.

But on that northwest corner across the street, in 1859, Henry Austin Sr. bought the property, which extended west along Lake Street almost to Marion and north to Ontario, where the park known as Austin Gardens is located. The Austins originally built their home roughly where the

Lake Theatre now stands. At the corner, they left the one-story frame building for public use, renaming it "Temperance Hall."

Henry Sr., an enthusiastic teetotaler, famously bought out the last tavern in town and took an axe to the last barrels of booze in stock. Oak Park stayed "dry" all the way through Prohibition and up until 1973.

The Women's Christian Temperance Union used the hall for meetings, but it also hosted "public rallies, dances and church services," according to Philander Barclay, who included an 1885 photo of the building in his famous turn-of-the-last-century collection of snapshots.

The hall became known as "the cradle of churches," with Congregational, Baptist, Presbyterian, and Episcopal congregations holding services there until their respective churches were built, eventually lining Lake Street so that Oak Park became known as "the place where taverns end and steeples begin." Early African American residents also met there before Mt. Carmel Church was completed on what is now Westgate.

Barclay noted that in Temperance Hall, "Virginia reels were danced and amateur plays given within its doors. ... Until 1900, when it was torn down, it was one of Oak Park's most famous landmarks."

You can see Barclay's photo at the Historical Society's new Oak Park River Forest Museum, 129 Lake St. "The wood frame holding the photo was made from the front door casing, the only thing left from the school house," according to a photo caption in the Oak Leaves on Dec. 4, 1968, showing Wallis Austin, Henry Sr.'s grandson, presenting the framed photograph to members of the newly formed Historical Society. Wallis' father, Henry Jr., started Oak Park Trust and Savings Bank in 1892 and in 1923 completed the familiar pillared edifice at the corner of Lake and Marion (now Chase Bank). For decades Oak Park Trust served as the financial cornerstone of the community.

Barclay gave the framed photo to Henry Jr. in 1935, with the stipulation that "at the proper time, the bank would turn this relic over to the Oak Park Historical Society."

In the mid-'30s at the height of the Depression, Oak Park Trust, like a lot of banks, was in trouble. To keep it afloat, Henry Jr. sold off the Lake Street frontage all the way to the corner of Lake and Forest. He had his house moved north (roughly where the Austin Gardens Environmental Education Center is now located). The Lake Theatre opened on the Lake Street site in 1936.

According to a map of that area, by 1950 a service station existed to the east of the theater, followed by a small surface parking lot, and a corner lunch counter. The Oak Leaves carried an article with a rendering of a $1.5 million shopping center planned for the site. Construction was set to start in March of 1950. It never came together, but it may have inspired Oak Park resident Willard W. Cole, president of Lytton's (aka "The Hub") to have a similar structure built on that corner and relocate from 1035 Lake (the general vicinity of The Book Table across the street) which Cole's store had occupied since 1927. Lytton's, in fact, was the first "State Street" store to open in Oak Park, preceding Marshall Field's.

The new Lytton's building was designed by the architectural firm Shaw, Mertz and Dolio and at the groundbreaking in May of 1956, among the notables in attendance was President Eisenhower's brother, Earl. In May of 1957, the store's grand opening was a big enough deal for the Oak Leaves to devote an entire special section to it.

Sometime in 1985 or early 1986, just shy of Lytton's 100th anniversary in Chicago, the store closed and the building was converted to nondescript office space with ground-floor retail (and for a time, the Visitor Center gift shop).

Frank Lipo, executive director of the Historical Society, says the history of downtown Oak Park is "layer upon layer of buildings."

It's possible another layer is about to rise ... high.

I'm not proposing a monument to Lytton's or the Austin family or to Temperance Hall. But the opposition to Albion has been making the case, and making it well, that there is more to development in Oak Park than merely the economic kind. This corner encompasses Oak Park's earliest history, its school history, church history and commercial history — and now, perhaps, its high-rise history.

If and when Albion gets built, it won't be the end of the world. If it doesn't get built, it won't be the end of the world either. It won't even be the end of the story, which is ongoing.

But before we take any step, we should know what we're stepping on.

May oaks find safe arbor (1999, 2014)

I think that I shall never see
An oak among our downtown trees...

The Downtown Oak Park Business Association recently sponsored an Arbor Day contest titled, "Ode to an Oak."

I'm too old to win and the deadline is past, but I'm a sucker for promotions like this.

School-age kids were asked to wax eloquent about "what trees do for you," a refreshingly pastoral notion for a business organization whose main job is promoting commerce.

Arbor Day itself is one of those charmingly obsolete annual calendar notations that got a boost from the environmental movement a quarter-century ago when they tied Earth Day to it. Tomorrow is Earth Day while Arbor Day falls on April 30. You could also call it "Tree Appreciation Day," as it has traditionally been a gentle reminder to keep planting these dinosaurs of the plant world to offset the relentless rape of our remaining forests by loggers who try to satisfy our relentless exploitation of wood.

Oak Park is located in a forest — an "urban forest" — but mature trees are nothing to sneeze at (unless they're in spring bloom) no matter how they got there.

Trees, in fact, are our single most important natural resource, which is reflected in the town's very name. And that's why people around here were so uneasy when the Emerald Ash Borer showed up in Chicago. We need to be especially vigilant because the village has already been through one tree trauma — the Dutch Elm devastation of the 1960s and '70s.

Authorities, who had the foresight to plant elms along our parkways once upon a time, which resulted in spectacular cathedral canopies over our side streets, did not, alas, have the foresight — or the arboreal acumen — to know that a tiny beetle could easily move from bough to intertwined bough, wreaking havoc and obliterating these blessed shade-casters.

But there is safety in diversity, we discovered, even before we made the commitment to human diversity, and our foresters now plant a wide variety of species to replace the old elms, and now the green ash trees, as they die.

But what about the oaks of Oak Park?

As of 2014, there were an estimated 170 pre-settlement oak trees left in the village. A group called Historic Oak Propagation Project (HOPP), spearheaded by arborist Kathryn Jonas and environmental activist Julie Samuels, in conjunction with the Morton Arboretum in west suburban Lisle and the Openlands West Suburban TreeKeepers program, have collected acorns from 200- to 300-year-old native Oak Park bur oaks and planted them on private property and village parkways. So there's hope

Which doesn't get us any closer to our ode. The tree that once dominated these parts doesn't even crack the top five species in our tree surveys. I haven't spotted many oaks in the downtown business district. Downtown Oak Park is one of the few relatively treeless plains in the village — hence the bastardization of Joyce Kilmer at the top of this column.

The contest instructions were pretty general: Discuss "What do trees do for you?" in a poem, essay, or short story, a thousand words or less. I settled on oaks because we settled under oaks:

An Ode to Oaks
Called "old growth,"
Pre-settlement,
Heritage oaks,
Some were here
Before Kettlestrings arrived
Before Scoville discovered the high ground
Overlooking the low-lying basin
Where wild onions sprouted
In the garden where Chicago grew.
Every summer, oaks shield from scorching rays,
Curling branches simulate
Settings from some Gothic fairy tale

Evoking mystery and majesty,
From other centuries.
Every winter they play possum,
And every spring, defying logic,
Greenery explodes from rigid surfaces.
They ruled savannas before invasive plants arrive,
Gave their lives to embellish doorways
And chairs supporting our derrieres.
Inhaling pollution, returning oxygen,
No scolding or strings attached,
Producing the most beautiful seed on the planet.
When autumn wanes and branches empty,
Oak leaves cling, desiccated, withered,
Rustling in the wind one season longer,
Making squirrel highways, perches to rest wings,
Buffering us from sky's awful emptiness
A testament to silence and endurance.
May they always find safe arbor in this,
Their namesake park.

Buying more than a house (2002)

A new family is moving in on the 200 block of Forest Avenue. The house isn't quite ready yet. It's being rehabbed on the inside pretty extensively — a task made necessary by the fact that the previous owners had occupied it for 55 years.

The house is an unassuming grey-blue four-square with white sashes and shutters, nestled in a stand of towering craggy oaks, sandwiched on one side by a Victorian painted lady and a Frank Lloyd Wright gem on the other.

Don't know anything about the newcomers except they have kids, which is always good for a neighborhood — keeps the area young and vital. Don't know where they came from or if they have any sense of local history, but it turns out the house they bought is probably more significant than the architectural pedigrees on either side.

That's because the previous owners were the Folletts, Dwight and Mildred, who had as big an impact on the course of Oak Park history as anyone in the second half of the 20th century. Milly, the last remaining Follett to live in the house, died recently, which is why the house went on the market and why a new family is now occupying it.

In Oak Park, you buy more than a house. You also inherit its place in the community. The Folletts moved into this house in 1946. Dwight had just returned from World War II to settle into the family business — Follett Publishing Company, specializing in textbooks. The Follett social studies series was so popular that most of us probably used it in school.

But the Folletts' biggest contribution came in the late 1940s, when they spearheaded a political revolution against the stagnant status quo — Republican machine politicians who had ruled Oak Park for decades. Dwight Follett led a quiet revolution that produced the Village Manager Association and promised a new era of "good government." The Village Manager form of government was adopted by voters in 1952, and a new generation of energized, progressive public servants laid the groundwork for the Fair Housing Movement of the 1960s and Oak Park's successful four-decade experiment with managed integration.

This village is a very different place today because of the Follett family. Many of the early strategy sessions to plot their revolution took place in the unassuming house on the 200 block of Forest Avenue. The current owners, I'm guessing, were drawn to Oak Park largely because of what went on a half century ago at the dining room table in their new home.

Many people joined forces to make us what we are today. But Oak Park's first village manager, Mark Keane, who went on to become president of the International City Management Association, when he visited Oak Park just a couple of years ago called Dwight Follett "one of the greatest civic leaders I've ever encountered. He was a selfless guy but with political savvy, and he was dedicated to Oak Park. He was great at working with people."

Most of us are blissfully unaware of how this town got where it is today. We may recognize in a general way that we owe it to those who came before and appreciate the efforts but don't know the particulars.

A village endlessly evolves. Residents come and go. One generation gives way to the next and bequeaths whatever progress they've managed as a silent gift, a quiet legacy.

It's up to us to tell the stories of those who once lived here and what they added to the community.

Once upon a time, Dwight and Milly Follett came to live in a house on Forest Avenue in Oak Park — and changed the course of village history. The new owners may not know that.

But, like the rest of us, they're benefitting.

Testaments to love and memory (2012)

Scoville Park at Oak Park Avenue and Lake Street takes up just shy of 4 acres, or one square block. It doesn't look big, but there's a lot going on here. The park is collared by trees and almost every tree tells a story. This is the epicenter of the park district's memorial tree program, dedicated to individuals, living and dead.

In honor of Memorial Day, I took a self-guided tour and found 56 plaques, not counting the ones on the World War I memorial, most of them planted at the foot of an oak, crabapple, elm, horse chestnut, hackberry, pine or redbud. They testify to our need to remember and to cherish — "in loving memory" being the most commonly repeated phrase.

If you think Twitter is compact, you should see these plaques. Yet they still manage to tell a story.

Under the low-hanging boughs of a ginkgo tree, an older plaque reads: "In loving memory of dear husband and father, Dr. Emanuel W. Demeur, 1898-1982." Zigzagging north through a shady grove dotted with practitioners of benign indolence, who recline at various angles of repose on blankets, chairs, or an unmediated interface with thick green grass, the plaques multiply:

"Charles R. Navolio, 1920-1998, We'll always love you, Dad."

"Our friend, Harry Talmage, 1916-1986."

"Celebrate Life, Florence A. Navolio, 2001."

"Joseph M. Cheney Sr., Beulah A. Cheney, in loving memory, Joe, Jim, Ann."

Under a large, spreading maple: "In memory of Barbara Downs, 1939-2010, Gardens were her pleasure."

Beneath a red oak: "Best friends, Jimmy Krenzer, from Pat Berggren."

The oldest plaque dates back 85 years: "Presented to the Park District of Oak Park by the Garden Club of Oak Park and River Forest for use as a permanent Christmas tree, May 1, 1937." This is not, interestingly enough, the tree the park district strings with lights each December.

The most elaborate tribute can be found at the foot of an ornamental pear tree near the corner of Oak Park Avenue and Ontario Street:

"A fiery horse with the speed of light, a cloud of dust, and a hearty 'Hi, Ho, Silver!' Dedicated to the memory of Peggy Stallone and champions of justice everywhere." The Lone Ranger rides on.

Close to the sign for the Continental Divide (no kidding), which runs diagonally through the park, there is a white oak, tall and true, the truest tree you know, located kitty corner from the former location of Ernie's museum (until it closed in 2017). The plaque reads, "In memory of Ernest Miller Hemingway from his sister, Madelaine M. Miller."

Hunting memorials is a surprisingly interesting way to see a natural refuge like this. I have traversed this park myriad times, but I have rarely "visited." Under a chestnut tree, covered by grass clippings and close to the tennis courts, is the second oldest plaque: "In honor of Col. H.R. Brinkerhoff, 1836-1921. This tree was planted on Nov. 5, 1939 by St. Mihiel Auxiliary to Col. Brinkerhoff Post V.F.W."

Nearby is one dedicated to a former village president: "My treasures – gardens, trees, people. Barbara Furlong, June 1, 2002."

Beneath a young maple (perhaps a second planting) is a plaque honoring the "10th anniversary of the United Nations, 1945-1955," almost certainly the handiwork of the late, great Elsie Jacobsen.

Under a pine tree, thick with soft needles, on the slope that once served as the front lawn of James Scoville's mansion, you'll find "Lived well, laughed often, loved much. Terrance W. Stone," which makes a good epitaph. To its right, an older pine, the one the park district did deck with lights the past few Decembers, commemorates "the distinguished service of Clarence W. Schilke to Oak Park," a former village clerk and the last male to hold that office.

A nearby hawthorn recalls "Bill Stone. His love, smile and a wink blessed us all." Never underestimate the power of a good wink.

Directly west of Peace Triumphant (aka "the war memorial") by the walkway he traversed each morning and evening on the way to and from the Green Line (until cancer prematurely took this noble seeker of justice from us) is the majestic elm dedicated to "John Lukehart, committed to a diverse village."

On the west edge of the park now, heading south:

"In loving memory of Peter M. Constantinides, Oct. 21, 1952 – Feb. 15, 1985. To live in hearts we leave behind means not to die."

"Nick Allabastro, 1973-1999, to your giving heart."

"Robert A. Papp, Eileen L. Papp, Two souls soaring on together."

"What a Wonderful Life, Kenneth Van Wieren, July 8, 1931 – Feb. 17, 1995."

"In our hearts forever, Michael A. Powell, dedicated 2006."

A beautiful breeze is blowing. Parents and kids cavort in the expansive meadow. This place, surrounded by memorials to those who have died, couldn't be more alive. In the shadow of the main library, several trees honor word-lovers:

"Barbara Ballinger, librarian, friend of reading, 2001" (another date can now be added, alas: "2022").

"In loving memory of Peter Saecker, author, editor and library friend, 1935-2001" (and travel companion on the Hemingway Foundation excursion to Cuba in 2000).

"Sue Blench, reader, gardener, friend. Moms Book Club, 2002."

The place is thick with testimonials:

"Edy Eul, we'll always remember you."

"Richard A. Murphy, a giving man who lived, loved, laughed always."

"David Pintor, beloved father, florist and friend."

"Mondi Fosco III. Like this tree, our love shall always grow. Grandma Gloria."

On the south edge along Lake Street, "Gerry's Tree" is "dedicated to him by his friends and fellow park district employees for a dedicated guy who always appreciated a good joke, a good cigar and a job well done, 5/31/94."

"Morris Buske, teacher, author, historian, Oak Park advocate, May 11, 1996."

A red oak for Carolyn Poplett, "a dedicated volunteer, calls others to serve." (She died in 2022)

I never would have guessed that the best way to see Scoville Park is tree by tree.

It made for a memorable afternoon.

* * *

In Scoville Park last week, I spotted a single yellow rose imbedded in the ground by its stem beneath a crabapple tree near a plaque dedicated to "Martha W. Conn, 'Mi Chiamano Mimi,'" followed by the word "Inspirit." It's easy to forget that we're surrounded by memorials, memory being our best shot at a kind of immortality. The word "inspirit," I learned, means "to infuse spirit or life into; enliven." Memorials are not just about mourning. They also recall joy.

I figured there was more to that story, which Warren Conn, Martha's son, filled in with a follow-up note:

"We dedicated the tree and stone in Scoville Park," he wrote, "on Thanksgiving Day — our favorite family holiday — the week before your 'walk through the park.' This was the seventh anniversary of my dear mother's passing, '7' being a spiritual and symbolic number. Martha W. Conn's spirit lives in the things she loved, surrounded by nature, the library, historic monuments and architecture, lovely shops, summer concerts and sporting events. This will be a place for reflection and meditation — and the occasional picnic!

"'Mi Chiamano Mimi' was my mom's favorite aria from Puccini's *La Boheme*. She studied voice before, during and after college, and had she not had three children and lived in a different era, might have gone on to some operatic success. She could sing the entire score — all parts — from memory, and beautifully! We played the aria at her memorial service in November 2002. 'Inspirit' was and is so apropos."

Warren said his sister, Meredith, lives with her family in Oak Park, where she runs the Farmers Market and works as a consultant for the YMCA.

"My mom," he added, "lived in River Forest — and continues to live in our hearts and in Scoville Park."

The yellow rose I happened to spot that day functioned like an internet link that amplifies and expands, when you click on it — a link to a wider world beyond the text you're reading.

Stories abound and surround. As I take my daily stroll up and down Oak Park Avenue (which is how I spotted the rose), I'm certain I could stop anyone along the way and within a few questions, enter a world that would link to larger worlds. The internet is just a digital metaphor for the reality we inhabit — infinitely rich, endlessly fascinating, dense with potential. All we need to do is click — or ask.

I don't recall ever meeting Martha Conn, but hearing her son's amplification made me feel that much richer, more human, more sure that the vast majority of my fellow human beings are worth getting to know.

As Mimi sings in *La Boheme*:

> *My story is brief. ... I am contented and happy, and it is my pastime to make lilies and roses that have such sweet enchantment, that speak of love, of springtime, that speak of dreams and of visions, those things that are called poetic. Do you understand me?*
>
> *They call me Mimi. ... I live alone, quite alone in a little white room. I look upon the roofs and the sky, but when the thaw comes, the first sunshine is mine. The first kiss of April is mine! A rose opens in a vase. Petal by petal I watch it, that gentle perfume of a flower. ... About me I know nothing else to tell. I am your neighbor who comes to bother you at the wrong moment.*

When the first kiss of April brings blossoms to the crabapple trees in Scoville Park, I will think of them as Mimi's "Outspirit."

We live in remarkable villages in a remarkable world.

It's easy to discover.

All that's required is paying attention.

Romancing the sidewalks (2020)

Having walked many, many miles around Oak Park the past 30 years, I've become a connoisseur of sidewalks. Oak Park is a pedestrian-friendly town. On almost every street, there are two sets of sidewalks, divided into squares — thousands of squares, each a potential canvas. When I walk, I look around, but just as often I look down, my head tilting as I follow a train of thought, or take a deeper dive and lose myself in the stream of consciousness.

I've studied sidewalks for three decades now and, as an object of contemplation, they are more rewarding than you might imagine. What initially seems blandly uniform is anything but. Concrete has gone through stages — from coarse, dark and highly textured to fine-grained, white and smooth. Sand and gravel was the formula once upon an earlier time. Some squares actually include seashells, the sand in the mix coming from some forgotten beach on some forgotten shore.

Not all of our sidewalks consist of concrete. Sandstone panels and even slate slabs survive, recalling an era closer to the beginning of the last century, closer to the founding of the village in the 1800s.

As squares crack and decay, they are replaced, hence the variety. Walking some blocks is like tracing sedimentary layers of the Earth itself — or a museum exhibit on concrete's evolution. We take for granted the flatness of our walkways, but the remarkable power of tree roots can dislodge these slabs like some annoying nuisance, creating trip hazards, though municipalities now have machines that grind down the protruding edges, angling them back into conformity, exposing a patchwork of imbedded limestone, mosaic-like, beneath the surface.

Concrete when it's wet is irresistible to living creatures, judging by the imprints left behind, from shoe to paw prints to squirrel tracks to leaf fossils. If you appreciate textural diversity, Oak Park sidewalks offer a smorgasbord. If you pocket your magic rectangle and do nothing but look at the sidewalk, you'll find beauty as well as mystery.

Mystery, you ask? Yes, because there is also a fair volume of sidewalk script if you care to decipher it. Humans are immortality seekers, initials are legion, sometimes united by plus signs, proclaiming romantic coupledom. In the newer pavement where Rick Meegan's newsstand operated for many decades, tucked under the overpass, away from the elements near the corner of Oak Park Avenue and North Boulevard, Greg and Flo Wood left their marker. Close by, an admirer of Iron Maiden, Pink Floyd and Led Zeppelin (abbreviated to Led Zep) attest to someone's faithful fandom. Along Erie, north side of the street, near Kenilworth Avenue, "Ginkgo Tree B&B" testifies to the former use of the grand Victorian on that corner and the giant ginkgo tree in the backyard. Makes a wanderer wonder about the backstories.

But the biggest mystery of all is the inscription located 14 squares west of Oak Park Avenue along Erie, north side of the street, north edge of the square: "I still love Nan"

Hmmm, "still"? The word leaps out.

Who is/was Nan? And who scratched this into the wet cement, helpfully dated to August of 1977, almost a half-century ago? Someone saw a fresh square of cement and an opportunity. Something so private, yet so public. Was Nan present when he did it (presuming "he") or was Nan already "gone"? Was the author thinking about the past or the future? Maybe he looked at her and said, "When someone spots this 40 years from now, if I'm still alive, I will still love you." Has that prophesy come to pass?

Whatever the circumstances, the scribbler felt strongly enough to set his love in stone. Not forever, but as close as we come — until the square is replaced or the words erode to illegibility.

Does this mysterious romantic, in fact, still love Nan? Does Nan still love him? Are either still alive?

Was she already dead — perhaps tragically and too young — and could he no longer contain his longing? Did it continue to console or haunt him every time he passed this way or did his feelings fade over time? Would he, later in life, shake his head or smile when he saw it, amazed by love's youthful intensity? Did he eventually stop looking as he passed? Did he sometimes leave a single blossom on the grass, unobtrusively honoring her memory or the memory of their love?

Or did he move away and never see those words again? Did she move away, too, then return much later in life, and come across the message, never having known it was there, at a loss over how to find her missing lover?

Maybe the story is less romantic. Perhaps they broke up years before, but he never quite got over it and needed to leave this message behind, frozen in time.

Four words that seem to say so much.

Ernest Hemingway, famously known for being a writer of few words, once responded to someone's challenge to write an entire novel in just six words. Here's what he came up with:

"For sale: baby shoes, never worn."

It breaks your heart, and the novel writes itself in your mind — or tries to. Hemingway described his literary efforts as the tip of an iceberg, 7/8ths of which lies beneath the surface, unspoken.

"I still love Nan" is a four-word novel etched in concrete. I suspect it was written by a young man, but a friend believes it was an old man at the end of a long, loving life together. Only death could part them. He had a hard time getting down on his knees to inscribe the words, but he had to.

He just had to.

Because the only thing greater than the intensity of youthful love is the depth of long-lived love.

Forty-three years have passed. For 30 of those years, I walked past this square on my regular path without noticing it.

Who says sidewalks aren't romantic?

Happy Valentine's Day.

St. Edmund's bells are calling (2008)

Ring out the old, ring in the new,
Ring, happy bells, across the snow:
The year is going, let him go;
Ring out the false, ring in the true.
Ring out the grief that saps the mind
For those that here we see no more;
Ring out the feud of rich and poor,
Ring in redress to all mankind.

Alfred Tennyson

The bells of St. Edmund, I hear they are calling ...

We're a long way from the world that produced the 1945 Bing Crosby film, *The Bells of St. Mary's*, but once in a while, living across the street from St. Edmund Church, it's easy to feel sucked into that time warp.

Maybe it's the gothic architecture, church and school — refreshing to the eyes, with its ascendant verticality and devotional ornamentation (including gargoyles) instead of the usual row upon row of mortared, clay brick.

I live as close as you can get to St. Edmund Church, an institution to which I'm beholden. My parents married there over 70 years ago, so it played a significant role in my very existence.

Some might find it a bother living across the street from a church with a bell tower, which goes off every hour from 9 a.m. to 9 p.m. Real bells, tolling the hours, starting with nine, then 10, then 11, then 12 powerful, resonant reverberations each morning — a very old-world, almost medieval vibe. It gets your attention. More than once I've been on the phone with someone who asks, alarmed, "What is that?!"

With funerals, there is a steady, measured, doleful tolling of the bell. Don't ask for whom it tolls, John Donne sagely advised. But even without his classic poem, we know the answer. It tolls for all of us, a reminder that thou art dust and unto dust thou shalt return. So the bells can send chills up the spine, though reminders of mortality have their uses.

But not all is downbeat. After morning (and mourning) takes its toll, and again in the evening, the St. Edmund bells put on a show, a throwback to an epoch when bells marked the day's progress for the faithful, and called them to prayer, as it still does in monasteries across the country. If you walk outside just after noon or just after 6 p.m., you'd think it was Victory in Europe all over again — a free-wheeling joyful pealing emanating from that silver steeple, a monument to first pastor Monsignor Code's hierarchical devotion over a century ago. If you're standing directly across the street when it starts, the sound overwhelms.

Lately, though, the pealing has paled. At noon and 6, there is only a monotonous, sing-song ring that fails to stir the soul.

Don Giannetti, St. Edmund's self-described "parish hysterian," says one of the bells needs fixing. They don't actually swing back and forth as in *The Hunchback of Notre Dame*, as it turns out. Mechanized clappers sound the gongs. So one clapper is in the crapper and the gong is gone, but the sonic bath will return soon enough, Giannetti says.

The three bells (one large, two smaller) were originally a gift from a parishioner named Gore who, once upon a time, served as governor of Puerto Rico.

The bells remind me of New Melleray Abbey in Iowa, the monastery I visited each October for 20 years, where the ringing is integral to the daily routine (including the 3 a.m. wakeup call).

Not everyone around here appreciates them, but Don and I, at least, still find them a-pealing.

Violano's virtuoso performance (2010)

It has 123 separate functions, roughly 1,500 individual parts and 27 miles of wire (each the thickness of a human hair), and it's all crammed into a mahogany and glass cabinet — along with a violin, a piano harp and hammers, two rollers, and a 110-volt DC motor.

And this contraption played Bach's "Air on a G String" — beautifully — for a delighted and intrigued audience last week at Pleasant Home, the once-upon-a-time residence of Herbert S. Mills, whose company manufactured this ingenious mechanical music device known as the Violano Virtuoso.

The occasion was the annual meeting of the Pleasant Home Foundation, dedicated to the restoration of the George Maher-designed mansion. And this machine could help.

The foundation used its annual meeting as a "coming out" party for the Violano (a hybrid term combining, like the instrument itself, a violin and a piano). The instrument was donated by Evon's Nuts owner Jasper Sanfilippo, of Barrington Hills, who possesses more of these mechanical marvels than anyone.

Laura Thompson, executive director of the foundation, was on the job just one week when she and her husband attended a fundraising event at Sanfilippo's mansion back in 2004. She mentioned Herbert Mills' Oak Park connection, and Sanfilippo offered to donate one of his 52 machines to Pleasant Home. All the foundation had to do was pay to have it restored, a multi-thousand-dollar proposition in its own right.

The finished Violano finally arrived at Pleasant Home in 2009, though it needed some tinkering and tuning before it was ready for public appreciation. The foundation still needed to raise $8,000 as of a week ago Tuesday. Then a donor called and offered $4,000. Thompson is hoping someone will match that gift.

To mark the formal unveiling, the foundation invited Terry Haughawout — the man who painstakingly restored this and over 700 other Violano Virtuosos over the last 35 years — and Bob Brown, who holds the rights to the Mills Novelty name (millnovelty.com) and the inventor of a computer interface that allows the machine to play over 7,000 tunes via wireless computer hookup.

In addition to Bach, listeners that night were also treated to Violano versions of "Rocky Top" and "Tumbling Tumbleweeds."

Brown and Haughawout talked not only about the machine but its history, checking periodically with three of Herbert Mills' descendents, who were in attendance — two granddaughters, Corinne O'Brien James and Judy O'Brien Nordstrom, and great-granddaughter Julie James O'Brien — for confirmation.

Herbert Mills, it turns out, was every bit as intriguing as his machines. The youngest son of Mortimer Mills, who started the business back in 1891, Herbert bought the company in 1895 and changed the name to Mills Novelty Co. By the 1920s, the 375,000-square-foot facility at 4100 W. Fullerton was among the largest employers in Chicago, churning out over 600,000 "arcade" machines (slots, jukeboxes and mechanical music devices).

"Slot machines were the bread and butter of the company," said Brown, but Mills was always in conflict with the government, which wanted to limit access to gambling devices. To make them look more family-friendly, Mills reportedly invented the fruit symbols that still adorn slot machines to this day.

Endlessly inventive and resourceful, it was said that he could walk in on Monday with an idea and by Thursday, his wizards would produce a part to make it happen. Sixty percent of the patents Mills owned were never produced.

"They were extremely inventive people," said Brown, noting that at the height of the operation in the 1920s, Mills Novelty employed more mechanical engineers than General Motors. They also produced the first refrigerated coin-operated vending machine for Coca-Cola.

The inventions didn't always go over so well. An early video machine that showed a "girlie" film (tame by today's standard, Brown said, but lurid for that era) landed Mills in jail for several months. The county was lenient, allowing him to go home on the weekends, but while he was incarcerated, he endeared himself to many of his fellow convicts by generously handing out money, and he even paid to have the drab facility painted.

When he got out, he threw a big party. Mills had lots of parties, his descendents attested, and the granddaughters confirmed the longstanding rumor that he had the dining room table at Pleasant Home wired so that, with the push of a button, he could deliver a small electric shock to his guests when they touched their silverware.

"It livened up the parties," said one of his granddaughters, who now lives in Mills Tower, built on the grounds a few decades back and overlooking the mansion.

In addition to shocking silverware, Mills also had a Violano Virtuoso in the family living room. The person who owns that particular machine now, in fact, visited Pleasant Home the afternoon before the annual meeting. The Violano currently in the home was built in 1929.

In 1904, Henry Sandell approached Mills about manufacturing his new invention and by 1909, the U.S. Patent Office ranked it as one of the

"Eight Greatest Inventions" of the 20th century's first decade. Mills Novelty morphed that distinction into a marketing slogan, "Eighth Wonder of the World," to describe their marvelous mechanism.

Mills also manufactured a Double Violano (two violins), as well as a Viol-Cello and a Viol-Xylophone. The machines ran on electricity, which had only been in homes for a decade by the time the Violanos started rolling off the assembly line. The music was recorded on paper rolls or wax cylinders, which are still usable. Nowadays, a restored Violano would probably cost $50,000 with the computer interface. Sanfilippo owns so many because "if you pay too much, they find you," said Haughawout.

The device originally cost $2,000, which was a lot of money back then, but the merchants who put Violanos in their cafes and ice cream parlors reportedly recouped that amount in one year — one nickel at a time.

This was the era before radio and jukeboxes (which Mills Novelty also specialized in). So having something like this in your house was a big deal.

"People were tickled to death to hear anything," said Haughawout.

Peering into the cabinetry, watching the hammers strike the piano harp on the back wall and the wheels spinning against the violin strings, it was obvious that people are still tickled by the Violano Virtuoso.

12

Walkabouts

"One foot in front of the other — through leaves, over bridges," says Newt to Catharine, in Kurt Vonnegut's romantic tale, "Long Walk to Forever."

"They add up — the steps," says Catharine.

Newt is AWOL from Fort Bragg. Catharine is a week away from her wedding ... to someone else. It's crazy, she tells him. They say goodbye, but ... (spoiler alert) ... end up in one another's arms.

For 32 years, I've been on walks to forever in Oak Park. An excellent way to see the town, see the people, become part of the seen-ery.

One foot in front of the other. The steps add up.

The more you see, the better you see. Observation leads to perception, even to perceptiveness.

I see people walking dogs, such as Kris Lenzo wheelchair athlete, with his faithful companion, Beyonce the beagle, whom he always tries to give away. Conversations with passersby who don't pass by but stop to talk are one of the rewards of a good walk.

If you don't care where you're going or when it ends, and you'd be happy if it never ended, then you're on a walk to forever.

This walk has lasted three decades; here's some of what I found:

How to take a walk (2009)

Step 1: Leave your confines behind.
Step 2: First one foot, then the other.
Step 3: Repeat. Endlessly.
Step 4: Don't hurry. You're going someplace, but you have nowhere to go. Don't "take" a walk; let the walk take you.
Step 5: Unlock your senses. Each is a sponge, soaking in your surroundings. Notice the way sunlight and the wind take turns making love to the trees.
Step 6: Make a clear distinction between sounds and noise, scents and smells: tar from a newly paved street, the whine of an air-conditioner, a jet rumbling overhead, a train rattling past a block away, birds' sweet solos, a passerby's trailing wake of perfume.
Step 7: Register the echoes of other eras — what it was like in this spot once upon many times, how these buildings catch the light just so, just as they did then. When the din dies down, the world resembles what it once was. On any given mid-summer afternoon, when everyone is somewhere else and the back streets deserted, you can feel the ripples of another time, dissolving the thin membrane between past and present.
Step 8: Pass through a "passive" green space, where squirrels approach in halting fashion, hoping to find in you an easy mark, where children chase and pull and push and tumble and sit. Compare their lyrical laughter to the cardinal's bright, clear chirp overhead.
Step 9: Note the breeze hissing through tree branches, the machinery pounding at a construction site in the distance, a siren gradually drawing closer, eclipsing all other sounds as it races toward a nearby retirement facility.
Step 10: Enter the downtown business district, feel the heat rising from pavement, savor the aromatic overtures, a cloud of roasting garlic from a nearby restaurant, pay close attention to the shadows of leaves dancing on the bare shoulders of a woman reading on a bench, wave

away the cigarette smoke drifting from an alcove where a shop clerk takes her break.

Step 11: Stop to chat with someone you've known a long time about how this summer measures up to seasons past.

Step 12: Come back to the present. If you aren't careful, you can get lost inside the long hallway of your head. There's plenty of time to inhabit your memories. Don't exhaust them. The present is the only place where memories are made, a highlight reel of the here and now.

Step 13: Observe trees being pruned, flowerbeds being watered. Let the vibrant reds and whites and purples of front-yard gardens pierce your pupils. Admire the fluttering of butterflies and porch flags.

Step 14: Flow along a busy avenue filled with fellow walkers, human and canine. Listen for intriguing conversation fragments, a few words in passing, that offer a window into other lives.

Step 15: Remind yourself, neither this day nor this season seem to be in any hurry. Why should you?

Step 16: When you reach a point where you wouldn't mind if this walk never ended, then you're getting somewhere.

A summer evening's stroll (2008)

Several evenings recently, I've taken the long walk to Hole in the Wall. If you're not familiar with Hole in the Wall, 901½ S. Oak Park Ave., it's a grand summer tradition among overheated Oak Parkers. The name refers to the narrow, half-storefront that houses this cramped, seasonal ice cream shop, which once specialized in what was called "frozen custard," then "soft-serve ice cream," and now "low-fat frozen yogurt." Or maybe it's all of the above.

I prefer "low-fat yogurt," easier to rationalize. That and the long walk helps me justify a summer evening's treat, applied to a waistline that doesn't need further encouragement.

But the "treat" goes well beyond the smooth, frozen chocolate-peanut butter-swirled concoction in my cup. The walk itself is the main course.

Oak Park Avenue is a busy street, but still feels surprisingly residential. Many single-family homes along the way have porches, and the residents are out enjoying them, eating dinner or chatting with neighbors, schmoozing amicably on their front lawns.

It's about a mile to the shop from my place, so as I stroll along, I begin to lose myself in the surrounding tableau. I spot a couple standing on the parkway carefully studying the exterior of their house — a home improvement project just started, just completed, or somewhere in between.

Avenue Ale House is abustle, front windows flung open. The stroll usually takes place around sunset, when the sky becomes a fluid entertainment medium, as clouds shape-shift and sponge up the remaining light. I look forward to crossing the bridge over the expressway canyon where the sky opens, unobstructed by trees and buildings.

Just past the bridge, there's almost always a line snaking down the sidewalk outside Hole in the Wall, which creates its own mini-theater. Three pre-adolescent girls in front of me are lost in animated discussion until one realizes, "We don't have any money!" They spy an adult from the neighborhood and wave cheerily, perhaps sensing a loan in the offing.

Parents and kids hang out on the corner, flush with the pleasure of sweet slush on the tongue, until the whole group aggregates and moves off toward home, imprinting sweet memories, available for future withdrawal, with interest, when needed in some low-ebb portion of their future — rising to the rescue when least expected.

I return home by a different route, East Avenue being the road less traveled. Corner parkway gardens tower with Queen Anne's lace and purple coneflowers, the prairie's testament to high summer.

Dusk gathers more quickly under a canopy of old elms.

The yogurt is mere memory.

The evening's treat, however, lingers.

Open porches, cluttered lawns (2017)

Former Oak Parker David Axelrod, political strategist and advisor to President Barack Obama, and former Oak Park resident Peter Sagal, host of the NPR quiz show, *Wait, Wait, Don't Tell Me!*, who were the first two guests in a series of interviews conducted by Public Square's Charlie Meyerson at Dominican University in River Forest this fall (sponsored by the local newspaper), focused on "frontage" in defining what they liked about living in Oak Park.

Axelrod called Oak Park "a front-porch community," as opposed to the "back-deck" western suburb he moved to later. By "back-deck" he meant prioritizing privacy over the upfront interface of front porches. Spending time on the front porch makes us visible, encourages interaction, exposes us to neighbors and other passersby. It makes us more transparent. Our homes are not just some refuge, sanctuary, or moated castle. We dare to live in the open. We aren't hiding from one another.

Oak Park has a wealth of porches — if not by design, then by good fortune. Our housing stock is old and porches were popular back when. If you buy a home in Oak Park, there's a good chance a porch comes with it.

Sagal recalled that when he was looking for his first home, he favored Oak Park partly because the front lawns were liberally littered with the detritus of family living — toys, sports equipment, etc.

His version of "curb appeal" was a well-cluttered front yard, more informal, "lived in" and therefore "neighborly," people who don't mind lived-on lawns and may be comfortably cluttered themselves.

Front porches and front yards, then, are metaphors for upfront, down home, and open — qualities Oak Parkers like to brag on.

Porches, however, can be ignored and front yards obsessively manicured, with warnings to "Keep Off the Lawn," so I put these metaphors to the test and took a walk — up Grove and down Kenilworth, between Erie and Division — on a surprisingly balmy first weekend in December, a severe test, to be sure, this being the "inside" portion of the year.

I did find a few fronts fenced, but none of the fortress variety. Several had gates shut, mostly in the "estate" section on Kenilworth, but one remained amiably ajar. "Invisible fence" signs reassured passersby that off-leash bowser wouldn't bother them — while perhaps also putting the nefarious on notice that a dog lives on the premises. Homeowners, after all, aren't about to leave their "private property" unprotected. In fact, the most common lawn signs were for security services.

But not by much. "Hate Has No Home Here," "In This House We Believe," and "Black Lives Matter" signs were common, along with those pledging allegiance to various schools. Our front lawns speak, sending multiple messages. The only "Beware of Dog" sign I saw also boasted membership in the OPRF High School "Huskie Wrestling Family." If you get past the dog, you'll have to contend with the wrestler.

One intriguing sign urged, "Let's Love Like #yourfamilyismyfamily (www.ahouseinaustin.org)" and two others admonished motorists to "Drive Like Your Children Live Here."

Christmas decorations don't really count for the purpose of this survey, but lawn ornaments remain a clutter for all seasons. A large stone owl sentinel hovered over one lawn while a cherub and a gargoyle dressed up a couple of others. A well-worn desk chair leaned against an even older elm tree, inviting scroungers to whisk it away, which is likely to happen since a number of unofficial "recycling agents" regularly patrol our streets and alleys.

Not all front yards can be described as "lawns." Many have moved their gardening efforts out front for passing eyes to peruse. One cultivator was out thinning the brittle brush, the gardening remains of Summer Past.

"There are plenty of lessons to learn," she brightly offered when asked if this chore represented the "downside" of green thumbery.

Some lawns feature "Free Little Libraries," tiny cabinets perched atop wooden posts. The message engraved on one makes a good slogan for egalitarian, communitarian living: "Want? Take. Have? Give." Other lawns feature lamp posts and other fixtures for the evening hours. A large goal and soccer ball coexist peacefully with the residue of a roof tear-off ongoing overhead.

A few houses have pavered or flag-stoned a section of the front lawn to serve as a patio, complemented by chairs and small tables or stone benches or metal love seats and even firepits. Birdhouses hang from tree limbs and wind chimes from porch overhangs. Banners proclaim country and college and even celebrate winter itself.

Adirondack chairs are popular, plopped directly on the grass or in a dedicated alcove. Next to one robin's-egg-blue pair, a rake is propped, its tines fat with speared leaves as if the owner were interrupted, mid-rake, and never returned. One frontage accommodates a small netted goal, two abandoned field hockey sticks, a frisbee (in the bushes) and assorted balls. A nearby sidewalk is flanked by a tennis ball on one side and a baseball on the other, serving as sportsy bookends.

One family arrives home with a fir tree tied atop their car, which attracts the attention of a young friend who shouts from across a busy street, and heads in their direction, with Dad in tow, to celebrate this momentous occasion. The friend shouts, "We got our Christmas tree!" loud enough for the whole neighborhood to hear. News travels fast.

Post-Halloween pumpkins gently implode on stairsteps or on the ground, well-gnawed by squirrels, whose fatness suddenly becomes more understandable. Half of a Sean Spicer head, Trump press spokesman, peers out from a bush, bogeyman style. A green plastic watering can has been left out by someone who is still living in another season.

Most porches are open-air, but a few are screened. Some are half-porches or porticos, or merely a widening of the stairs at the top to allow for a bench or a couple of chairs. Few porches have been abandoned, however, even now. A good number still have cushions in the wicker furniture or cast-iron rockers. And, of course, many feature swings. On one porch, six chairs surround a table, indicating that the residents haven't quite given up on the possibility of one more al fresco dinner this year. There is even a double-decker porch furnished with outdoor furniture on both levels. On the lower level, a ceiling fan hibernates till next summer while a candle sits on the ledge awaiting some windless, mild, early winter evening.

And what to my wandering eyes did appear, on one porch near

Holmes School, but a well-bundled woman idling away the late afternoon — on Dec. 1!

The verdict is in: We are indeed a front-facing, forward-thinking population. Then again, most of these houses have alleys, offering ample opportunities for backyard connections as well.

We are, indeed, a village of lived-in porches and comfortably cluttered front yards.

Oak Park was built for connection.

Pandemic pedestrian (2020)

I see friends shaking hands, saying, 'How do you do?'
They're really saying, 'I love you.'

Louie Armstrong
What a Wonderful World

Well, maybe not shaking hands. Bumping elbows. Or a friendly wave. But the question has taken on new urgency, deeper meaning.

"How are you?"

A good friend used to bristle at that question. He saw it as shallow, lazy, insincere. "How are you?" in his mind was a profound question deserving a real answer, and he didn't think most people wanted a real answer.

But things are different now, as you may have noticed. Impossible not to notice, really. We're using words like "isolation," "quarantine," and "lockdown," which send shivers down the spine. "Social-distancing" is a kinder, gentler euphemism, and "shelter in place" which sounds positively benign, though it also sounds like "running in place," a metaphor for expending a lot of energy to go nowhere. My friend would have called that an apt description of our society — before this global pandemic altered (permanently?) the world we live in.

And how we live in the world.

So how are you? Are you well? Are you coping? Are you thriving in spite of circumstances? Are you down? Struggling to adjust?

I feel for high school and college seniors whose last semesters have been cut short. The final semester should be a golden time of savoring, looking back, and eagerly anticipating what comes next. I feel for athletes whose encounter with a bigger stage has been canceled after years of extraordinary dedication to their sport — high school and NCAA basketball players, baseball players on the brink of making the major leagues, teams that might have won championships, hundreds of Olympic athletes around the world.

I feel worse for those who live paycheck to paycheck and have been furloughed or laid off, and those who will lose businesses over this. And those, in the wealthiest country on Earth, who still don't have adequate access to affordable health care.

I worry about those who are frail and fragile and most at risk. I worry for everyone because we're all vulnerable. No one is exempt; no one's privilege can protect them.

But after I work through these emotions, I look around and notice what's happening and what's not happening.

Distractions have been reduced. Consumerism is based on distractions, exploiting our impulses, our willingness to serve our appetites. With so many businesses closed, distractions are reduced — radically. With less hustle and bustle, noise has been reduced.

We can hear ourselves think.

We're all in, people are saying, but we're also out. Normally when I'm walking, the only people I encounter are attached to dog leashes. Now whole families are ambling, taking their time, taking it all in, going nowhere in particular. It's like every day is the day after Thanksgiving. We're in permanent holiday mode as the economic engine idles — without the afterglow of celebration.

But we have been given the gift of time. Not short-term "time off" but time with no end in sight. Time to remember or, for the first time perhaps, realize what's important and what isn't. Time enough maybe to think about what is unnecessary in our life and in our world. Time to imagine a whole new world. A world in which we are not reduced to bowing at the altar of capitalism and serving the 1% priestly caste.

Or as Rebecca Solnit said in her *On Being* interview last Sunday, "There is so much other work that love has to do in the world. ... What if we can be better people in a better world? ... Unpredictability is better than certainty. It creates an opening, but you have to walk through it. ... We can become the storytellers rather than the person told what to do."

In ways we cannot yet see, our current cloistering could lead to a healthier, better world. A global time-out. These are "The Days the Earth Stood Still," and like that sci-fi classic, it has the potential to bring us all to our senses. We have time to think about the world we've created and wonder whether we can't do better.

As my columnist colleague John Hubbuch recently said, "This is an opportunity not to be wasted."

Most of us now have enough toilet paper — our security blanket — to last us the rest of our lives. Grocery stores have become our new community centers. Mostly we're sheltering in place, but we're reaching out to one another, sending emails, using our hand-held devices as actual telephones.

And we're asking the most profound question of our times:

How are you?

I've been walking quite a bit lately. You too? It's a gratifying experience. I've never been thanked so often for going out of my way to avoid people. And I've never been so tempted to use my favorite line from the end of every Lone Ranger episode: "Who was that masked man (or woman)?"

Feels good to get out, though, if only to survey the display of seasonal flowers, which seem to thrive in our chilly, not-in-any-hurry spring. The daffodils are dazzling, nodding as if to say, "We're cool." They shine like yellow glow sticks. Even the magnolias, burned by sub-freezing temps and burdened by two snows, have shown real hardiness, struggling through and even thriving.

Flowers are vulnerable but not fragile. There's a lesson in this.

Sidewalks are a-bloom with chalk pastel bouquets. Hopscotch is making a major comeback. Creative expression abounds. Front windows are full of teddy bears and encouraging messages. My favorite is "April distance means May existence."

And speaking of creativity, I never expected to be singing "What a Wonderful World" to my grandsons on a computer "platform" called Zoom.

Here's a quote I found in an old notebook attributed to Chekhov:

"Any fool can get through a crisis. It's this day-to-day that's killing me." But what happens when the day-to-day is part of the crisis?

Another, attributed to Oscar Wilde: "It is because humanity has never known where it is going that it has never been able to find its way."

Or Henry Ford: "Failure is simply the opportunity to begin again more intelligently."

Plenty to think about. Plenty to ponder.

Nothing has ever been so dangerous for the status quo — or the status quo's guardians — as so many people having so much time on their hands to contemplate the flaws and unfairness of the current system.

Maybe a revolution is building.

The powers-that-be desperately want the economic engine restarted — mostly as a distraction — because the longer this goes, the more clearly the inequities come into focus. No wonder the privileged are in such a hurry.

Never before have so many families spent so much time together. You see them out on front lawns, whole families, mid-day, mid-week. Kids today will be telling stories about this extended recess when they are grandparents themselves.

We shouldn't be in too much of a hurry to reopen. Never underestimate the power of a pandemic to reorder priorities. What's important ... and what isn't? We've been given a great gift: slowing down so we have time to think ... about the world we want to live in, a world where the economy and the powers-that-be serve us instead of the other way around.

April social distance means May co-existence.

Maybe the lockdown will set us free.

Pollution is fading. Gas prices falling.

Justice calls for system overhauling.

We're all in eLearning.

Is fairness returning?

A revolution is brewing, a revolution that begins with revelations.

Think about it. You have the time.

Who are all those masked men and women?

It's us, the Lone Rangers.
Just keep thinking:
What a wonderful world this could be.

The far side of day (2021)

I'll be looking at the moon, but I'll be seeing you.

Sammy Fain, Irving Kahal
I'll Be Seeing You

In a pandemic year of many walks, the sky features prominently. Open sky offers welcome balance to the confines of walls and rooftops and leafy trees during months of sheltering in place. During the day, the sky is an abstract expressionist canvas, painting and repainting itself in blues and grays and whites and, at the ends of days, in brilliant golds and pastels, with great broad strokes in shifting shapes.

But the night sky offers true companionship. In the heavy glow of urban streetlights, the sky is a desert of starlessness, so anything in the great vault that shines brightly is likely a planet. This year, Saturn chased Jupiter across the southern sky, like a younger, smaller sibling pursuing an idolized older brother, never quite catching up — until December, when it sat smugly atop in triumphant convergence, jewel upon jewel, for a few precious nights in the afterglow of sunset.

Halfway through the year, Mars, imperial in its march directly overhead, joined the procession.

The moon, meanwhile, took turns dallying with each, and served as a fine companion for walks home, alone in the dark. Though usually facing away, more interested in chasing its solar master, the once monthly moon turns its round, direct gaze upon us:

> *Walking home*
> *Late*
> *After talking with a friend*
> *Accompanied by our only moon,*
> *Full-faced,*
> *Present and presenting*

After several nights in hiding,
Waiting to bestow
Its far-flung glow.
Not the cold dead moon,
Stuck,
A slave to its orbit,
But this living moon,
Of secret rendezvous.
Not the same moon
That kept my mother company
During her last years on Earth
Through her bedroom window
Late at night or just before dawn,
The moon she called "my buddy,"
Which she also called my father
Whom she believed waited
Somewhere beyond.
This moon,
Close to that moon,
Mirrors the sun,
Dancing in and out of view,
Thin clouds streaming past like steam
From some percolating mystery.
This moon,
Somehow,
Has absorbed life's departed
Held there, aglow and warm
Even now.
This moon, keeping watch,
Keeping company
On my walk through the village,
Past the lit windows of the living
Down this long sidewalk to the bedroom
Where I sleep

Not quite alone
Thanks to this moon,
Out my window,
Three days' journey away
Yet so close to the eye.
Who could feel alone
Walking wordlessly
On the far side of day,
With this rear-view-mirror,
This moon,
Wiped clean by tissue-thin clouds,
Pretending preoccupation
With Earth and Sun?
Keeping me company
Through this village
Of many seasons
That holds so much
And so many,
All vital,
Some only in memory,
Somehow now
Contained in this moon
Of many dear faces
Beaming back to this heart
Of many dear loves.

13

Time Capsule

The Grover's Corner time capsule in the play *Our Town* includes a copy of the New York Times and the Grover's Corners Sentinel newspaper, a Bible, a copy of the U.S. Constitution, and a copy of William Shakespeare's plays. The stage manager says he's going to include a copy of *Our Town* itself, so people in a thousand years will know, "This is the way we were in the provinces north of New York at the beginning of the 20th century. This is the way we were: in our growing up and in our marrying and in our living and in our dying."

What about here in the provinces west of Chicago in the first decades of the 21st century? What do we want people to know about us going forward?

Well, Oak Park once had stately elm trees lining every parkway, creating a lovely green cathedral arch over each street. But Dutch elm disease taught us our first painful lesson in the benefits of diversity. We no longer put all our seeds in one basket.

And the replacement trees of many varieties have had a half-century to grow and flourish and our mature trees are once again the envy of those who come to visit.

So trees go into our time capsule — along with the pedestrian mall on Lake Street, an ill-fated but courageous innovation in the 1970s and '80s, meant to redress the great economic downturn that afflicted Oak Park's once-vaunted shopping district, which suffered from the sprawl of large suburban malls and the highways that took shoppers there post-World War II.

Every town, if it wants to survive, must evolve. And many elements of life that residents took for granted for so long have become casualties of time and trendiness and ended up discarded by the wayside, fading in the rearview mirror, or locked in the musty vault of memory.

Rick Meegan's last stand (1997)

The New York Times driver arrives over an hour late. The regular driver's father died, reports Rick Meegan, who has operated the newsstand at Oak Park Avenue and North Boulevard every Sunday for 25 years.

But people still walk by and ask, "When did they put in a newsstand?"

"I have to laugh," says Meegan. It used to be located across the street. He doesn't remember exactly when they moved the grey wooden shack to the southwest corner under the railroad embankment to protect it from the elements.

It's April, but the kerosene heater is still running. There is a dusting of snow on the ground, but the sun is starting to break through the clouds, and business always picks up when the sun comes out.

A Cadillac proudly flying a Green Bay Packers pennant pulls up, and Meegan's daughter, Kathy, pops out of the shack, decked in boots and a heavy coat with a fur collar.

Running this newsstand is pleasant during the summer when

Meegan's children and grandkids (eight of the former, going on 21 of the latter) sometimes join him, but they're not so motivated in winter, and lately business hasn't been so good.

Rick has been driving a Tribune delivery truck for 45 years this July. The newsstand was a way to pick up a little extra income. His kids liked working the stand growing up because they could make some spending money, Kathy recalls, but now her siblings have too many other obligations and interests, so she and her fiancé are the main support crew now. She'd like to see her dad give it up, "but you can't change a zebra's stripes." Kathy works for an architectural firm and lives in Westchester. Rick has been an Oak Parker for 60 of his 62 years.

Business is down because people pick up their Sunday papers at convenience stores now or via home delivery. It's hard to compete "unless you sell dirty books like in Berwyn," Rick laments. The village of Oak Park requires over $400 in liability insurance, though the annual permit is only $10.

Rick used to sell 250 to 300 Tribs on a Sunday. "Now we're lucky to break 190," he says. He makes 29 cents for every Trib sold, 23 cents for a Sun-Times, and 55 cents for the New York Times. He arrives a little before 5 a.m. and stays open till about 1.

Cars pull up around the corner on North Boulevard or on Oak Park Avenue. Sometimes a northbound car will make a looping U-turn, he says, and a vehicle does just that as he mentions it.

Many of the cars are large, Cadillacs and Chryslers. Rick estimates that 80 percent of his customers are older. The newsstand is a tradition for them and they're financially secure, so they don't need to pinch pennies.

Before and after Mass at nearby St. Edmund, there's a rush, but Rick thinks there are fewer people attending church these days. Owners walking their dogs are another important part of his client base. And the breakfast bunch often buy papers before heading into Erik's Deli, George's or some other local eatery.

Rick and Kathy know many of their customers by sight (or by car) and the drivers call out their preferences as they pull up. Rick's peripheral vision is keen, detecting customers well before the uninitiated observer.

Today is a $20 bill day, he notes, as he fishes for change in his pocketed apron. Some days they get more tens and fives. And the quarters are going fast.

A regular customer walks up and Rick greets him with "New York, New York?" The customer responds on cue, "What a wonderful town," as he hands over his money. At regular intervals, the rapid transit or Metra trains rush past on the tracks overhead, kicking up wind and a flurry of snowflakes. That and the faded wreath attached to the side of the shack prompts Rick to wish passers-by a Merry Christmas.

Business goes in spurts and lulls. If they run out of papers, he walks over to the nearby White Hen and buys them at full price just to keep his customers happy and coming back.

A man in a green Boston Celtics jacket picks up his New York Times, and Rick mentions the death in the driver's family.

"I had someone working for me who had three grandmothers die," the customer quips.

Start spreading the news.

Rick Meegan suffered a stroke in 2007. His grandson kept the stand going for a while and then an assistant to one of the delivery drivers took over. The old news shack was finally shut down and removed in 2010. Rick died in 2015 at the age of 80.

Pieritz Bros. and talismans from the past (2017)

Among the numerous family totems in my apartment is a "Vintage Remington Rand Model 5 Portable Typewriter" from the 1930s.

You can find these for sale online, but I'm not interested in selling.

Two venerable book sets also echo my childhood: The 1949 Childcraft series (wonderful artwork in the well-thumbed *Storytelling and Other Poems*), the 1959 Random House Landmark series (*The Swamp Fox*, about Revolutionary War hero Francis Marion, and *The Adventures of Ulysses*, a retelling of the Odyssey were among my early "great reads"), and a worn copy of *Grimm's Fairy Tales*, which also had a powerful impact on my developing imagination.

The books and sundry other keepsakes are displayed behind glass doors in my parents' china cabinet, which formerly anchored the front hall of the Gunderson house at Elmwood and Jackson, where I grew up.

My twin grandsons, age 4, are a little young for the books, and the other items are only of passing interest, but they enjoy playing with the typewriter, which I have sitting out on a side table next to the couch.

It belonged to my maternal grandfather, Pat Mooney, a self-made man and larger-than-life figure, an almost exact contemporary of Ernest Hemingway, with whom he had some parallels. My Papa died of cancer just two years after Papa Hemingway, who spent much of his adulthood hammering away on manual typewriters like this one. In 1940, about the time Ernie took up permanent residence in Cuba, my grandfather moved the family to Oak Park from Cicero, inaugurating our 77-year history in the village.

The Remington 5 spent most of that history gathering dust in my parents' attic until 1999, when they downsized, and I confiscated it. The ribbon was dried out so the boys didn't see much of a result for their pecking efforts, so one afternoon last October, I grabbed the typewriter and drove over to Pieritz Office Supplies at Ridgeland and South Boulevard.

If you haven't been there, it's one of those businesses you swear can't possibly still exist in the 21st century (which is more a comment on the 21st century than on Pieritz).

Whenever I go there, which isn't often enough, the place feels Brigadoon-ish. I can't help feeling that this storefront springs into existence only when I darken their doorway, and as soon as I leave, it vanishes into the mists of some Scottish Highland.

When I entered, the shop looked like a manual typewriter museum, so I knew I was in the right place. Not quite believing it possible, I asked co-owner Deborah Pieritz if I could get an inked ribbon for my Remington 5 so my grandsons might see the letters of their names on paper when they pressed the keys.

"Sure," she said matter-of-factly, taking the typewriter, whose condition I apologized for. The next day, I picked it up, found the ribbon inked and the typewriter carriage dust-free (a minor miracle). She only charged me for the ribbon, restoring my faith in humanity and random acts of kind customer service.

I rolled a piece of paper under the platen, and the boys were thrilled to see this ancient mechanism actually function — though they still prefer pressing as many keys as possible at the same time so the spindles stick together and have to be pulled back by hand.

Someday, maybe they'll appreciate this talisman of the past, this charm, this amulet, this thing capable of working wonders, which is how the Oxford English Dictionary defines "talisman," a magical figure capable of benefiting its possessor.

Someday, they may possess such clan totems, or at least fondly recall them. And maybe they'll also read the Childcraft and Landmark books too.

Perhaps possession will benefit them as much as it still benefits me, reminding me of the people I came from, how I got here, and how I came to be the person I am.

There is power in these otherwise inanimate objects. They are part of my "canon of beauty," a reminder of the richness of the life I have been gifted.

If nothing else, the Remington might help the boys — men someday — remember that, once upon a time, there was a writer in the family.

You never know, perhaps two writers … or maybe even three.

After 125 years in the office supply business, Pieritz Bros. closed in 2020. The corner of Ridgeland and South Boulevard will never be the same.

May Madness (2002)

Our best street festival has lost either its innocence or its mind — maybe both.

This was the 12th May Madness, formerly known as Midnight Madness, and it just isn't the same. How could it be? My son was 7 that first year. Now he's 18.

He was there the other night — saying goodbye. He's off to college this fall, probably won't look back for a while, but when he does, May Madness may be one of the highlights of his Oak Park childhood.

This annual rite of spring became part of Oak Park's annual rite of passage. It marked incremental independence, the ties that bind less and less each year.

This is where many Oak Park kids got their first taste of freedom. It happened in stages. First, the buddy system. Have a trusted friend with you at all times. Designated check-in spots, every hour, then every two hours, then "touch base once in a while," then "tell us what your plans are" and finally, "don't be late getting home."

Kids move in migratory herds — late elementary, middle school, high school. They frolic, chase and check each other out. At an event like May Madness, they can feel secure and adventurous at the same time, making memories by the minute.

This year African drummers performed on the south stage as distinguished scientist Carl Spight, a drummer himself, stands to the side, bobbing his head in appreciation. In the background, the setting sun reflects off the silver spire of St. Edmund Church and saturates the out-leafing, post-blossom pear trees. A giant inflatable figure jiggles like Greek warriors holding a victory celebration inside the Trojan Horse.

Adults grab a beer and brat and find a table or section of curb near one of the stages and schmooze or simply listen. Nearby, Charlie Robinson wields his spatula, flipping ribs. In front of Erik's Deli, Village President Joanne Trapani hugs a cop. Marinated chicken sizzles on a large grate over hot coals in front of Winberie's at Oak Park Avenue and Lake Street. Parents and kids stand toe-to-toe in the street, negotiating the length of the leash.

May Madness is where divisions dissolve. It's the only time all year when this many teens can be found in such close proximity to so many adults. It's also the only time this many kids from Austin can be found in such close proximity to kids from Oak Park. That's healthy — or should be, if only fear didn't rear its ugly head.

The kids from the Austin neighborhood where the western edge of Chicago meets the eastern edge of Oak Park are well behaved but skittish. When a scuffle breaks out, the police react quickly, but the disturbance sets off a small stampede. For the second year in a row, the party is shut down before 10 p.m. That's a shame.

The group on the north stage was just drawing a crowd. In Scoville Park, the youth band doesn't get to show off the finale they worked so hard on. You can tell a successful street festival by the crowd it draws. But this festival may become a casualty of its own success.

Maybe they should put the best bands on at 8 p.m. and offer "wind-down" music after 9. Maybe they need a new name — like May Meandering, since that's what most people do. And the police need to figure out how to quell disturbances without causing a stampede.

May Madness or May Meandering? May we keep this going?

Project Unity's place in our story (2020)

The group officially came to an end on March 8, 2020. Two dozen Oak Parkers of color and those who fall into the ethnic catch basin known as "white," gathered in the social hall at Euclid Avenue Methodist Church (the one with the large banner outside proclaiming, "Jesus Was Radically Inclusive") to celebrate, reconnect and bring Project Unity to closure.

The "project" will never really end, of course, but its beginning dates back 28 years to 1992 when the Longfellow School Parent-Ed Committee met to discuss a disturbing trend. Several of the parents were either in interracial marriages, had adopted children of another race, or both. They were concerned, as their kids wound their way through the school system, that they might not fit in with kids of either race. They and others moved to Oak Park specifically because of its reputation for openness and diversity. They wanted their children to benefit from that diversity, not be hampered by it.

The perceived problem was that, while students of different races mingled well in elementary school, they started to separate in middle school and high school. The committee held a forum and asked students to talk about the issue. The kids didn't really see a problem, but if there was one, they pointed out, it was more with the parents, who weren't exactly setting a good example of racial interaction.

Becoming better role models, then, was the motivation behind Project Unity, which formed in 1993 and peaked with a membership of 130 households (235 adults). Consciousness-raising was certainly a priority. Book groups formed and evolved into discussion groups. Some lasted two decades. But the driving force was socializing, getting to know one another and, above all, having fun. Dances and potluck dinners brought them together.

"Project Unity was about fostering friendship among people of different races," said Pat Winters, who chaired the social committee. Improving communication through cross-racial dancing is another way of putting it.

And it worked. Friendships formed that continue to this day. But as with many social organizations, Project Unity didn't attract enough young couples to whom the torch could be passed. Energy waned, kids grew up, nests emptied.

To truly measure Project Unity's success, the attendees agreed, you need to ask the kids. Did our modeling have a lasting impact? Those kids grew up in a country that became increasingly fragmented and polarized. Racial tension is a more complex issue now than it was then. There is a need for a national "Project Unity" and not just for Black-White relations. We are a much more diverse country (and village) but less unified. U.S.A. now stands for Uneasy Silos of America. Not enough communication, not enough interaction.

And not enough dancing.

At the final get-together, members shared reflections.

"It built community for me," said co-founder Karin Grimes. Her biracial daughter eventually wrote her college admission essay about what it meant to grow up in Oak Park. Karin is now a member of the village's Community Relations Commission and runs the potluck dinner program, continuing one of Project Unity's most successful activities.

Co-founder Cheryl Capps said she came to Oak Park from Pittsburgh to "interface with other kinds of people. Project Unity was that bridge for us." When asked if it shifted the conversation within her family, Cheryl noted that her daughter would probably say it didn't make a difference, "but she lived it. She didn't know any different. In college, she had to say whether she was White or Black. She doesn't feel different here."

Pat Healey was taking a class called "Race Relations" at the University of Chicago when she heard about Project Unity. She started attending so she could write a paper for the class. Her Project Unity discussion group was still meeting as of 2010. At the time, she wrote, "We have examined our racial, religious, gender, ethnic and political views. We have challenged one another. In doing so, we have sometimes surprised ourselves with our deeply-imbedded stereotypes. We have celebrated and mourned together. We are friends."

Her son is currently teaching a diversity class in Evanston.

Yasmin Ranney said, "Project Unity was moms and dads. There was no other agenda. It was free-flowing, evolving organically. It helped build community without intending to." Steve Ranney added, "Our kids were accepted here. Thanks for everything."

Carl Spight was thankful for the "intensity and intentionality" of Project Unity's annual Kwanzaa celebration. "You guys pulled me in. I miss it."

My involvement started when I showed up at the first public meeting in December 1992, partly because I had a son at Longfellow and partly because I hoped to write an article about it.

Until that time, I talked a good line about the importance of racial diversity and Oak Park's history of promoting it, but it was mostly talk. Project Unity provided opportunities to walk that talk. I needed the structure, and my interactions expanded my comfort zone dramatically.

In 2014, when Michael Brown was killed, and Ferguson, Missouri erupted, it was a rude awakening and forced me to enlarge my comfort zone by another order of magnitude. At first it was discouraging, discovering too many hidden biases and acknowledging my shortfalls.

But I was thankful for the wake-up and the humbling, I credit Project Unity with laying the groundwork that made this self-examination possible.

Joining this group was one of the best things I've ever done. Project Unity was a chapter in our evolving sense of community that should never be forgotten.

And maybe, just maybe, our current crop of Oak Park parents will consider starting their own version in the future — Project Unity 2.0.

A Great Books group that led to a revolution (2018)

The Village Manager Association (VMA) disbanded last week, going out, not with a bang, but not exactly a whimper either. More of a whisper. The VMA has been in decline long enough that many Oak Parkers no longer even know what it stood for — the initials or the convictions.

The VMA officially came into existence in 1953 when their first slate of candidates swept into office, and they dominated local politics for the next half-century, but that wouldn't have happened without a group calling itself Education for Democracy and the Revolution of 1949.

Prominent citizens, such as Wallis Austin (from the family that gave us Austin Gardens) and textbook publisher Dwight Follett were fed up with the corruption and ineptitude of the Republican machine politicians who had been governing Oak Park for far too long. Also fed up were members of a local Great Books discussion group, which included Jean Moore, daughter of Oak Leaves editor Otto McFeeley; her husband, Gene; Chuck Seabury; and Cy Giddings.

When I interviewed Giddings (who died in December of 2002), he recalled that the group was inspired by the ideas of Aristotle and Plato about the nature of power and how it corrupts. The group discussed the concept of good government and how Oak Park's government came up short. Those discussions led to Education for Democracy. The new organization decided to challenge the incumbents in the 1949 election.

Because they had never run for office, one of their members, Robert Kubicek, campaigned for state representative in 1948 to learn how it was done. By 1949, they had learned enough to run a slate dubbed the Village Independent Party, which included Stuart Cochran for president and Bruce Bell, Timothy Durkin, Giddings, Lyle Hicks, Kubicek, and Kathryn McDaniel (daughter of OPRF High School Supt. Marion McDaniel) for commissioner (as board members were known then).

The establishment slate, known as the Non-Partisan Civic Party, whose slogan, believe it or not, was "Keep Oak Park As It Has Been," beat them handily, but during the campaign, the upstarts pioneered a number of innovative grassroots techniques that generated coverage in the Chicago papers: Home meetings, which branched out pyramid-style (each attendee was asked to hold similar meetings with their friends); a babysitter corps so couples with kids could attend the meetings (one of the babysitters, Sara Giddings (later Sara Bode), became Oak Park's first female village president in the early '80s); a dishwashing brigade to relieve attendees of that chore on the night of the meetings; and Operation Phone Book, with 300 volunteers each taking a column so that every name in the book was contacted.

Here's a sample of their rhetoric: "A little over a year ago, a group of Oak Park men and women, facing another decision in another election, resolved to make democracy work right here at home by challenging the rule of political bosses and supplanting it with active participation of rank-and-file citizens in government. ... They awakened a new interest in affairs of government in thousands of people. They exploded a heavy charge beneath the decaying structure of the local political machine, from which it is still tottering. ... Will you exercise your priceless heritage as a citizen of a democracy — where ultimately everything depends on you? ... Will you, as voter and citizen make the positive, active choice, investigating candidates and issues thoroughly and voicing your wishes strongly for the guidance of those you elect? Or will you make the passive, inactive choice which permits lesser men to rule by default? You, your friends and neighbors hold the real balance of power. It's up to you to say what you want, and you will get it."

They took a big step, positioning themselves for the next election. That came in 1952 when Education for Democracy put a referendum on the ballot calling for a village manager form of government, a recent innovation, pioneered in Cincinnati, that was, as Cy Giddings put it, "rising from the soil" in Illinois. It took the nuts and bolts of political governance out of the hands of machine politicians and put it in the hands of a professional administrator. Evanston adopted it in 1952. Fed up with political cronyism, so did Oak Park voters. They chose not to "keep Oak Park as it has been."

Education for Democracy renamed itself the Village Manager

Association, and, with Dwight Follett and Arthur Kaiser as co-presidents, slated Homer Brown, Whitney Campbell, R. Emmett Hanley, Edwin Rittmeyer, Leo Shea, and Clifford Westcott for trustee — and for village president, Herb Knight, a capable, respected, older leader, who unfortunately also had a heart condition. On doctors' orders, he stopped campaigning midway through and J. Russell Christiansen filled in for him. After the entire slate was elected, Giddings said, Knight promptly resigned and Christiansen was appointed as his replacement.

The first thing the new board did was hire Mark Keane as village manager. When Oak Leaves publisher Telfer MacArthur sent over a stack of parking and traffic tickets incurred by his staff, on the assumption that Keane would "take care of them," along with a helpful list of village hall staff from the previous regime that he felt should be retained (or fired), Keane sent back a polite reply informing him that things wouldn't be done that way anymore.

Keane went on to become head of the International City Management Association in Tucson, Arizona for many years, and returned to Oak Park in 2003 to honor the VMA's 50th anniversary. He described the early VMA as "really outstanding people. I've never had a better group to work with."

Russ Christiansen ran for re-election in 1957 because "he wanted to win under his own name," Giddings said. Then he stayed on for a third term from 1961-65, this time as a trustee.

When Keane left for another position in 1962, Harris Stevens, his finance director, was hired as village manager, and distinguished himself during the Open Housing Movement and the beginning of racial integration, leading up to and beyond the passage of the Fair Housing Ordinance in 1968.

Keane said his proudest achievement was hiring a tree expert from Michigan State as the village's first professional forester who addressed the onslaught of Dutch Elm disease. Their efforts diversified and saved our frequently honored, and now largely taken for granted, "urban forest."

"We changed the tone of government," Keane said, which transformed the public's attitude from suspicion to respect. As the respect increased, so did civic involvement. Keane called Oak Park "a model democratic process."

You just have to be willing to get involved and make it happen.

A torch to pass (2018)

They're older now, but in their prime, they stepped forward and got involved. Sunday afternoon they gathered at the Carleton Hotel, some 60 strong, for a valedictory sendoff. The Village Manager Association, now officially dissolved and disbanded, threw itself a retirement party.

"When you look at the history of Oak Park over the last 66 years," said former VMA president Bob Kane, "what we did mattered. We changed the course of our community."

They have a torch to pass.

They just don't know to whom.

"There is still a need for leaders who will steward good government," Kane said. "The simple truth is that in today's world, running an all-volunteer campaign every other year is simply too much.

We wore ourselves out."

Newer Oak Parkers, he said, "want to live in a community like the one we helped create and do not seem to care that all of the goals were not achieved. We needed to be vocal about the next cause and we were not." But over six-plus decades, the VMA "turned Oak Park from a place to be 'from' to a place where you want to be."

The torch they want to pass is the torch of good government, which sounds quaint (even boring) in an era when so few Americans believe in government anymore or its potential to be or do "good." But the VMA proved it was possible. They eliminated corruption, uprooted machine politics, and governed with integrity for over half a century. Some claimed that, because 90 percent of their candidates were elected, they turned into the very political machine they were working to prevent.

The VMA never became corrupt. They were simply citizens who stepped forward and got involved. Amateurs. Volunteers. They did not accrue and consolidate power. When their time passed, the VMA passed — quietly.

But while they existed, they stood for "accountable and responsive government." And for the most part, that was what they delivered. If and when they came up short, it was as amateurs, not as professional political operatives.

What did good government accomplish? Their greatest achievement was a comprehensive public-private approach to managed, ongoing, and inclusive diversity. Without that, Oak Park would have been no different from any other community. With it, the village set itself apart, served as a role model, proved it was possible when few other communities even attempted it. The Fair Housing Ordinance in 1968. Equity assurance, to calm jittery property owners. Working with the Housing Center to encourage diverse neighborhoods throughout the village, especially along the eastern boundary with the West Side of Chicago. Building a new village hall at Madison and Lombard as a statement of confidence in our ability to integrate border to border to border to border. Actively recruiting LGBTQ residents and passing first the Domestic Partnership Ordinance and later the Domestic Partnership Registry, signaling the village's support, decades in advance of national acceptance of same-sex marriage.

As the longtime Community Relations Dept. director, Sherlynn Reid, pointed out in her remarks, we never became a town divided into pockets that were all-White and all-Black. Instead of all-anything, we are all-everything. We worked to become an integrated whole. Not perfect. Still a long way to go. But further than most comparable communities have ever come. And that's because the VMA and its partner agencies were committed and intentional about managing diversity. It just doesn't happen on its own. And it doesn't continue to happen, Reid pointed out, unless we keep working at it.

The VMA also backed "balanced and sensitive economic growth." In 1959, the VMA issued a resolution opposing high-rise apartment buildings. Now, in the post-VMA era, high-rises have become the engine of economic growth as impatience with the VMA's slow-and-steady approach became the last straw in the organization's demise. Yet the current acceleration of economic development — represented by the election of Village President Anan Abu-Taleb, followed by the defeat of the entire

VMA slate in the last village election — could never have occurred without a base of economic development to build on.

And that was laid over many decades by the VMA. Probably their most important move was allowing liquor licenses after a century of being "dry," which created a restaurant industry in Oak Park. Government partnership also facilitated development of the Frank Lloyd Wright/Ernest Hemingway tourism industry.

Lynn Kamenitsa, the last VMA president, noted, "It's easy to lose sight of what we've done." There is much more. They recruited citizen candidates for over half a century, she said, "who were dedicated to the entire village, not their own self-interest." And those citizen boards worked to further Oak Park's "diverse, distinctive and desirable image." They resisted populism and its "simplistic solutions to complicated problems." They found quality people, not just "haves" pulling all the strings from their ivory towers, but a sincere, good-faith effort to find candidates who represented all of Oak Park. To underscore that, the VMA used to print a map showing the geographical distribution of the trustees' residences.

In the past, the VMA did a much better job of "selling" their good government efforts. A display board on Sunday, assembled by Historical Society Director Frank Lipo, included fliers proclaiming, in 1968 for instance, "Vote Up! You've Got Good Government Now — Keep it Up!"

They stopped selling it at some point. Maybe because Americans in general lost faith in the concept of good government. That lack of faith has become a sickness in this country and a self-fulfilling prophecy. But the VMA proved it was possible. Government we can trust, which must be proven over and over and over again.

Doug Wyman, a young 90, claiming to still have 10 to 15 good years left in him, recalled that soon after he moved to Oak Park in 1963, there was a knock on the door. It was Dominick Meo, recruiting volunteers for the United Way (then known as the Community Chest). He said something Wyman never forgot. "Every generation has to build its own courthouse."

"The next generation will build its courthouse," Wyman predicted, and when they do, "they may even ask for help from you and me."

If so, he and the other remaining VMA stalwarts have a torch they'd like to pass along.

It's easy to write off the VMA as a staid relic whose time has passed, but before we relegate it to the trash heap of history, we should acknowledge what they brought to Oak Park: improved governance, political integrity, citizen involvement, and progressive ideals. They even saved our trees.

Without the VMA, Oak Park would be a very different place today, and not a better one.

We have Cy Giddings, Russ Christiansen, Dwight and Millie Follett, Mark Keane, Rupert Wenzel, John Gearen, Hazel Hanson, Harris Stevens, and so many other principled men and women over the past 66 years to thank for that.

The VMA's time may have passed, but governance with integrity is timeless. We still need good government, we need to believe it's possible, and we need to get involved to make it happen.

Disrespect for, and disbelief in, government is a self-fulfilling prophecy that we can no longer afford.

The VMA's demise proves we can't "keep Oak Park as it has been," but its enduring legacy is that good government is possible and should be our North Star.

Magic Tree's open windows (2012)

It all started when someone left the window open.

Storefront display windows add old-world charm to the most charming block in Oak Park, the 100 block of North Oak Park Avenue. The Irish Shop windows are filled with Waterford Crystal and Belleek china. Il Vicolo Ristorante offers inviting white tablecloth-covered tables. Filoni features fashionable fancy.

And Magic Tree Bookstore, the dean of independent shops in Oak Park (27 years in business, 23 on Oak Park Avenue), displays a rotating array of seasonal children's books, pegged to the next holiday or visiting author. If you walk up and down this street as much as I do, you look forward to the eye candy, which accessorizes the surrounding streetscape.

But Magic Tree's latest display is altogether different. A worn, multi-paned wooden window frames the words, "It all started one day when someone left the window open." On the shelf in front is an open book. Paper vines seem to be growing out of bird-shaped holes carved into the pages. And those bird shapes appear to be ascending in a cloud, skyward. In their midst are strange papier mache shapes: an old sailing ship appearing in the mist, a nun sitting in a hard-back chair in mid-air, a knife poised over a glowing pumpkin, and a house that is blasting off into space.

Not your average display window. An intriguing mystery.

Actually 14 intriguing mysteries, for those who recognize the allusions. Understanding the references means you're probably a fan of children's book illustrator Chris Van Allsburg, best known for books like *The Polar Express* and *Jumanji*. He's known for mastery of artistic technique married to a vivid imagination, never more evident than in his 1984 book, *The Mysteries of Harris Burdick*, which contains 14 illustrations, each capturing a single moment in some arresting, magical fable, none of which is completed in that book. They leave the reader hanging, piquing our imagination.

One illustration depicts an open window. The wallpaper covering the adjoining wall features a repeated pattern of birds in flight. One of the wings has come loose as if it were making a leap into the third dimension. An empty space next to it indicates that one of the birds has already departed. The caption at the bottom of the page reads, "It all started one day when someone left the window open."

"That's my favorite," says Bethany Fort, a part-time employee at Magic Tree, who is responsible for the window display, featuring birds taking off from the pages of a book. "It epitomizes the subtlety of his imagination."

The publisher of *Harris Burdick* (Houghton Mifflin) recently came out with a sequel. Fourteen authors — including mystery maestro Stephen King; Gregory Maguire, author of *Wicked*; Lois Lowry, author of *The Giver*; and Jules Feiffer — take a crack at telling the stories behind the illustrations.

To promote the new book, *The Chronicles of Harris Burdick*, the publisher sponsored a nationwide bookstore window display contest. The winner would get a visit from Van Allsburg himself. Fort's creation didn't win, but they were named one of three runners-up, for which they will receive a complete library of Van Allsburg's books, autographed by the author.

The contest also required partnering with a local educational institution. Lincoln School agreed to host an essay contest, won by Alyssa Hirshman.

Fort moved to Chicago from Texas two years ago. In college, she was an education major with an emphasis on reading. She worked for Barnes & Noble in the city, but really wanted to work for an independent bookstore. She met Magic Tree owners Iris Yipp and Rose Joseph through various publisher-sponsored author dinners.

"I begged for a job," she recalls.

And why not? Magic Tree became famous for hosting one of the nation's first Harry Potter book release parties in 2003, which was attended by thousands of young fans, who took over the 100 block of North Oak Park Avenue. The event made the front page of the New York Times.

Fort says she loves organizing book-related events and "theme-decorating." She designed a couple of windows last fall at Magic Tree, but this is her most involved effort to date.

"I worked on it for five weeks," she said. "We got it up two days before the deadline." That was Dec. 30, she says, noting that December is "the worst time to do a display window" because of holiday madness.

Fort was inspired by Sue Blackwell, an artist who regularly incorporates books into her artwork.

"What could be better than pages of a book?" she thought.

The window frame came from Rose Joseph's garage.

"I wanted something three-dimensional," Fort said, "to give the display depth."

To create the flock of ascending birds and images from the book, she rigged marionette sticks overhead and attached fishing line. It took an entire day to put up the 30-35 strings and tape the birds to the lines so they would appear to be flying. The papier mache (covering wire frames) figures were harder to balance, "but I wanted to have more than birds," she said.

The nun in the chair, for instance, refers to the illustration, "The Seven Chairs." It shows a seated nun suspended in mid-air in a great cathedral. Two priests on the ground below look up in disbelief. The caption reads, "The fifth one ended up in France." Intriguing to say the least.

Ironically, Fort had to destroy three books in the process of creating her window display. The first was an old, decrepit copy of Chaucer's Canterbury Tales, which turned up at a thrift store.

"It's blasphemy," Fort admits, "but I didn't think he would mind."

The second book was a relatively new technical manual.

"I wanted different textures and shades to add more character."

The bird cutouts came from an old novel.

"It took me 15-20 minutes to find the right book." She wanted a plain cover, no photos or illustrations inside, thick enough to cut into and big enough for the bird shapes.

She used a box cutter. "I still have slivers of paper all over my apartment," she noted.

The most elaborate shape was the old ship, which took the longest, but was worth the effort.

"I love old ships."

When all was installed, they had trouble taking photos for the contest submission, because of the glare from the windows. At night, the lights from the store overwhelmed the electric lights Fort imbedded in the papier mache shapes.

And she contacted Van Allsburg's publisher to make sure they didn't get the wrong idea.

"I was afraid they would think I cut up one of his books."

The display has been up for two months, longer than most of their windows, but it has generated a lot of interest from passersby. Many poke their head in to ask about it or extend a compliment. One merchant from down the block asked if she would design a window for her.

Magic Tree keeps selling out their supply of the two books, so from a marketing standpoint it seems to be working.

"I'm glad it brought attention," says Fort, who is applying to graduate school to study children's literature in the fall. "The books deserve it. Harris Burdick is my favorite. It's the most brilliant picture book I've ever seen."

All it took was leaving the imagination open.

Magic Tree Bookstore closed in October of 2018 after 30 years on Oak Park Avenue.

The symphony comes full circle (2001, 2003, 2008)

Oak Park's diversity story started with the Symphony of Oak Park-River Forest. Not exactly where you'd expect Oak Park's integration experiment to begin, but on Feb. 17, 1963, diversity struck the symphony — and the rest of Oak Park — like a thunderbolt.

Once upon a very different time ...

In November 1962, Milton Preves, music director of the Oak Park Symphony, invited an African American musician named Carol Anderson to rehearse with his orchestra for the upcoming Feb. 17, 1963 concert. Preves had been director of the organization for eight years and brought in a number of new players, often by way of his other orchestra — the North Side Symphony of Chicago.

Conductor Milton Preves congratulates Violinist Carol Anderson after Oak Park concert

Anderson had been playing with North Side Symphony, so she was a proven performer. And she had the resume to back it up: playing violin since she was 4 years old and a graduate of the Boston Conservatory of Music.

Preves, meanwhile, was principal violist for the Chicago Symphony Orchestra, so he didn't feel any particular need to notify the board — then known as the Oak Park-River Forest Symphony Association — whenever he wanted to bring in a new performer.

This rankled the board, but they didn't make an issue of it — until Anderson showed up. The board chair, Marie Dock Palmer, was also the principal cellist of the Oak Park Symphony. After the rehearsal where Anderson first made her appearance, Mrs. Gustave Palmer, as she was frequently identified in press reports from that more formal era, called Anderson and told her that her services would no longer be needed.

Here's how Anderson related the conversation when we tracked her down in 2003: "Mrs. Palmer told me she was sorry, of course, and that she was sure I was a nice girl, but if I stayed it would mean that the community would withdraw its support of the orchestra. She said I would understand that, as a Negro, I would not be acceptable as a member of the orchestra in this community."

This was Mrs. Palmer's first season as board chairman, and it seems safe to say she was in over her head. In fact, as reporters of the Chicago daily newspapers quickly discovered, no doubt to their delight, Marie Dock Palmer was the motherlode of politically incorrect quotes.

No crusading

"We didn't know if anyone would object to the orchestra being integrated," she told Donal Henahan of the Chicago Daily News, who broke the story, "but we weren't about to find out on our own. We're not a band of crusaders."

Once the story got out, of course — although the Oak Leaves studiously avoided mentioning the controversy — Chicago reporters had a field day with the quotable Mrs. Palmer.

"Nothing is integrated in Oak Park as yet," she said. "And we felt that we were only abiding with what already existed in town. If [Preves] wants something like this, let him start it in his own community. As long as things are so quiet and peaceful, there's no sense in bringing it up."

When a reporter pointed out that African American scientist Dr. Percy Julian lived in Oak Park, she responded: "Yes, but he is not very active in Oak Park. And he doesn't try to promote his own race. He hasn't tried to bring other negroes in." She admitted the symphony board "didn't actually know if anyone would object to the orchestra being integrated. We might have been able to take 10 of those people in. But we weren't about to find out on our own."

Mrs. Palmer crawled even further out on the limb, observing, "You know, once we had a Semitic problem out here. Now that seems to be conquered. Some people have asked us, for instance, 'Why do you have a Jewish conductor?' Some have asked, 'Why couldn't he be grateful for that?'"

When a reporter asked if Mrs. Palmer could ever imagine a Negro soloist performing with the orchestra, she allowed that "a person like [opera performer] Marian Anderson would be very well received. Of course, we couldn't afford her."

They could, however, afford *Carol* Anderson, and Preves said that if the symphony refused her services, they could do without his as well. "I do not wish to be associated with and particularly known as head of an organization which practices the discrimination of excluding any person because of color," he wrote in his resignation letter.

That was fine with the Symphony Association, which had just about had it with Preves' unilateral decision-making. Robert C. Ransom, who was then executive secretary of the board, told Preves in a letter that "you have no authority delegated to you by the board to say who shall be a playing member in the orchestra." Ransom's son, Robert M., says the protocol issue was probably the main thing for his father, who was himself from Mississippi originally and often had as many Black clients as White. And in fact, Ransom Sr. described the controversy to a Chicago reporter as "a minor thing and definitely not a racial incident."

No one else was buying that, but it's pretty clear from Mrs. Palmer's vocal distaste for Preves that it wasn't entirely a racial incident.

"Milton Preves is at the bottom of this," she was quoted in a Chicago paper. "He is using this incident in order to wreck [sic] vengeance on us." She called him "money-minded and vindictive," accusing him of pouting after the November concert because he wasn't consulted about the hiring of a soloist, which meant he "could not get his cut of the fee."

"I just can't understand," she added, "why a person would come in this town and gladly take the money we offer and bring us his problem."

Preves retorted, "There are about 35 community orchestras in this area, and the competition for good musicians is fierce. When I am in trouble, I sometimes have to call up a teacher and say, 'Send me a violinist in a hurry.' I can't stop to find out what color he is or to wait to have a board clear it."

Mrs. Palmer insisted, "There is no prejudice against Miss Anderson. She is a fine person and a fine musician." It was the principle of the thing, she said.

"We just thought we were not the organization to crusade and pioneer a controversial subject in the community." The orchestra would not be integrated, she maintained, "until I can see that a consensus of the community is in favor of that."

Community consensus

Though Mrs. Palmer couldn't see it, consensus in the community was already building — in the orchestra, too, where 25 of the 83 musicians threatened to quit in response to the incident.

Residents wrote letters to the Chicago papers decrying the symphony board's discriminatory action. "Is Oak Park in Mississippi?" asked OPRF High School teacher Jack Rossetter. "I should judge from your article that the Oak Park you refer to would not even permit colored television!"

Another wrote: "What Mrs. Palmer fails to realize is that all persons of good will, and especially those in positions of influence and authority, have crucial roles to play in the continuing fight for racial justice. To wait for 'community opinion' is to relinquish the right to make one's own moral decisions, and act upon them."

The Oak Park establishment responded quickly. Elsie Jacobsen, then president of the OPRF High School board, went public and threatened to evict the orchestra from the high school facilities if they continued to practice discrimination. "We are in charge of renting [the auditorium], and we would not want discrimination in our school," she stated.

Local clergy took it a step further. Twenty members of the Oak Park-River Forest Council of Churches, led by Rev. Charles Jarvis of First Methodist Church and Rev. Oliver Powell of First Congregational (now First United Church of Oak Park), signed a declaration condemning the decision and arranged a meeting with several members of the Symphony Association at the Oak Park YMCA.

The board had planned to cancel the concert because of the controversy, but the ministers convinced them to go through with it — and to reverse their position on Carol Anderson.

That same evening, the Oak Park Village Board of Trustees adopted a "statement of concern" about the incident.

The ministers, along with many members of the media, attended the final orchestra rehearsal before the concert. Appropriately, it took place on Lincoln's Birthday. Also in attendance was percussionist John Staunton, who secretly taped the proceedings and captured most of Milton Preves' address to his musicians. The tape reveals an impassioned Preves talking about how he was attempting "to build this orchestra" by bringing in good musicians, not using it to "force an issue." He read several quotes attributed to Mrs. Palmer (who, wisely, did not attend the rehearsal and never played for the symphony again), and demanded the statements be retracted or he would not conduct the concert that coming Sunday.

Some people, he noted, had asked him, "You mean to say you'd let a colored girl cost you this job?" Yes indeed, he replied, and he'd hold his head high about it. He complimented Oak Park for taking a stand against the action and singled out the clergymen who led the way.

One of those clergymen then stood up and negotiated a compromise with Preves on the spot. If Mrs. Palmer and the board issued an apology to Miss Anderson for the hurt and discrimination she had experienced, would Preves agree to conduct? "The community must have the chance to express its repudiation and its approval," the clergyman reasoned.

Preves consented, and Mrs. Palmer, to her credit, made the call and apologized to Anderson. "We thought it would be the right thing to do," she said afterward.

A packed auditorium

The controversy was certainly good for attendance. Over 700 people showed up that Sunday, almost twice the normal crowd. Among the attendees was Dr. Leon Anderson of Wilmington, Delaware, Carol's father.

When it was over, Preves shook hands with his concertmaster as is customary; then he shook hands with Carol Anderson. The audience gave them a standing ovation.

Afterward, Anderson told the press, "I think much has been accomplished. If another Negro ever plays here again, I don't believe this incident will be repeated. I've received many letters, all supporting me. Everyone has been very nice."

Although she was invited to stay, Anderson never returned to play for the Oak Park Symphony, and Preves never conducted there again. Anderson said she joined the orchestra because of Preves and if he were leaving, so was she. In June, a headline in a Chicago paper noted that Carol Anderson had joined the Summer Symphony in Wheaton. The conductor of that orchestra? Milton Preves, of course.

Preves ended up playing viola for the Chicago Symphony for over 50 years, and he did return to Oak Park in the mid-1980s to play with the Symphony of Oak Park-River Forest. He died in 2000 at the age of 92.

A catalyst

While many people viewed the incident as a black eye for Oak Park, many others, including the press, commended the village for its response and what it likely learned from the fiasco.

"The Oak Park incident can serve as a constructive demonstration," declared a Daily News editorial, "that the pressure of a community, educated to an awareness of the cruelty and immorality of this prejudice, can prevail against the remaining areas of its prejudice. ... Perhaps it will serve a good purpose. It demonstrated the volume of support on tap for fighters against discrimination; it provided an example of the rebuke awaiting those who attempt to impose their prejudices upon the rest of the community."

Rev. Robert Schumm of River Forest Methodist Church saw it in even more elevated terms. "The citadels of isolation and segregation have been broken," he told his congregation.

Rev. Jarvis, who at the time was serving as president of the Council of Churches, said, "We've learned a lot about how to deal with a situation like this. I think in general the Protestant approach — privately making a decision and expressing ourselves as individuals — is not enough. We have to mobilize all community forces for the right."

John Staunton, who has been with the symphony for 51 years, is the only current orchestra member who played that 1963 concert. Today, percussionist Mike Daniels is the only regular Black member. Thanks to Staunton's diligence in clipping articles (not to mention taping that dramatic rehearsal) an excellent record exists of one of the watershed events in Oak Park history.

As a result of the symphony incident, community forces were indeed mobilized. The following year, a full-page ad appeared in newspapers, paid for and signed by over a thousand Oak Park and River Forest residents, declaring "The right of all people to live where they choose."

Open housing advocates began marching along Lake Street in 1966 to protest discriminatory real estate practices and lobbied the village to pass a Fair Housing Ordinance, which passed on May 6, 1968.

Finding Carol Anderson

In 2003, we decided to see if we could track down Carol Anderson, the Black violinist who, unbeknownst to her, had started the Oak Park integration story. She played one concert and was never heard from again around these parts.

But through the generous assistance of Boston Conservatory of Music's Alumni Services, we found Carol Anderson Neff living in a suburb of Portland with her husband Tom and two sons, Chris and August, and managing the Metropolitan Youth Symphony in Portland.

When we spoke to her, we found out something quite surprising: Carol Anderson had no intention of playing in that 1963 concert. When she heard Milton Preves was planning to conduct Tchaikovsky's Sixth Symphony, a work she had always wanted to learn, she asked him if she could sit in during rehearsals.

She came to one rehearsal and later that night, received the fateful call from Mrs. Palmer disinviting her. Since Carol wasn't even planning to play in the concert, she shrugged it off. But when she mentioned it, in passing, to Preves, everything hit the fan.

"I was really astounded by how it exploded," Carol said. "I just sat back and watched [Mrs. Palmer] put her foot in her mouth."

She played the concert because it was the only way to get Preves to conduct it.

Carol's father read about the incident back in Delaware and flew in for the performance. She got so much media attention, "I felt sheepish. All I did was accept a phone call."

When told about the impact she'd had on Oak Park history, she said, "I'm flattered and amazed. I figured everyone in Oak Park had forgotten."

The symphony finds its 'Place'

In January of 2001, the Symphony of Oak Park-River Forest assumed a central role in celebrating our town's diversity history when they performed *A Symphony of Place*, an original composition by James Kimo Williams, commissioned by the American Composers Forum for the Continental Harmony Project, funded by the National Endowment for the Arts.

Several hundred residents packed the high school auditorium for the Jan. 27 event. Emceed by WFMT's Carl Grapentine, an Oak Park resident, other performers included the Oak Park-River Forest Children's Chorus, Heritage Chorale, the OPRF High School Jazz Band, the Oak Park Area Community Gospel Choir, and dancer Sarita Smith Childs.

The event honored the 1968 Fair Housing Ordinance, the local legislation that set us apart from other American localities.

It's a story that hasn't truly been told — not often enough, not fully enough, not to enough people. Since a village keeps changing, as residents leave and others arrive, we have to keep telling that story, with shifts in emphasis, generation after generation.

When the local paper told the entire story a few years back, the bare bones came from the Historical Society's files. That was about the time Camille Wilson White and the Oak Park Area Arts Council submitted their proposal to the Continental Harmony Project.

Though this story has many heroes, Rupert Wenzel, Elsie Jacobsen, Bobbie Raymond and Sherlynn Reid were chosen to tell it that night. Several minutes onstage as a prelude to the symphony performance, however, didn't allow much attention to detail, but the passion of the storytellers was impressive. We have many wonderful tales to tell from our history, but none more important than the story of Oak Park's intentional efforts to become a diverse community.

The story isn't finished, of course, so they would tell how we reached this juncture, from the past for the present, and we must retell it from time to time for the future.

A Symphony of Place

On the appointed Saturday evening in late January, the high school's auditorium was packed. Searchlights fanned back and forth over the curved edge of the OPRF Field House as the crescent moon, accompanied by Venus, set in the west. A red carpet directed streams of residents into the building, where they were welcomed by gloved ushers.

Inside, some 1,500 chronologically diverse residents gathered to satisfy their curiosity and hear a premiere performance, composed expressly about Oak Park, the tape soon to be archived in the Library of Congress.

Tuxedos mixed freely with sweaters and evening gowns. Kids sat up front. On that night, it was the place to be.

But before the symphony, the story — of one village's growing pains, opening itself to diversity, blossoming, making it official through the Fair

Housing Ordinance in 1968. Some in the audience knew the story well, some knew it in generalities, and some heard it for the first time.

A dance depicting the darkness of discrimination, a song about healing, and an orchestral arrangement about coming home punctuated the narrative.

A brief intermission, then the centerpiece of the evening: the commissioned work. Complicated, many-faceted, melodious, a challenge to pull together, like diversity itself, accompanied by three local choruses, merged and rising to the occasion, soloists singing a lyrical argument about change, jazz strains mixed with grand, Copland-esque themes, a harp, percussive dissonance, Harriette and Mac Robinet, early African American homeowners, reciting portions of the Village Diversity Statement, and finally, a gentle sing-along, ending with the gathered community humming harmoniously, peacefully, reverently.

At the reception afterward in the school cafeteria, June Heinrich sat alone, taking it all in. She had written the text for the double-page newspaper spread in 1964, signed and paid for by Oak Parkers and River Foresters, upholding "The right of all people to live where they choose," which started the open housing movement that led to the 1968 Fair Housing Ordinance.

"You have to fight for good," she said quietly. "It doesn't just happen." You try things, she added, and you never know which will have an impact.

Looking around the room, she said, "This one did."

And with that, the Symphony of Oak Park-River Forest came full circle at last.

14

Winter

Getting reacquainted with the white stuff (2013)

Never dreamed we'd reach a point where I would stop taking snow for granted. Chalk up another unintended consequence to climate change. Snow, which hadn't settled on us for the better part of a year, once again feels enchanting. Waking to unexpected snow this past weekend waltzed me back to the wonder of childhood.

Snow is that soft idealizer, godlike in its perfection, descending upon the world, momentarily obscuring the world's imperfections, which all too soon gain the upper hand, turning this perfect precipitation into a sloppy swamp of slush.

Over the years, I gradually stopped marveling at snow's unadulterated whiteness, its ability to profoundly transform the surrounding landscape, the way it accommodates itself to surfaces, chameleon-like in its conformity, miming and lining the graceful swirl of tree branches and accentuating the regularity of clay tile roofs.

Snowing has always been preferable to having snowed. Looking out from my windows, I am soothed by the peaceful aimless descent of flakes, the sudden sideways minuets, choreographed by capricious winds. But I came to dislike living with snow. With each step we sully the stuff, subjecting it to the original sins of our man-made artificiality, turning it gray with soot, debris, polluting effluence. We tromp it down, compressing and converting it to tricky, treacherous, uneven ice.

In the country, whole fields and forests remain un-fouled by boot soles and rubber tires. There snow creates an alternate reality, not easily found in citified environs — with one exception this year: Scoville Park, fenced off for renovation, was reborn this past weekend as an unblemished snow reserve. No dogs pranced through this comfortable coverlet with puppy-like rejuvenation. No child sledded pathways down its gently sloping ridge. Squirrels may lightly jostle the un-mottled mantel, but it suffers no mammals more disruptive. Like some promised land, it tantalizes with the luster of mid-day, just beyond reach behind the awkward, hastily assembled, chain-link fence that contains and protects it.

Inside the coffee house across the street, a babbling toddler stands on the adjacent stool, pointing to the park, then turning to me, as if instructing. I understand perfectly. We're seeing with the same eyes. Her dad says, "That's the library, isn't it?" But I know it's not what she's focused on. Books come later. Right now she is absorbed by the wintry wonder of snow. She has lived a lifetime without snow.

Until recently, I didn't miss it one bit. Like an ex-lover, I am well acquainted with how difficult it can be.

But while it is falling, all is forgiven. Utterly disinterested in where it settles, snow is gravity's greatest admirer. Every good snowfall surrenders to Earth's irresistible magnetism.

Eskimos, I've been told, have names for 40 different kinds of snow, and so should we. There is lazy snow, snow that snarls traffic, picture-postcard snow, snow that completely shuts us down, snow that covers the grass but melts on pavement, snowman snow, good-packing snow, snow that sticks, snow that piles, snow that drifts, snow that stubbornly resists melting, snow that hangs around for weeks and obliterates all memory of the ground beneath, overnight snow that gives plows a head start on the morning commute, snow that forms large crystallized conglomerates as it descends, small-bore snow driven like a blitzkrieg by an angry wind, snow that binds and snow that blinds.

Indiscriminate, snow plays no favorites, shuns no one and nothing. Snow is the ultimate disciple of democracy, proof that all men and women are coated equal.

I don't miss the logistical complications of snow, but I do miss the kind of severe winter that magnifies the ecstatic euphoria come spring. If climate change deprives us of that hard-earned payoff, I will miss even the slog that precedes it.

I savored the snow that visited last weekend — just deep enough, covering what should be covered, leaving clear what needs to be clear, light enough for easy brushing and shoveling, the kind that glistens in the sunlight. Snow that alights and delights.

The kind of snow you just can't take for granted.

The Snowmaritan Hall of Fame (2008)

Snow again. Beautiful from a certain angle, but that angle shouldn't be on your back, looking skyward from the sidewalk. It's not the snow that causes slippage but the ice that follows when the snow settles in. When someone doesn't shovel, snow gets stomped down by boots, then melts a little, then refreezes and suddenly you've got people walking in the streets to avoid the sidewalks altogether.

It's been a great winter for snow, but a bad winter for ice. When snow is removed from sidewalks, it's not a problem. The downside of living communally is that some people do and some don't. Some can't, and some apparently won't, pay a local kid to shovel for them. There's no legitimate excuse for leaving sidewalks un-shoveled. Older residents should definitely not be shoveling, but the whole point of block parties and progressive dinners and living in an interactive utopia like ours is that every senior citizen on every block should know at least one family nearby with kids they can call and pay to shovel their sidewalks. Maybe the village could provide vouchers to low-income seniors to pay for the service.

But that, alas, doesn't happen, and it especially doesn't happen with houses along east-west streets, which is where a lot of pedestrians would like to pedestriate. It's a special pain keeping walks clear along the side of a corner house. I grew up on the northeast corner of Elmwood and Jackson, and it was my job and personal mission to make sure that incredibly long stretch of sidewalk remained free of snow. No one ever congratulated me for doing my civic duty for hours under streetlights long after midnight (well, not really, but it felt that way).

Maybe, in addition to the "stick" of a snow-removal mandate, the village should add the "carrot" of municipal recognition for corner-dwellers who keep their sidewalks clear.

And maybe one other honor: Lately, I've seen the unmistakable signs of "Good Samaritanism." On certain blocks, judging by the continuity and evenness of the track, some kindly neighbor with a snowblower is removing snow, not only from his/her own property, but most of the other properties as well.

Shovelry is not dead.

Those helpers deserve a special pat on the back — official or otherwise. If you have a good-hearted neighbor to congratulate publicly, there should be a hotline at village hall to nominate a neighbor for the Good Snowmaritan Hall of Fame.

On Oak Park Avenue, I regularly see a woman of very advanced years, dressed as if she had just been transported from another century. Her back bent badly, she shuffles along, pushing a modified walker, cut so it operates at a 45-degree angle to accommodate her spinal curvature. She moves so slowly you wonder how she ever gets where she's going.

I have no idea how she traverses stretches of neglected sidewalk in the winter. How she survived this winter is anyone's guess. Watching her move is perhaps the greatest testament to the indomitability of the human spirit I've ever witnessed.

She should be our poster elder for those who don't believe local government should tell them how to manage their sidewalks. Scofflaws shouldn't be fined. I propose community service, which would include walking this lovely lady up and down the street on her appointed rounds each day for a week. One trip would likely lead to a permanent humanitarian conversion.

And while we're on the subject of snow removal: One drawback of heavy snowfalls is that it forces all our drivers onto the main streets at the same time — some Type A, some Type B, some Type C (for Cellphone because, during their conversation, the car seems to be driving itself). The combination is maddening. Oak Park drivers are notorious "short-cutters," avoiding main streets whenever possible, which at least siphons off some of the more annoying drivers (but watch your step on those side streets).

After a big snow, however, we're stuck with one another on the main streets — the absurdly slow drivers, those who feel compelled to shave seconds off their trip, and the clueless. The driving can be harrowing.

All the more reason to encourage "snowmaritanism".

Living in a snow globe (2021)

It's a badge of honor to get through a Midwest winter. But the bright side of a severe winter is that it intensifies the spring euphoria when it finally arrives. And that's worth waiting for.

Last winter, we got off lightly, and this year looked to be even lighter — until the last week of January. In past years, we hardly had measurable snow cover at all and when we did, it didn't last long. Kids settled for sledding on brown snow or solid ice. The thermometer yo-yo'd and the poor park district kept trying to put up temporary ice rinks in the parks, but the temperature wouldn't stay below freezing long enough to last.

This year was headed for the warmest winter ever — and then it started snowing. And snowing. And snowing. Three weeks later, over 40 inches has fallen, covering everything.

Everything.

Kids probably couldn't believe their good sledding fortune. Cross-country skiing is popular again.

The snow has settled slightly, but none of it melted because we never got above freezing for almost a month.

It is as beautiful as it is brutally frigid, but not as many people are commuting these days because of the pandemic and most of us were already staying close to home. Life is slower, giving us a chance to appreciate this astonishing snowscape — with plenty of shoveling for exercise.

A terrible beauty is born, as Yeats put it, referring not to the snow but the recurring catastrophe that was the Irish independence movement. During a snowy winter, this terrible beauty is borne — endured, managed, and even, to a surprising degree, enjoyed — as serene as the poets always depicted it:

> *Damn ice dams,*
> *Beauty bordering grotesque,*
> *Ice floes,*
> *The polar opposite of flow.*

Like inverted petrified flames,
Stalactites in the open air
Melt against sun-warmed bricks,
Seeping through mortar,
Infiltrating the kitchen,
Endless drips from window frames,
Caught in buckets, drumming and thrumming,
Then a plaster avalanche from a closet ceiling,
Cold fingers of winter
Working their invasive mischief,
In the deep recesses of breached shelter.
Elsewhere, frozen cascades of savage teeth,
From gutters and eaves almost reach the ground
Like entries in a deathcicle competition.
Smothering snow
Buries every memory of other seasons
Beneath a shining-white comforter,
Unsettling settling
Layer upon layer
Totaling tons,
Giant dump trucks carting mountains
Away to vacant lots,
Lots of lots.
Snowplows leave graded hillsides
Like burial mounds.
Sheltered yet vulnerable,
We battle our way out,
Wondering is this the worst
Or best of times?
Soft savagery or savage softness?
Hemmed-in by semi-passable narrows
Once known as roadways,
A graveyard of piled-on cars,
Wait for shoveling archaeologists,

To sift through sedimentary layers.
Pity the package delivery drivers,
Strangling already bottlenecked blocks.
In Thatcher Woods,
Deer feed on greens and grains left by the caring,
Skiers glide across meadows, weave through woods,
Dogs bound with delight,
Tethered to snow-shoed companions,
A tough trudge,
Across seductive undulating curves
In undisturbed fields.
Life in a snow globe:
Deep snow, deep nights, deep dreams,
Deep in the heart of winter.

Living in the snow globe of February 2021 evokes nothing so much as the ending of James Joyce's famous short story, "The Dead":

"A few light taps upon the pane made him turn to the window. It had begun to snow again. He watched sleepily the flakes, silver and dark, falling obliquely against the lamplight. The time had come for him to set out on his journey westward. Yes, the newspapers were right: snow was general all over Ireland. It was falling on every part of the dark central plain, on the treeless hills, falling softly upon the Bog of Allen and, farther westward, softly falling into the mutinous Shannon waves. It was falling, too, upon every part of the lonely churchyard on the hill where Michael Furey lay buried. It lay thickly drifted on the crooked crosses and headstones, on the spears of the little gate, on the barren thorns. His soul swooned slowly as he heard the snow falling faintly through the universe and faintly falling, like the descent of their last end, upon all the living and the dead."

15

Eulogies

In the powerful third act of Thornton Wilder's *Our Town*, Emily Gibbs has just arrived in Grover's Corners' Cemetery high atop a hill overlooking the town. From this lofty perch, the dead do not keep an eye on the living. They sit in straight-backed chairs, facing away, the better to accomplish their central task: weaning themselves from life.

Oak Park has no cemeteries, but we do have a pantheon of sorts, remembering those no longer with us except through their impact on our community. Like most towns, we have our memorials — names on brass plaques, memorial rocks and monuments, and sides of buildings.

The high school has a "wall of fame" that lists its many accomplished alums. They call it the "Tradition of Excellence," and each year a few more names are added to the list. Some of them return to visit their alma mater and address the students.

The Historical Society of Oak Park-River Forest has an exhibit on former Oak Parkers who achieved notoriety in their lives and/or made significant contributions to the wider culture. The society also sponsors an annual "Tale of the Tombstones" graveyard walk in neighboring Forest Park, which boasts an abundance of cemeteries, during which actors research and, in period costume, embody the dearly departed, recalling their contributions.

There is also a growing collection of statuary around town: Percy Julian (outside the public library), Bobbie Raymond (in front of the Oak Park Art League), Frank Lloyd Wright (at the northeast entrance to Austin Gardens), and Ernest Hemingway (Oak Park Public Library's Hemingway Archives, Special Collections). The memorial tree program, meanwhile, remains popular in our parks.

At any point in its historical development, each town owes, and sometimes expresses, its debt of gratitude to the many who came before and helped make this the place it has become.

The following is a sample of those we came to know and admire because they made a difference — and from whom we have not yet weaned ourselves.

Common threads of lives well-lived (2009)

Some funerals are sadder than others. The really sad ones mourn life cut short in its prime. Others are more upbeat — tributes to a long life, well lived.

The memorial service for Bill Cassin was, in many ways, an ideal funeral — beautiful program, lovely music, inspiring readings, a moving eulogy, a large and loving extended family who knew how good they had it, and many friends and admirers filling the pews in support. The kind of funeral we probably all dream of.

I knew Bill pretty well — well enough to know the tributes were authentic and earned. I always feel privileged attending such gatherings because the love is tangible and the outpouring reassuring. When your life has had an impact, people recognize and acknowledge it. In Bill's case, it included overcoming health challenges in his youth, combat in Europe during World War II (including liberating a death camp), instilling in his children a love of the natural world, and providing the kind of dedicated partnership that assisted his wife Ginie's long career of civic involvement.

Photos on display, accomplishments cited, foibles fondly teased, anecdotes retold, meaning measured, and wisdom woven like veins of precious metal shining along the walls of life's course. Sadness and laughter complement on occasions like these. It is not a euphemism to say that many funerals are "celebrated." Even at their saddest, loved ones make an extra effort to highlight a life ended too soon. And in so doing, the individuals come "alive" even as they have departed from us.

But short or long, sad or celebrated, after a while, you can see commonalities in well-lived lives. The celebrated life is usually characterized by integrity, devotion to someone, some group, or some larger cause, frequently putting others' needs ahead of their own, working hard at something they love and deeply believe in, having an impact on others' lives, setting an example that others want to follow, making loved ones feel loved, actively engaging in the wider community, keeping the kid inside alive, and enjoying life while helping others enjoy theirs.

Do they enjoy life because circumstances turn out well or do their circumstances turn out well because they know how to enjoy living? If they enjoy life regardless of circumstances, what is that magical gleam in the eye and where does it come from — divine providence, personal determination, a fortunate fluke of body chemistry? All of the above?

Personalities vary widely. Some of the departed were warmer and more approachable than others. Some were adored, some quietly appreciated. No one was a saint, but their shortcomings and oddities tend to be more endearing than alienating.

And finally, a tribute to a life well lived inevitably leaves us with a desire to try harder in our own lives.

On the back of Bill's memorial card, the Cassin family included a quote that bears repeating:

> *To laugh often and love much;*
> *To win the respect of intelligent people and the affection of children;*
> *To earn the approbation of honest critics and endure the betrayal of false friends;*
> *To appreciate beauty;*
> *To find the best in others;*
> *To give of one's self;*
> *To leave the world a bit better, whether by a healthy child, a garden patch, or a redeemed social condition;*
> *To have played and laughed with enthusiasm and sung with exultation;*
> *To know even one life has breathed easier because you have lived —*
> *This is to have succeeded.*

Poet Mary Oliver's admonition, "Listen, are you breathing just a little and calling it a life?" does not apply to a life well lived.

Often I leave funerals and memorial services feeling not a sense of loss but a sense of gain.

They make me take a deep breath — and resolve to start living a fuller life.

Jack Levering's empty bench (2006)

This park just isn't the same without Jack Levering, who died last month at the age of 85. Jack was a CCOC (colorful, cantankerous old coot) — in the best possible sense of that term. Though suffering from various maladies, he embraced life more completely than possibly anyone I know.

Most of the time, I found him sitting on his bench in Austin Gardens feeding the squirrels and pigeons — seed, nuts and water — the last being most important, he insisted. Many of those who feed animals, he said, don't think about how thirsty they are.

Pointing to the bare patches on the tails of certain squirrels, he noted that they were mothers, using their own fur to line the nests of their young. It brought him to tears.

As did poetry. One of the first times we talked, he quoted English poet Rupert Brooke, who perished in World War I. "Death will find me long before I tire of watching you," he said, his voice cracking with emotion. "Isn't that the most beautiful thing you've ever heard?"

He did not fear beauty or feel ashamed of the emotion it aroused. And he loved all creatures great and small — except for those he couldn't stand, mostly of the human variety, usually of the excessively religious persuasion. He had a deep suspicion of organized religion and its "salespeople" and was himself a devout humanist. He could be quite irreverent, but more than anything, he was humane.

He wore a button on his cap that read: "Still horny after all these years." He was the only octogenarian I know who wore his hair in a ponytail. He cackled in a high-pitched voice when he laughed (which was often), and when any two-legged critter passed his bench, he would bark out with a smile, "You're late!" For some it was unsettling. Others smiled back. A few stopped and chatted. I stopped and sat down.

In World War II, he casually mentioned, he was assigned to an engineering battalion where he served as assistant to the commanding officer who invented the attachment that allowed tanks to cut through the thick hedgerows of the Normandy countryside following D-Day. I've read enough about WWII to know this was one of the major turning points of the campaign. It allowed the Allies finally to break out and start moving with speed toward Germany. Jack shrugged it off, but he had seen his share of history.

Knowing him was a blessing, but the sandhill cranes were his gift. Every March 10 or so, right around his birthday when the weather conditions were right, he told me, sandhill cranes fly over Oak Park on their migratory journey northwest to Wisconsin (and again, southeast, each fall). He taught me to listen for their insistent, distinctive bugling. I didn't think much about it until the following March when I was taking a midday walk and suddenly heard the strangest, distant racket. Sandhill cranes fly at high altitude, rising on the warm thermals of early spring, so you can't always see them with a casual glance at the sky, which is why most of us miss them. But on March 10, 2000, I stood in the middle of Austin Gardens, craning my neck (so to speak), squinting my eyes, and suddenly hundreds of wings came into focus circling high overhead — a breathtaking sight.

Death will find me long before I tire of watching them ... or of missing Jack Levering.

He didn't want a memorial, but I'm pretty sure he'd approve of this:

> *Oh! Death will find me, long before I tire*
> *Of watching you; and swing me suddenly*
> *Into the shade and loneliness and mire*
> *Of the last land! There, waiting patiently,*
> *One day, I think, I'll feel a cool wind blowing,*
> *See a slow light across the Stygian tide,*
> *And hear the Dead about me stir, unknowing,*
> *And tremble. And I shall know that you have died,*
> *And watch you, a broad-browed and smiling dream,*
> *Pass, light as ever, through the lightless host,*
> *Quietly ponder, start, and sway, and gleam —*
> *Most individual and bewildering ghost! —*

*And turn, and toss your brown delightful head
Amusedly, among the ancient Dead.*
Rupert Brooke

Elsie Jacobsen: Matriarch of Oak Park (2003)

Printed on tiny paper flags embedded in the jade plant pots given out at Unity Temple, were the words, "Live well, inspire others, do good work."

The other side marked the occasion: "In loving memory of Oak Park's Elsie."

No need for a last name. Everyone on hand knew Elsie Jacobsen, and they turned out on a cold night to give her a warm send-off. A Viking funeral would have been appropriate, given her Nordic background, but not realistic under the circumstances, so family and friends gave her the next best thing — a tribute and reception at Frank Lloyd Wright's Unity Temple, one of the many Oak Park heirlooms she helped save, revive and restore.

Her daughter Ellen read the epitaph that will adorn Elsie's final resting place:

"She always strove to make the world, and especially Oak Park, the very best place it could be. A respected member of her community, no task was too big to undertake if the cause was right. She left a legacy of human understanding, peace, and education of the world's children."

Summations are important, especially for lives as well lived as Elsie's was.

But epitaphs should be brief. "Live well, inspire others, do good work" would also suffice.

Elsie's unfailing warmth and good humor inspired others to get involved in much the same way Tom Sawyer inspired friends to whitewash his fence. She made it look fun — and, in fact, she made it fun.

During the reception afterward, people commented not so much on all she had accomplished, although that list is long — first woman president of the District 200 high school board, raising funds to build more than a dozen schools in Third World countries, founding the Historical Society of Oak Park-River Forest, helping to save the Oak Park Conservatory. Instead, they testified to how Elsie had gotten them involved by gently twisting arms. Before they knew it, they were chairing a committee.

We're in a "sendoff" stretch of our 20th-century leaders. Within the last 12 months, we said goodbye to Cy Giddings, Jim Devine, Lee Ellis, Dr. Greg White, Bill Furlong, Ellis Fields and Carol Warner Shields. All made significant contributions to these two villages, and all lived well, inspired others, and did good work.

To honor Elsie's legacy, and all the aging heroes who helped make us what we are today, we should officially adopt hers as the village motto: The town that lives well, inspires others and does good work.

My favorite epitaph, by the way, appears on Nathan DeVore's headstone in neighboring Forest Park's Waldheim Cemetery. DeVore, who died in 1934 at the age of 48, had the following inscribed: "I have studied the stars too long to fear the night." I found a slightly different version painted on a post along the walkway south from Trailside Museum by the Des Plaines River.

> *Though my soul may set in darkness, it will rise in perfect light;*
> *I have loved the stars too truly to be fearful of the night.*
> (Sarah Williams, from her 1868 poem, "The Old Astronomer")

Having studied and loved the stars of community service this long, I no longer fear the night of their absence.

Inspiration, as Elsie Jacobsen well knew, is infectious.

Peter Blakemore's moment in the sun (1995)

The only time I ever laid eyes on Rev. Peter Blakemore, he was sitting in a lawn chair in Mills Park during Exalt, a worship rally held last summer by Christian churches from the western suburbs, which is all about praising the Almighty, mostly through music and dance.

It was a diverse crowd, racially and chronologically, but a familiar crowd. There was plenty of hugging, hand-clasping, arms on shoulders as they listened, singing and swaying to hymns. The movement of wind-blown branches overhead mimed the choreography below. This wasn't your downbeat fire-and-brimstone sort of worship experience.

No berating our sinfulness, no political agenda, no condemnation of alternative lifestyles. It was sweet and uplifting. "Jesus, Jesus, Jesus, there's just something about that name like the fragrance after the rain."

As the name implies, Exalt accentuated the positive — interspersed with testimonials about God's impact on people's lives. Peter Blakemore delivered one of those testimonials.

Wearing a straw sun hat, he looked frail as he walked slowly up to the stage. Someone nearby said she'd heard he was pretty sick, and, indeed, he had the look of someone undergoing treatment for cancer.

He stood out as a low-key presence in a high-key setting. Cancer, I imagine, does that to a person, making them feel a step removed from the day-to-day concerns and elations the rest of us make such a fuss about. Facing death puts everything squarely in perspective.

In unassuming fashion, he talked about his illness and how his faith helped him deal with it. He also mentioned the importance of courage. His words were remarkable for their lack of hyperbole, self-pity, sentiment or melodrama. Without raising his voice, he spoke with considerable authority. When a cancer victim talks about courage, people pay attention.

He was an oasis of calm, bringing a reflective moment to a gathering charged with emotion.

But what I remember most about that day was the sight of his two daughters before he went up to speak, one standing next to him, the other sitting close, looking as if they couldn't get enough of him, almost luxuriating in his presence. They likely knew he was dying, or would likely die, perhaps soon. He didn't seem the kind of father who made up fictions to shield his children from reality or to foster unrealistic hopes.

No one is lucky to get cancer, but in that moment I envied him. There must be nothing quite so close as family members who know their time together is short.

Turns out they had another 14 months together. He died on Aug. 27 at the age of 42. Occasionally over the past year I had wondered about him, wondered what it's like to know you're dying, but I could never work up the nerve to give him a call. I didn't have the courage.

Rev. Peter Blakemore was pastor of Harrison Street Bible Church in Oak Park, like his father for 40 years before him — a small, close-knit community by all accounts, in no small measure due, no doubt, to the efforts of their pastor.

It's hard losing someone who's had a powerful impact on your life — as several church members attested. It takes as much courage as faith to face that kind of loss. Maybe Peter Blakemore wasn't talking about himself when he spoke of courage that day in Mills Park. Maybe he was talking about those who go on living without those who tried so hard to show them how.

So to the Blakemore family, made painfully incomplete by this loss, I offer one vivid mental snapshot, tucked away in memory, of a loving father resting in a folding chair on a beautiful June afternoon, his daughters close and attentive, as if they couldn't get enough of him.

They were right.

We can never get enough of one another.

Redd Griffin, village visionary (2012)

With Redd Griffin there was no such thing as a short conversation. He knew too much, and it was all hyperlinked in his expansive mind. He could take you to the rise in Scoville Park overlooking the intersection of Oak Park Avenue and Lake Street, and suddenly you saw it — and the entire village — as the juxtaposition of old-world European architecture and new-world Prairie-style design.

And you heard about James Scoville, resting on that ridge (a continental divide, for heaven's sake) of what is now the century-old Scoville Park (designed by famous landscape architect Jens Jensen) and deciding to settle there. Suddenly you saw the entire life span of the village, stretching out before you.

You saw the Oak Park that Redd Griffin saw — and lived in and celebrated — the village where everything is an intersection.

Redd died unexpectedly of a heart condition, Nov. 20, at Rush Oak Park Hospital. He was 73.

It is difficult to encompass most people in an obituary. With Redd Griffin, it is impossible.

He taught history at Morton East and West high schools. A lifelong Republican, he served a term as state representative in Springfield in the early 1980s. He was Oak Park's great champion of Ernest Hemingway, serving on the board of the local Hemingway Foundation, which he co-founded in 1983, and the development of the Hemingway Museum. He also co-founded the Wright Preservation Trust in the 1970s and the Historical Society of Oak Park-River Forest in the 1960s. He was married to his loyal life partner, Mary Jo, for 42 years. They had two sons and two grandsons and lived in their home on Kenilworth Avenue with the back deck where Redd held court with guests late into the evening (and early into the morning).

And this doesn't begin to define him.

When he was born in West Suburban Hospital, his mother shared a room with Sunny Hemingway, Ernie's younger sister. He attended Bishop Quarter Military Academy, located in the building that first housed Oak Park High School at East Avenue and Lake Street, a truncated portion of which now serves as the home of Stephanie Clemens' Academy of Movement and Music. During his time at Bishop Quarter, Redd commuted from Chicago State Mental Hospital (now Chicago-Read Mental Health Center) on North Oak Park Avenue, where his father was the superintendent and the family lived on the grounds.

He attended OPRF High School for two years in the mid-1950s, then gained early admission to Shimer College, an experimental school based on the ideas of the University of Chicago's legendary president, Robert Maynard Hutchins. There he became a lifelong devotee of Hutchins' Great Books program.

Serving in U.S. Army Intelligence in Berlin during the early 1960s, when The Wall went up, he had a unique perspective on the Cuban Missile Crisis in 1962 and attended Kennedy's "Ich bin ein Berliner" speech. During his time in Berlin, he experienced a profound spiritual conversion, which he described as a mystical experience. He was anything but your ordinary soldier.

When he returned, he worked for WTTW Public Television in the 1950s, and arranged a private conversation with Frank Lloyd Wright while the master architect waited for a televised interview. On a trip to California, he managed to track down and visit author John Steinbeck. He was still on the WTTW Community Advisory Board when he died. And he even served a stint with the City News Bureau.

Redd was the most unlikely of combinations: a Republican who was also a proponent of alternative medicine and vegan restaurants and cultivated friendships, and long discussions, with local liberals like Tom Ard and columnist Frank Walsh. He became state rep just as the effort to ratify the Equal Rights Amendment to the U.S. Constitution came to a head and vote.

A public school teacher, he was an active supporter of Alcuin, the first Montessori school in the village, where they enrolled their two sons. After retiring from Morton, he taught philosophy courses at Triton College and Holley Court Terrace (now Brookdale) and enjoyed an avid following. He also delivered presentations through Elderhostel.

A longtime board member of the Illinois State Historical Society, he was just about to join the board of the Chicago Literary Hall of Fame, and was a recipient of the Senior Citizens Center's Ulyssean Award for his commitment to lifelong learning.

Redd wrote and produced readers theater productions and led Hemingway discussion groups for the foundation. He established personal relationships with the Hemingway and Wright family and coordinated visits to Oak Park and River Forest by members of both — when he died, he was planning the visit of Ernie's grandson, Sean Hemingway.

The problem with Redd is it takes so long to describe him, you never get around to saying how you felt about him. But here are a few testimonials:

"Redd was one of the smartest, most vibrant people I have ever known, and I feel like a huge hole has opened up in the world that will be impossible to fill," said Sue Mosher, one of the students in his Triton philosophy class.

"I will surely miss our conversations, and listening to his ideas on the continuum linking Jeffersonian democracy, the legacy of Hemingway and Wright, and Oak Park's past, present and future values." (Mike Iverson)

"Redd Griffin was a wonderful human being, the kind of man who gave Oak Park a good name." (Christine Vernon)

"Redd's intellect and warm, generous spirit will be terribly missed. He understood as well as anyone the sense of place and character that define Oak Park, and he worked relentlessly to preserve those qualities." (Kathryn Jonas)

"He had high standards in his teaching and his work with many organizations. It's hard to visualize the Ernest Hemingway Foundation without him." (Maryanne Rusinak)

"Redd cared so deeply about so many things. That's why he talked so much," noted Martha Swisher, who hosted him on many a porch night.

Redd Griffin was a lifelong learner, a lifelong educator, and a master interrogator and integrator of our past and present, finding value and meaning in all of it.

His heart was as expansive as his mind.

If only it hadn't given out so soon.

John Philbin's rules for good governing (2012)

Maybe it's because he was in office when I started working for the local paper, but John Philbin has always been my prototype village president.

Witty, intelligent, unflappable, and comfortable in his own skin, he had two qualities that every future village president should inculcate: He never took himself too seriously and he had a thick enough skin to let the barbs bounce off.

Of course, you never know how thick your skin is until you step into a role like that.

Some past presidents have been afflicted by excessive seriousness. Some tended toward taciturn, or even caustic.

But Philbin was a delight. Eminently quotable (and available), he didn't view the local press with wary suspicion because he understood that everyone at this level of governance is basically on the same side. Everyone wants good governance.

He served as trustee, then president, and just before he left office in 1993, we interviewed him in our offices. A few of his responses highlight why John Philbin was in a class by himself:

Asked how he got into local politics, he replied: "One of my wife's thousands of old boyfriends asked me one day if I wanted to do some work for The Party," which is how he referred to the Village Manager Association (VMA), whose members would cringe if anyone referred to the organization that way today.

"Not even old Richard Daley had as much success as The Party," he added.

He talked about the relationship between village boards and village managers as "the yo-yo effect." Sometimes the trustees wanted someone they could dominate and sometimes they wanted "a take-charge guy."

The Philbin prescription was: "The village manager should be doing 80 percent of what's needed. The board can't set new policy every day of the week."

On the subject of Oak Park's notoriously opinionated populace, he opined: "For the most part, people have class. I've only gotten two hate calls in 10 years of service [one about the fire department and one about the handgun ban]. You'll get some complaining letters, but you also get a lot of complimentary letters. It's a class community where it isn't just people carping.

"Probably the biggest problem with a literate, educated community," he added, "is on the part of some people who disagree with the village and have an arrogance. Some people think they know everything about everything but don't really know what the facts are."

On Oak Park exceptionalism: "There are people who live in Schaumburg — whose last experience with Oak Park might have been 10 years ago — who say, 'How's Oak Park doing?' which is what you usually say to a cancer patient. Oak Park is a high-visibility community. Whenever the metropolitan press wants to do a story about what the suburbs are doing on this or that, automatically one of them says, 'We'd better find out what Oak Park is doing.' It's sort of a burden that keeps you breathless because everybody expects you to be light years ahead of everybody else."

On the benefits of the arts, tourism and diversity: "Hopefully it impacts on people to want to visit here, or they're making a decision on whether to move here. It can tell people what life's like in the community.

"That nervousness about diversity? There was always a rule of thumb that there was a tilt point. Sociologists would say, well, 20 percent or something. But there's less emphasis, I think, on a tilt point today because people are looking at more than numbers and more at what else the town has to offer."

John Philbin took everything in stride and was wise enough not to get too riled up or take anything too personally. He was refreshingly honest in a way that was easy to listen to. He inspired confidence. Future trustees and presidents would do well to study his style.

Don't take yourself too seriously; let the barbs bounce off: That should be inscribed in the good government playbook for future candidates. And it's something for all of us to keep in mind as we head toward next April's local election.

Call it "The Philbin Rule."

John Philbin died in 2012 at the age of 89.

Val Camilletti and the soundtrack of our lives (2018)

Though she lived in Cicero, for many people Val Camilletti, 78, was the most recognizable face in Oak Park.

More than anything else, she was associated with music, beginning in the late 1960s when she ran record stores, first on Ridgeland Avenue, then on South Boulevard just east of Oak Park Avenue, and finally at 239 Harrison St. in the Oak Park Arts District. She started with vinyl and ended with vinyl, the majority of her sales in recent years coming from used records, as a new generation discovered LPs.

Her store, Val's halla Records was a play on Valhalla from Norse mythology — as were the names of her dog, Halla; her cat, Woden; and Halla's successor, Loki, who were omnipresent. And for many customers, it was indeed a kind of mythical paradise, especially during rock 'n' roll's heyday of the 1960s and '70s. It was the place to go, and kids flocked there. As baby boomers grew older, they remained loyal even as the music industry morphed dramatically with digital technology. One of her most devoted customers was TV and film actor John Mahoney, during his long tenure as a resident of Oak Park.

Her musical knowledge was encyclopedic and her storytelling was, well, legendary, which made frequenting her store more than a shopping experience. The shrine to Elvis alone was a mecca for many.

She was in charge of music during the May Madness streetfests on Oak Park Avenue during the 1990s and early 2000s. For a couple of years, she emceed the Church of Beethoven concerts, which gave music lovers a Sunday morning alternative to traditional church worship, and she even penned an entertainment blog for a time in the local newspaper.

But Val's halla Records wasn't the institution — Val was, with her gravelly voice and big glasses and bushy gray hair. You couldn't miss her.

But we're missing her now.

In 2012, when those music industry changes took a toll on her business, it looked as if the shop might close, but the community rallied. Children's musician Jim Gill and his wife, Sue, threw a benefit concert at their house, which raised enough to "keep the lights on."

"From the moment I first wandered in," Gill said, "I fell in love with that place. You can't separate falling in love with the place from falling in love with Val. The store is more than a store for her. It really embodies all she knows about music. Val's is a place where music is more than bought and sold. I don't think the community is ready to give that up."

Val was 72 at the time, but she wasn't ready for retirement.

"I'm not sure how to spell that word," she said. "It's so much a part of my identity. I don't know how to describe it any other way. We don't just talk about music. We talk about everything. I'm interested in anything. That's part of the real joy."

She described her store as "a unique musical landscape."

Andy Mead knew her as both an employee and a friend, which pretty much went hand in hand.

"If you spent time at the store," he recalled, "you either became a friend or you were scared of her. She had a big echo. She was like musical Velcro. She could talk about everything from Maria Callas to the Beatles, from film to food. If you talked to her, you talked for 45 minutes. Music was her lifeblood."

Mead worked at the store from 1988 to 1998 and "we very quickly became friends. I was 23 and she was 48, but we combined well."

Working for her was like everything about her: "Very intense. If you collided with Val, you didn't forget it. She stuck with you. She was demanding, hilarious, generous, passionate, charming and loud. If you could roll with that intense interaction, you became a lifetime customer. It was like working in a family. She was a friend, not a boss."

Val Camilletti grew up in the Austin neighborhood of Chicago, graduated from Austin High School, then moved to Oak Park for a while before finally settling in Cicero. She landed a job with Capitol Records on Michigan Avenue in 1962, doing record promotion, working with radio stations, organizing sock hops, etc. Two years later, the Beatles landed. It was a crazy time to be part of the record industry, but she passed up her one chance to meet the Liverpudlians when her boss went to pick them up at the airport for their concert at Comiskey Park in 1965. He asked if she wanted to go but she said no.

"She hated all the screaming," Mead said. "If she couldn't hear them, she didn't want to go. She said she had no regrets."

In 1967, she started working for NMC Discount Records, a chain that had a store in Oak Park. Val managed the various stores, but when they went out of business in 1972, she took over the Oak Park shop on Ridgeland, which soon moved to South Boulevard and became Val's halla. She migrated to Harrison Street in 2006.

"She weathered everything from the Big Box stores to the internet," Mead said, even as record stores everywhere were closing. "It was the force of her personality. She just pushed through. That store was her and she was the store."

But she also had a full life beyond the store.

"She loved kids and animals," Mead said. "She was a huge advocate for the Animal Care League for many years, emceeing their annual auction. She loved golf and played at Columbus Park just a couple of weeks before she went in the hospital.

"She lived fully. She told me about one weekend in the '70s when she went to see David Bowie, the opera, and a rodeo, all in one weekend. Louie Armstrong to Taylor Swift, she could span all that. She was very involved in the folk scene in the 1950s and early '60s. John Prine used to come in the store and show her his latest record. She knew Steve Goodman.

"She was always a little ahead of the curve. As one friend put it, 'She was always cool.' She didn't show her age. I forgot she was 78."

Laura Maychruk, owner of The Buzz Café, said, "My relationship with Val began when she moved to the Arts District. From the beginning, she was a force who injected new energy into our district. She has been an active member of our board from the very beginning. To say she is a legend is an understatement. She has shaped thousands of lives through her passion for music over her nearly 46 years in business. She was a friend and fellow Arts District champion and fought alongside us as we forged the Arts District that you see today. She will never be forgotten."

Terri Hemmert, the longtime radio personality on WXRT-FM posted this about Val on Facebook after she died:

"We've lost a great friend. Val Camilletti passed last night. Yeah. That Val. The Val's halla Record store Val. The woman who has been enabling those of us who can't get enough music in our collections. For almost 50 years people have been making the trip to Oak Park to spend quality time in those bins of records to see what they could find. But the real draw was Val herself. A lot of us music nerds can talk for hours about our favorite songs, but Val even more. She was a friend and mentor to countless people. Especially young people. She supported musicians, venues and kids who were crazy enough to want to work at a record store. I was one of those kids. It was 1969 when I was still in college that I found her and her marvelous store.

"We quickly became friends, and the next year, after I graduated, I moved to Oak Park, four blocks from the Oak Park Arms Hotel because I was determined to work there at WGLD. Took a few months but finally landed a job. I could walk to work since I couldn't afford a car. In fact, I couldn't afford to buy Christmas presents for my family, so Val said she needed extra help for the holiday rush. I'd work 9 to 5 at the station, grab a sandwich and walk over to Val's to work 6 till 9. With my employee discount I was able to give my parents and siblings records for Christmas. They were thrilled.

"When I started going to New Orleans for Jazz Fest over 30 years ago, Val would let me crash in her hotel room. We had great times at the Lion's Den watching Irma Thomas. Val would get recognized more than myself on the street and at the fest. Val was a star. And a true friend.

"We both got cancer around the same time. We were our own support group. I lucked out. She didn't. But a lot of people didn't even know she was sick. She showed up at the shop every day till last week when things went bad. I'm just glad she lived large these last two years. Even last fall we were meeting every Monday night at the Hideout for the Flat Five's residency. They showed up yesterday to serenade her. Bless their hearts for that. She was unresponsive but I know she heard every marvelous note. She loved music but she loved us even more. We were her family. My love goes out to everyone who knew her. Listen to some music. She'd want you to."

I asked her once if she were going to sing a song at a Karaoke bar, which would it be? Her reply was telling:

"'If Love Were All' by Noel Coward, one of my favorite songs of all time. It has one great verse: 'I believe that since the world began, the most I've had is just a talent to amuse. Hey, ho, if love were all, I would be lonely.'"

But as one of Oak Park's most recognizable people, she was seldom alone for long.

Of her local renown she once said, "I guess you get old, you get famous. It just never really penetrated that that meant anything. It's not part of my nature to think in those terms."

Sergio Quiano and the community covenant (2018)

After reading about the murder of Sergio Quiano — and testimonials in the local paper — I wondered, "How did I miss this guy?" After all, he was frequently sighted walking the streets of Oak Park, the same streets I've been walking for the past quarter-century. I thought I was familiar with all the "regulars" as I call them, solitary figures whose lives I often wonder about. I chastised myself for not meeting this kind, gentle soul — as most described him — who would start conversations with people and lift their spirits.

Then last week we ran his photo. I not only knew him, he was my next-door neighbor for a couple of years in the early 2000s. His apartment door was literally next to mine. Yet we never really connected. At that point in my life, following a divorce, I was pretty withdrawn. Being a sensitive soul, maybe he "read" that and let me be.

In the ensuing years, I saw him from time to time, but we didn't interact beyond saying hello, so I never experienced what an interesting person he was. My loss.

Sergio was still living in that tiny studio apartment on the 1000 block of North Boulevard when he apparently welcomed some deeply damaged human being into his place and paid the ultimate price.

His funeral was held last Saturday morning at St. Edmund Church, a parish that celebrates Mass for the indigent, unknown and unfamilied, an admirable part of their overall ministry.

Sergio may not have had family here in the U.S., but he wasn't indigent, nor was he alone in the world. This was his parish for the past three decades. And his St. Edmund family turned out on this occasion, some 50 strong, not only to acknowledge, but also to celebrate his life.

"We remember how you loved us," they sang. And, more poignantly given the circumstances of his death, "The Lord is my life and my salvation. Of whom should I be afraid?"

He walked humbly with his God, said Rev. John McGivern in a homily from the heart. Sergio's footprint on this world could hardly be seen, McGivern noted, "but we recall the ways he touched our hearts. He didn't have much, but what he had, he gave away, helping us understand bounty and abundance in a different way. That was the gift he gave us.

"God wants us to leave a mark, a gentle imprint," he added. "Sergio showed us how. These are the really important lessons that can last a lifetime. In the face of the cruel way he was taken from us, perhaps that is the redemption."

Wary of rhetorical overreach, he emphasized, "I want my words to match his beautiful, simple life."

St. Ed's Church is a treasure, with large stained-glass windows, dazzling in the early-spring sunlight. It features a low ceiling, unlike the high vaults of most Gothic-style churches.

Behind the altar three windows memorialize the savior's birth, death, and resurrection.

"I will break their hearts of stone," the congregation sang, "give them hearts of love alone. I will speak my word to them. Who shall I send?"

"Here I am, Lord. ... I will hold your people in my heart."

After communion, several attendees approached the pulpit to share memories. One young man, shortly after he arrived in Oak Park in 2001 from Florida, met Sergio and found himself having dinner with him in Chinatown.

Sergio's landlord, LaVerne Collins, said that, along with his rent check, he would send a letter of gratitude each month, naming names and promising prayers, for helpful services rendered.

"He was never selfish, always humble," she said. "He didn't just walk the streets of Oak Park. He also walked in the presence of his Lord."

Brian Slowiak, a retired Oak Park police officer, said he knew Sergio from his days working at Baker's Square restaurant. Slowiak said his daughter, a fussy eater, loved a particular soup on the menu, so Sergio would put aside several containers of it in the freezer for him to take home to her.

"A man never stands so tall as when he stoops to help a child," Slowiak said. "He was a good man and a good friend. Serge, I'm going to miss you — and so is my daughter."

A basket of bananas was placed on a table near the pulpit and everyone was encouraged to take one in remembrance of Sergio distributing them to customers in local restaurants in his effort to promote healthy eating. Nearby, a photo poster showed him at different stages of his life.

The people his life touched made sure he was known. Midway through the funeral, a frail older man in the pew ahead of us tried to kneel and couldn't get back up. After we raised him to a sitting position, his wife thanked us, and confided, "Sergio was his best friend."

Parishioners and non-parishioners alike drew close Saturday morning to re-enact an ancient ritual, one that defies death, defies even murder — that says violence may steal a life, but it cannot steal a life's meaning.

It is the covenant of community: We promise to be a witness to each other's life because everyone's life has value. We make a promise: You will be known.

Maybe that's why we left the church that morning and moved on feeling less diminished.

Because, at our best, we hold one another in our hearts.

Bobbie Raymond's feisty advocacy (2019)

She was short but seldom came up short. She was small in stature but left an outsized footprint. She went by a young-sounding name and had a young-sounding voice, but no one ever looked down on her (not for long, anyway) or took her anything but seriously.

And always, to the very end, she was Oak Park's fiercest advocate.

For a while early on, it looked like she might end up on Broadway or in Hollywood. Born in 1938, she was a hard-working child actor in Chicago, 1945-52, using the stage name Roberta Alden, appearing in NBC Radio shows like *Jack Armstrong, the All-American Boy* and *Cricket on the Hearth*. She did commercials, trade shows and television, including the soap operas *Search for Tomorrow* and *Love of Life*.

After graduating from Oak Park and River Forest High School in 1955, she toured the Catskills with the Stanley Woolf Players in 1958 and had a lead role in the pre-Broadway cast of *Tender Loving Care* with John Payne in 1960.

She answered the question, "How ya gonna keep her in Oak Park after she's seen the Great White Way?" by bringing her brand of show biz back home. Never one to shy from the spotlight, she turned her attention to a different stage.

After studying sociology at Drake University, the New School for Social Research, and Hunter College, she focused on racial integration and the Fair Housing Movement, joining the Citizens Commission for Human Rights, which spearheaded the effort to pass Oak Park's Fair Housing Ordinance in 1968. That led to Roosevelt University, where she wrote her master's thesis, "The Challenge to Oak Park: A Suburban Community Faces Racial Change," as a prelude to founding the Oak Park Housing Center, using office space provided by First Congregational Church (now First United Church of Oak Park) in 1972.

Based on the notion that "a community attempting to maintain integration had a better chance than a community that resisted it," the Housing Center, as stated on her Wikipedia page, "worked to encourage continuing demand from whites while opening new opportunities for minorities by counseling housing seekers to promote neighborhood diversity and integration."

Ever the advocate and innovator, in addition to welcoming people of color, Raymond and the Housing Center also actively marketed Oak Park to the LGBTQ community.

Her comfort in front of the camera paid dividends. She was featured in the documentary, *As Time Goes By: Oak Park, Illinois*, which premiered at the Lake Theatre in 1974 and was later shown on WTTW, the Chicago PBS affiliate. She wrote the winning presentation script for Oak Park's All-America City Award in 1976, was featured on CBS' *60 Minutes* in 1978, and appeared on the last *Phil Donahue Show* filmed in Chicago in the early '80s. All these and more gave Oak Park a higher profile and positive publicity nationwide.

In 1977, she was one of the founders of the Oak Park Exchange Congress, a national organization comprising member municipalities that met annually for 15 years to discuss ideas for maintaining stable diversity, which came to be called the "Oak Park Strategy."

That strategy included the recognition that Oak Park could not succeed if it remained an island of integration, so she worked to build bridges across Austin Boulevard by collaborating with the Austin Schock Historical Association to create the Austin Village House Tour, promoting the West Side neighborhood's historic homes. She also organized the Boulevard Run, a 10K race whose course ran through both Oak Park and Austin (including Columbus Park).

In 1996, she retired as executive director of the Housing Center, which by then was called the Oak Park Regional Housing Center, reflecting the wider scope and focus of their efforts.

But retirement didn't slow her down much. She served on the boards of the Oak Park Development Corporation, the Doris Humphrey Foundation, the Ernest Hemingway Foundation, and the Oak Park Art League, to name a few.

She established and served as president of the OPRF High School Alumni Association, which included a scholarship fund for educational travel.

Many of her causes did not put her center stage. In 1996, she connected with a 1938 OPRF grad named Lewis Pope, a star running back for the nationally ranked OPRF High School football team. When OPRF was invited to play another powerhouse, Miami High, in the Orange Bowl, Pope was prohibited from playing because of his race. Raymond brought him back to Oak Park and interviewed him for the oral history project, "Legends of Our Time." During his visit, Pope was also honored with the high school's Tradition of Excellence Award (Raymond was likewise honored in 1990).

In a series of articles in the Oak Leaves, she published the first history of early Black residents in Oak Park, dating back to the 1870s. And she was integral to establishing A Day in Our Village on the first Sunday of June.

An avid painter and gardener, she combined those passions, creating nature-based watercolors, some inspired by her backyard, some by the Oak Park Conservatory, and some by her frequent trips to Door County in Wisconsin. She was a longtime member of the Oak Park-River Forest Garden Club.

At the Oak Park Art League, she led the Sunday figure-drawing class for years and was one of the founders of Expressions Graphics on Harrison Street. A Francophile, she organized a long-running French Club conversation class at Good Shepherd Lutheran Church in Oak Park. And she was one of the organizers of the popular First Tuesday Club, bringing independent art films to the Lake Theatre.

And as an avid cross country skier, she loved a good snowfall.

Sandra and David Sokol, who moved to the village in 1972, said if you got involved in Oak Park, you inevitably crossed paths with Bobbie Raymond.

"She was a small, feisty person who spoke her mind," David recalled.

"She grew up here," said Sandra, "a real DOOPer [Dear Old Oak Parker]. She said OPRF was the best education she had. I did a lot of listening. She would say, 'You agree with this, right?' I did, mostly. I miss that. She had a brilliant brain."

She was opinionated and could be blunt, but she was also generous.

"People didn't know about it," David said. "She was happy to give money anonymously. She went way beyond the 'feisty redhead.'"

Bobbie's son, Charles Raymond, remembers that his mom seemed to be at a meeting every night. And not just when he was growing up.

"She would bake cookies and brownies for all these meetings. I would say, 'Come on, Mom, you're 80!' She would say, 'The meetings keep me going.'"

"She loved everything about Oak Park," he said, "its diversity, how beautiful it was. She was a huge fan."

He would like Roberta "Bobbie" Raymond to be remembered "as somebody who devoted her whole life to making Oak Park the best it could be."

Harry Parker and the very marrow of being human (2019)

Rev. Harry Parker delivered his last sermon on Reformation Sunday, Nov. 3, at First Baptist Church of Oak Park, where he served as pastor for 27 years. He knew it was his last sermon. The doctors told him six months ago he probably wouldn't make it to the holidays this year, though he held out hope that, with his family's help and our prayers, he might "prove the doctors wrong."

So pale, so frail, so mortal, he was no longer the reliable regular the Oak Park Runners Club knew — or the pastor who organized tours of Israel and Jordan. On this Sunday, he didn't have a lot left in his tank, but what he lacked in energy, he made up for in devotion.

I was the only non-Baptist in the bunch in 2006 when Harry led a remarkable spiritual journey through a troubled, holy land. We visited locations mentioned in the Bible and took turns reading passages aloud that pertained to those sites. It was like walking through a biblical hologram. We experienced the power of a windstorm sweeping in off the Mediterranean Sea at the end of the rainy season; the stillness on the Sea of Galilee (Lake Kinneret); the salt-caked sterility of the Dead Sea, lowest point on Earth and terminus of the Jordan River; the Golan Heights, fertile source of the Jordan River, gushing out of the rocks following the winter rains. Our pilgrimage took us to Bethlehem where we stood in a cave that served as a stable for the shepherds who still tend flocks there. We walked among the olive trees in the Garden of Gethsemane — or a reasonable facsimile — overlooking Jerusalem, and recreated the walk down to the old city, which Jesus entered on Palm Sunday to face his Via Dolorosa. Approximate locations in many cases, but grist for the mill of faith, which grinds exceedingly fine. The Bible never seemed more alive, much more than a roller-coaster ride through a religious theme park. I'm beholden to Harry and First Baptist for that journey.

What kind of sermon would you deliver if you knew it was likely your last? Pastor Parker's title was, "My Confession."

Quoting Winston Churchill, by way of Samuel Johnson, he said he was staring down the barrel of a .30-06 Springfield rifle. Johnson, he said, put it more succinctly: "When a man knows he is to be hanged in a fortnight, it concentrates his mind wonderfully."

Harry said he felt that increased concentration, and staring down the barrel of a terminal cancer diagnosis "woke me up."

In spite of the "Great Commandment" ("love God with everything you have and your neighbor as yourself"), he confessed that he loved some things more than God. "I'm guilty of loving myself too much," he said, "which is the heart of all other sins."

The sin of pride, for instance. He was thankful for his wonderful partner, Linda, and their three children, for leading this congregation for 27 years, for teaching in the seminary for 20, but the pride he felt sometimes led to "putting myself above others," sometimes without even being aware of it. "Pride is universal," he said. "All are guilty. The things we're most grateful for have a shadow side."

And finally, the sin of idolatry, i.e., loving the good things of this world with "a disordered affection. What I long for are the blessings of God: extended life, health, freedom from pain. I've been seeking the blessings of God instead of God himself."

Someday soon, he said, he would stand before God and be tempted to say, "But didn't I preach? Didn't I teach Sunday School? Didn't I attend all those meetings?" He had a pretty good idea what the answer would be.

But despite such sinfulness, he said, "This is where grace comes in. By grace we are saved. When I stand before God, what I want is never to have sinned at all and that everything sad will become untrue. I want to remember that if God is for us, who can be against us? That nothing will separate us from the love of God."

He was letting go — of ego, pride, desire. Dissolving the bonds that tie us to the physical world, including his own weakened body. He was standing on the precipice of a great mystery. Facing it, ready to let go, a man of faith to the end. Faith, of course, doesn't prove anything, but it surely comes in handy when the time comes to let go.

And let go he did on Nov. 22, following a nine-year struggle with cancer.

But before that, Harry put his affairs in order. He published a book titled, *Journey to Wholeness – The Path to God and Your True Self*, a summation of his own journey.

Speaking of the illness that claimed him, he wrote: "This disease set me out on a pilgrimage to deepen my spiritual life. I began a quest to sift through a small mountain of books from the second to the 21st century. I drank deeply from the wells of wisdom dug by spiritual giants of the past, both ancient and modern. I have not 'wasted my cancer'."

If there is an afterlife, he now knows. It might not be exactly what he expected, but whatever form it takes, surely the immense power of love will be central.

Harry's son helped him down from the pulpit so he could preside over communion one last time as the congregation sang, "Amazing grace, how sweet the sound." Afterward, congregants lined up to wish him well. If only they could wish him well.

In my few moments, I reminded Harry that the only other time I received communion from him was in Jerusalem, in a garden on a sunny, spring-like Sunday morning that closely resembled my own imaginings of what that open-tomb Easter looked like — minus the gift shop, of course.

Atul Gawande, in his book *Being Mortal*, writes, "The battle of being mortal is the battle to maintain the integrity of one's life — to avoid becoming so diminished or dissipated or subjugated that who you are becomes disconnected from who you were or who you want to be." That never happened to Harry Parker. "Whatever the limits and travails we face, we want to retain the autonomy — the freedom — to be the authors of our lives," Gawande wrote. "This is the very marrow of being human."

Frank Muriello and the race to justice (2020)

The word "avuncular" was created for people like Frank Muriello. He was a good uncle.

Frank was the first adult I beat in a foot race. One summer day in Crandon, Wisconsin, at Keeler's Resort as we were waiting our hour after lunch before swimming in Lake Metonga, I happened upon Frank and one of his sons toeing a starting line on the softball field. So I joined them — and won, which surprised me. A modest rite of passage to be sure, but it felt significant at the time. Uncle Frank didn't seem to mind.

Crandon was as close to paradise as I have known — three families, 20 cousins, three sets of parents at the center of that mini-verse, our tiny commune of cottages. The adults would gather each night in one of the cottages, tell stories, and laugh late into the evening as the lake lapped ceaselessly against the shore and we drifted securely off to sleep.

As I grew older, I was vaguely aware that Uncle Frank had become a figure of some note in Oak Park, but I didn't realize he dreamed up the notion of Equity Assurance during his tenure as village trustee (1981-85) until he died at the age of 92.

White flight was rampant from the 1950s through the 1970s — across the nation and certainly in the Chicago metropolitan area. Resegregation, as it's known now — panic peddling or redlining as it was known then — swept the West Side, heading directly for Oak Park. Would the village muster enough courage to resist White flight? That meant ignoring unscrupulous real estate agents who told White homeowners they'd better sell before their housing values cratered, a self-fulfilling prophecy that proved out across the West Side right up to Austin Boulevard, our eastern border.

Oak Parkers did resist those initial waves of White flight, thanks to intentional efforts and the stiffened spines of homeowners who refused to cave in to fear — people like the aforementioned three sets of parents who seemed so carefree each July in the North Woods during the 1960s.

But resisting the initial wave wasn't enough. Fear lapped ceaselessly against our shore. By 1981, when Frank was elected trustee, the situation was far from secure. If we were going to diversify, we needed integration everywhere, right up to our borders with other communities. Some 45 blighted multifamily buildings were in danger of resegregating. In 1979, the Oak Park Residence Corporation, an innovative public-private partnership, started buying those buildings and rehabbing them. Frank took over as executive director in 1986. Over the next dozen years, ResCorp, as it came to be known, rehabbed 25 buildings and sold them off or managed them. They partnered with the Oak Park Regional Housing Center, which marketed them with an eye toward maintaining stable diversity.

Calming single-family homeowners was another matter. Frank suggested creating an insurance policy to cover nervous homeowners against losing their investment if housing values crashed. They called it "Equity Assurance." The question was, would it work?

One Sunday morning a few years back, I was listening to an *On Being* interview with john a. powell (spelled lowercase intentionally), director of the Haas Institute for a Fair and Inclusive Society; professor of Law, African-American and Ethnic Studies at the University of California, Berkeley; and the author of *Racing to Justice: Transforming our Concepts of Self and Other to Build an Inclusive Society*.

As they discussed race and segregation, interviewer Krista Tippett said, "You told one story about Oak Park, near Chicago," she said. "Would you tell that story? I feel like these little stories are really crucial."

"They're little," powell said, "and they're big. Chicago's one of the most segregated areas in the country. Cook County has the largest Black population of any county in the United States, and a lot of studying of segregation takes place in Chicago. So here you have Oak Park, this precious little community. And there were liberal Whites there. Blacks started moving in. And they were saying, 'Look, we actually don't mind

Blacks moving in, but we're concerned that we're going to lose the value of our home. That's the only wealth we have. And if we don't sell now, we're going to lose.'

"[Village government] basically said: 'If that's the real concern, what if we were to ensure that you would not lose the value of your home? We'll literally create an insurance policy that will compensate you if the value of your home goes down.' They put that in place, and they haven't had to pay one policy. Whites didn't run. That's a stable community; it's been that way for 50 years."

Turns out Oak Parkers were better than their word.

Frank didn't do it all alone, of course. Village government took his idea and ran with it. However far we still have to go in overcoming racism, Oak Park became a model of stable diversity. And, yes, the finish line is still a long way off.

Frank Muriello, a solid Republican, grew up the son of an Italian immigrant, so he knew about discrimination because it was very real for Italians back then.

"My father taught me to always find the good things about people," Frank once told me. "The real strength of Oak Park is the melding of every nationality into being Oak Parkers."

I may have beat him in one race, but in the race to justice and a more inclusive village, I was looking at his back.

Thanks for the baton, Uncle Frank.

We'll take it from here.

What's real and what's not (2007)

Last week was as strange a week as I've lived through. The first half I spent trying to help unravel the mystery of John Dietz, or John Diaz, who claimed to be a decorated veteran. He was going to lead the July 4th parade, then didn't. The more we looked into his story, the less we knew for certain. Now it looks as if he might have fabricated much of his identity.

That would mean we were "taken in." Journalists aren't supposed to be duped. We're supposed to be more skeptical than the average person — for just this reason. Sometimes, I guess, you want to believe a story, so you let down your guard.

Nobody likes living that way, of course. We want to trust. We crave authenticity. We need to know what we can count on — and sometimes we wonder if there's anything we can truly believe in.

Then July 4th arrived, the day each year when I am most aware of the gap between our myth of America, which I love so, and the reality of the United States, which so often disappoints me. The gap between the two has never been wider, and many of us who remain patriots despite it all, can't help wondering if there's anything left of our founding ideals to hang onto.

The next day, my father died.

Quite a guy, my father. A graceful athlete and unshakeable man of reason, he grew up during the Depression, fought in Europe during World War II, raised six boys and put us all through college, managed the family business for three decades, coached youth baseball for more than 30 years, battled Parkinson's Disease to a draw for a quarter century, and attended daily Mass for 50 years until his condition got the better of him (though it never got the best of him). For 35 of those years, he opened the church five days a week, then went over and, frequently, woke up the priest to preside over 6 a.m. Mass. His entire life he rooted for the Cubs — through thin and thinner. He didn't live to see 2016.

Through it all, he never complained. Whenever we railed against the slings and arrows of outrageous fortune and asked how such an injustice could have happened, he would shrug and say, "Just lucky, I guess."

My dad didn't go in for bitterness though he had some reason to. He was the kind of guy who would look up at a gloomy sky and say, "It's definitely brightening up."

He always gave his best and taught us to do the same. With each stage of his illness, as he diminished physically, then mentally, he still gave us his best, whatever "best" was at that point, right to the very end.

Seeing my father's body last Thursday morning didn't shock or repel me, as I thought it might. What I felt was a tenderness unlike any I've ever known. Sadness, too, of course, along with some relief that his long ordeal is now over.

All in all, a very strange week: Getting acquainted with possibly the most inauthentic person I've ever met, then losing the most authentic person I'll ever know, separated by a holiday that raises more questions about authenticity than any other.

I feel badly about John Dietz and badly for him. I'm not the punishing type. Most people in the final analysis are more sinned against than sinning, as King Lear said. John seems to be a gentle old guy who, for some complicated set of reasons — perhaps even beyond his conscious control — needed to try on a different identity.

Like other well-intentioned people, it looks as if I was taken in. I'm embarrassed, but I don't feel angry or disillusioned. It doesn't make me question what's real or wonder if, indeed, anything is real.

I know what real looks like. I said goodbye to him last week.

My father made it impossible for me to be cynical. He was a wonderful father, an inspiring coach and a great teacher. When my brothers and I were born, we hit the Trifecta. How could we have been so blessed?

Just lucky, I guess.

A perfect match: Ginie Cassin and Oak Park (2020)

Ginie Cassin was a hard person to say no to. That's what a lot of people said, all those people she recruited as helpers to realize her visions for civic improvement. Once she slid her arm through yours, you were a goner.

But she was also a person who hardly ever said no. Her working motto as village clerk for 20 years was "I can do that." And she did, everything from the logistics for Farmers Market and A Day in Our Village to helping write Oak Park's landmark Fair Housing Ordinance.

Virginia "Ginie" Cassin died on Oct. 16, 2020 from complications of a very long, very full, very well-lived life in Oak Park, and then Baxter, Minnesota, where her family migrated and who surrounded her with love as she expired last week at the age of 96. In other words, she died as she lived: bringing people together for the betterment of her community.

She was happiest when she was useful, so the last few years were likely frustrating for her, but there was no way around it. A nonagenarian has to make a few concessions. She hated leaving Oak Park, but family closeness was her consolation.

While she was here in Oak Park for the better part of a century, though, Ginie left her mark. She was in the first wave of Catholics who got involved in local politics, back in the day when that ruffled some Protestant feathers. She and her life partner Bill got involved in the Chicago Archdiocese's Cana Conference like many young couples in the '60s. That engagement led to joining the League of Women Voters, which led to the village's Community Relations Commission in 1963, which boosted the Open Housing movement and led to becoming Oak Park's first female village clerk until she retired, then chaired the Ernest Hemingway Foundation board until age finally coaxed her into retirement ever so gently.

Twenty years ago, I found myself on a Hemingway Foundation-sponsored trip to Cuba with Ginie and Bill, and I let it slip that she reminded me of my mother. Well, she knew my mom from Cana, so she understood what a high compliment that was, which meant my cover as an objective, hard-edged journalistic word-slinger was utterly compromised. From then on, we bonded. But she *was* like my mom: warm, welcoming, gracious, intelligent and hospitable on the outside, tough inside — and very short in stature (physically only).

I wasn't the only one who had a hard time saying no to her. She didn't have to twist arms. All you had to do was surrender. She made it easy. It also helped that I believed in her cause — convincing a largely indifferent village of the mind-boggling literary legacy laid in its lap in the person of Ernest Hemingway, who was born and raised here.

The Hemingway Foundation's efforts greatly enriched Oak Park's cultural legacy, unique among metropolitan suburbs. A fitting memorial to Ginie Cassin would be to build a Hemingway Wing onto the Historical Society's Oak Park River Forest Museum.

Great people produce great towns. Or do great towns produce great people? Maybe both. At the very least, special towns make it possible for people with great potential to fulfill their promise. That was certainly true in Ginie Cassin's case.

"I'll miss the good feeling of being from Oak Park and being a part of Oak Park," she said in 2018 before moving to Minnesota. "I feel it has been an honorable place to live, representing a good community with a lot of good people in it.

"Most of my adult life, I have lived under very good government, which has espoused policies that are very much in line with the way I feel about things, whether it was racial diversity or the openness of the board and commission system where there are hearings and opportunities for people to put in their thoughts.

"I think people rise to the occasion of being an Oak Park resident or business owner. And this might sound a little funny, but I'm happy to have generally been on the right side of things. It means that you match the place where you live."

Oak Park and Ginie Cassin were, indeed, a perfect pairing.

Breakfast won't be the same without John Hubbuch (2020)

John Hubbuch and I had a good arrangement. Twice a month, I edited his column, which I always looked forward to, and in return, every other month or so he would take me out to breakfast, usually at Hemmingway's Bistro, where we ate our Bircher Muesli, sipped coffee, and held court for a couple of hours on a wide range of topics — from the achievement gap at OPRF High School, to philosophy, to youth sports, to the latest outrage in national politics, to the afterlife and the existence or non-existence of God, to the latest controversy in Oak Park, to films, to Indiana basketball, to our kids and, especially, our grandkids.

My brain slipped into a higher gear during these sessions and I always left feeling wonderfully, thoughtfully stimulated. His was an active life of the mind. John faithfully attended Redd Griffin's extended-learning seminar on Great Thinkers through Triton Community College for years, and when Redd died some years back, John kept the class going.

Originally, his plan, growing up in southern Indiana, was to become president of the United States (JFK was his early hero, Barack Obama later). By the time he and Marsha moved to Oak Park in 1976, he was content with serving a term on the District 97 school board in the late 1980s — though he always left the meetings by 10 p.m., saying he needed his sleep and they knew where to reach him if they took a late vote.

He was also a longtime member of the YMCA board and president of the OPRF High School Huskies Booster Club for 10 years — so he did become president after all — and he was proud of living in Oak Park.

"It was a place where people talked about important ideas," said Marsha. "He was very impressed by what Oak Park stood for."

And he wrote a column for this newspaper for roughly a quarter-century. He was funny, provocative and sometimes painfully honest — a truly independent thinker. He delighted in playing the contrarian and skeptic (but never cynic) and enjoyed getting a rise out of readers.

When I entered his name in our Search function, the following headlines popped up:

"Offended by Hubbuch's column"

"Hubbuch's column reveals classism, elitism"

"Hubbuch, get some Prozac and go to confession"

He fancied himself a curmudgeon, writing columns titled, "Confessions of a lapsed, liberal Democrat" and "Beware: This column contains alternative opinions." But he wasn't really. He was too upbeat to be a curmudgeon. His son Chris described him as "an optimist, but a realist." I would call him a realist whose optimism kept shining through. There was just too much sunshine in him.

We didn't always agree, but I always enjoyed reading him. I admired his brevity, wit and refreshing candor. He acknowledged his personal shortcomings more freely than most. He started one column: "What follows are the individual, non-expert thoughts of a 71-year-old male living in Oak Park, Illinois. Although I am pretty egotistical, I do not presume to tell anyone about anything."

The one area of his life where he was never the contrarian or skeptic was family. He described himself as a "C" lawyer, a "B" husband, and an "A" parent. He made time to coach his three sons in basketball (his first love, being from Indiana), baseball and soccer. He and Marsha were high school sweethearts, and they stayed sweet on each other. Though he never got around to assigning the grade, he was an A+ grandfather, down on the floor, crawling through tunnels, sliding down slides, landing on his butt. Grandparenting was a full-body contact sport. When the kids went down for naps, so did he. He left it all on the floor.

"John," Marsha said, "was the heart of this family."

His favorite moments were spending an afternoon on the golf course with his sons or watching the Bulls together in the basement during their remarkable run of six championships in the 1990s.

Every August for four decades, the Hubbuchs joined friends for a week in Watervale, Michigan. In a 2013 column titled, "Vacation: a philosopher's paradise," he wrote:

"This year I spent considerable time on the beach with Lily and Ava, my little granddaughters. I reveled in the moment when the waves crashed against them in my arms, and they came up sputtering, torn between joy and fear, just like their father and uncles so many years earlier on that very same beach.

"Each year I come away from Watervale with a renewed appreciation of the natural world. I am affirmed in my decision to put family at the center of my life. I grasp how very fortunate I am. Perhaps most importantly, I understand that life is filled with possibility, and it is up to me to make the most of it."

John made the most of it. He retired as early as possible (59) so he could spend more time with the people he loved. When the nest emptied, he and Marsha sold the big house on the north end of Oak Park and downsized to a bungalow south of the Eisenhower.

So much for being classist and elitist. He was, first and foremost, a silo-buster.

And he had his priorities in the right place.

"John always tells me that nobody has it better," said Marsha last weekend trying to buoy our spirits as we hoped against hope that Loyola could work a miracle on his torn aorta. But it was too much even for modern health care and, even though he was in excellent physical condition, his heart gave out.

For his grandkids the loss is huge. The older ones — especially his first, Lily, already showing promise as a writer — will need to remind the younger ones as they grow older what their grandpa was like, how special he was. Three-year-old Hazel calls him her best friend. So does Hazel's father.

He was a character. He loved wearing the color purple, gumballs, and disguises (especially his Captain Hook Halloween costume). In fact, that comprised his entire Christmas wish list last year.

"He was a purple shirt-wearing, gumball-chewing goof," said his son, Nick, "and the smartest person in the room."

John wasn't afraid of death. At any rate he wasn't afraid to look at it squarely, which he did in April this year when he wrote:

"I do appreciate the concern that everyone has for old people like me during these troubled times. But trust me, I have thought about death quite a bit as I have gotten older. I get it. I am more vulnerable to COVID-19, but then I am more vulnerable to heart disease, Alzheimer's, the flu, falling down the steps, etc., ad nauseam. Old people always are dying."

"If this is it," he said, as the paramedics wheeled him to the ambulance, "it was a great run." There was only one thing he didn't accomplish: dancing with his granddaughters on their wedding day. Other than that, as a father and a grandfather, his sons say, "He went out on top, like Michael Jordan."

"The most important thing he taught us," said his son, Phil, "is to be the best parent we can possibly be."

I will miss our breakfasts, but most of all his columns. I'm more of an essayist, but John was a true columnist. Get in, hit the nail on the head, and get out. That's how he lived, too. He made me laugh and made me think — or rather, pushed me to find out what I was thinking. But he never made me cry.

Until last week.

Chief Joe Mendrick: 'It's not that difficult to change' (2000, 2021)

There has been a lot of talk lately about police reform in this country. But it's not the first time for Oak Park.

In the 1980s, the department went through two very high-profile probes amid charges of excessive force (one of them led by soon-to-be bestselling novelist Scott Turow). In both cases, the police chiefs at the time departed and Deputy Chief Joe Mendrick stepped in as acting chief. In 1990, he was named permanent chief of police, and served until he retired in 2001.

Mendrick turned the Oak Park Police Department around. Police are now respected in this village and enjoy widespread support. But that doesn't mean the department isn't still in need of reform.

Police departments are always in need of reform.

In the wake of George Floyd's murder by a Minneapolis cop in 2020, and myriad other killings of unarmed people of color by police around the country, many are calling for systemic changes in policing.

That's not just the opinion of radicals. Joe Mendrick died in 2016, but if he were alive today, he would agree. In fact, he said as much during his "exit interview" back in 2000.

What he said then was remarkable — and even more timely 21 years later. His comments should be required reading by police departments in every American municipality.

"If you look at the problems they're having in L.A., Chicago and other major cities," Mendrick said, "they're putting the finger on bringing in too many people too quickly and not training them. That was a problem in this organization."

The Oak Park Police Department, he noted, doubled in size in the mid-'70s because fear of crime was rampant nationwide. Many of those new recruits (60-plus in a single year) were Vietnam vets, he recalled. Some had issues. They weren't screened, and they weren't adequately trained.

Not surprisingly, there were problems. When Mendrick became

permanent chief in 1990, some were skeptical at first, thinking he might be too "inside" to turn things around. Turns out he was exactly the right person at precisely the right time.

"The main thing you've got to remember," Mendrick said, looking back on his 11-year tenure as chief, "is that we are accountable to the public. Police, in general, are not trusted. That's why you have the Constitution. They put reins on us."

It's amazing how many police officers in other cities still don't understand this. Their attitude seems to be, as Mendrick put it, "We're the police. We can do what we want."

Under his leadership, that attitude changed. Oak Park was one of the first departments nationwide to institute a Field Training Officer (FTO) program to work with new recruits. As Derek Chauvin proved in Minneapolis, where he was an FTO, that alone is not enough, but, "We really screened our people," Mendrick said. "They're trained. Turning 'em loose on the street to run and gun, that's out."

Oak Park was also one of the first towns to embrace community policing, which Mendrick said was the real turning point in the 1990s. He remembered the lessons he learned when he was a young beat cop in the late-'60s, early-'70s, working the streets of Oak Park.

Lessons about building trust.

"It's not too hard to tell somebody why you stopped them," he said. "It's not too hard when you walk by somebody to say hi. It's not too hard to listen. It's not too hard to be empathetic. And it's not that difficult to change. You've got to be willing to understand that people will question. You've got to accept that, and if you don't, you're not going to go anyplace."

He was willing to change and the department did go someplace. It became a model. How did Joe Mendrick change things?

Transparency.

"We opened the doors," he said. "Come and see what we do. We were a closed environment before that. We opened up, not only to the newspaper but to the public. ... When we have problems, we're open about them. When officers have trouble, they go before the [oversight] board. ...

We're held to a higher standard, and I believe in that. An organization is based on ethics, period. Do the right thing. We're not in an occupation that is conducive to forgiveness. If there's something in the organization or atmosphere that's not up to the standards of the way law enforcement has to operate in today's society, then you leave."

I can't help wondering how many police chiefs in other communities, even today, would so freely espouse that.

"We opened our arms to the community and said, 'What's important to you? Where do you want us to put our resources and for what? We're willing to discuss it with you. We don't know all the answers.'"

Joe Mendrick put the "servant" back in public servant. He followed in the footsteps of the legendary Chief Fremont Nester, who talked residents down and prepared the way when African Americans began moving into town.

"You realize that you're just a community service organization," Mendrick said, "even though you are responsible."

And that has been the model in Oak Park since. It was carried on by Mendrick's successors, Rick Tanksley, Tony Ambrose, LaDon Reynolds and now Shatonya Johnson. Do the Oak Park police need reminding occasionally and does the model need updating? Of course, and that requires community input. But the core principles are intact, as articulated by a remarkable police chief:

"We are accountable to the public."

"We don't know all the answers."

"Do the right thing."

"It's not that difficult to change."

Can that model be used everywhere? Some will say, "Oh no, it's too dangerous in the inner cities." What's really dangerous, we now know all too well, is conducting law enforcement in an adversarial fashion, based on mutual mistrust.

"You're as good as the people around you," Mendrick said in 2000. "What I try to do is find people I have faith in — their values. That's what I look for in people — values, period. You can teach anybody to be a policeman.

"What you need to be is a good person."

Sherlynn Reid made us whole (2021)

Sherlynn and Henry Reid made history when they moved to Oak Park in 1968. They were the first black couple in the 1960s to buy a home using a conventional loan — which happened just after the adoption of the village's landmark Fair Housing Ordinance. You can hear Sherlynn's thoughts about that era in a video in the Fair Housing exhibit at the Historical Society's Oak Park River Forest Museum.

The Reids, along with the Robinets and the Registers — the 3 Rs of Oak Park integration — were the 1960s pioneers who paved the way.

The first thing Sherlynn did when they moved into the big house on Ridgeland Avenue was call Police Chief Fremont Nester and tell him he could reassign the squad car in front of her home, which was there as protection against, well, people with anger issues and poor impulse control.

Sherlynn wasn't worried. She told the chief they would take their chances. That could serve as a good slogan for Oak Park's Black residents and for that matter, the entire village:

They took their chances.

The next thing she did was get involved, in a big way, quickly weaving herself into the community fabric. She joined the First Tuesday Club, a group of remarkable women — including Joan Pope, Marge Greenwald, Ann Armstrong, Fran Sullivan, Bobbie Raymond, Trudi Doyle, Marie Kruse, Mary Ellen Matthias, Gloria Merrill, and Sandra Sokol, among others — who networked, researched issues, and started waking up a sleepy suburb.

By 1999 when Sherlynn retired after more than two decades as head of the village's Community Relations Department, she had served as chair of the League of Women Voters' Human Relations Committee, established a human relations workshop at OPRF High School, joined the Beye School PTA board and the Christian Education board at First United Church, was a Brownie Troop leader and served on the Girl Scouts Council.

Actually, she did all that in her first three years here.

She eventually got around to being president of the League of Women Voters and the 19th Century Club; was an active member of two African American social organizations, Jack & Jill and Links; helped launch the block party tradition in Oak Park; and started the "Dinner & Dialogue" program through Community Relations to increase the comfort level between White and Black residents. She was also a longtime supporter of the CAST arts program at Julian Middle School, which her husband Henry co-founded, and she raised money for that program's scholarship fund, which bears Henry's name. She even acted in some of the plays. And she was a member of the task force that founded the Oak Park Education Foundation.

Sherlynn Reid helped Oak Park come a long way from that grocery store where, according to a 1971 Oak Leaves article, a "gray-haired matron" came up to her and said, "Pardon me, Miss. I'm looking for domestic help. Can you spare a day for me?" And following speaking engagements when well-meaning members of the audience would gush, "You're so different!" Sherlynn would reply with the air of authority that came so naturally, accompanied by that gracious smile: "There are thousands of Black people exactly like me. I happen to be the only one you've met."

Oak Park is a different — and much better — community than the one Sherlynn found when she arrived in 1968, thanks in no small part to her efforts.

In that same 1971 article, Henry Reid said, "Only Whites can integrate a community. Blacks just desegregate it." But Sherlynn did integrate this community, in the true sense of the word "integrate," which is "to make whole."

The Reids, the Robinets, the Registers, and many other Black families and households helped Oak Park integrate. We have a long way to go, but thanks to pioneers like Sherlynn Reid, we're going together.

Sherlynn was born 2½ hours after her twin brother, Sherwood, emerged — with no one expecting her to show up. Her mother, Mary Dee, the first Black radio personality in Pittsburgh, reportedly told the doctors, "It's not over till it's over."

Well, Oak Park wasn't expecting Sherlynn to show up either, but she got here none too soon.

As Frank Lipo, executive director of the Historical Society, put it, "There is always a need for the Sherlynns of the world. She created systems of non-oppression."

By the age of 85, she had slowed down some and her eyes were giving her trouble. But her vision was as keen and clear as ever. Here's how she described that vision just before the turn of the millennium:

"We must look at new paradigms where people of all races, professions, sexes, religions, sexual orientations, ages, etc. are determined to live side by side in tolerance, if not love, with one another."

She did as much as anyone to make that new Oak Park paradigm a reality.

But she did more than that.

Sherlynn Reid made us whole.

Postlude

A day to say goodbye

No one knows what happens when we die. Most of us don't think much about it — or think too much about it. Far more pressing than life after death, some would argue, is life before death.

But what if there is an afterlife, and it included an opportunity to pay a return visit — a day of your choosing, part of your life review? Maybe a day in the present. Maybe a day from the past. Your past.

Would you do it?

That was the choice facing Emily Gibbs, the young wife who has just died as Act 3 begins in Thornton Wilder's classic American drama, *Our Town*. Despite warnings from the other "residents" of the Grover's Corners Cemetery — that going back will be too painful — she decides to return anyway.

What would it be like to make one final visit to life? Would Oak Park be revealed as Eden reborn, the kingdom of heaven itself, which we — and every other villager alive at this moment — cannot fully fathom because we're too busy living? Relieved of all tasks, responsibilities, details, worries, and minor dramas — relieved of life itself — how would our town look to you?

Would you stand astonished by the beauty of sunlight basting a tree out your bedroom window in the morning? Would you spend all afternoon mesmerized by clouds shaping and reshaping over Scoville Park, or listening to songbirds in Austin Gardens, or smelling newly-mown grass?

Would you notice people bustling toward the CTA Green Line station on their way to work, hoping to make the train? Or would you be captivated instead by the leaves of a graceful old elm swaying in the breeze? A kid nibbling on a breakfast burrito as he ambles down the sidewalk toward Gwendolyn Brooks Middle School? The simple elegance of a young woman reading in the park? The remarkable peace of the world when you're not in any hurry?

Would you see the town you thought you knew ... anew? Would you see more in your surroundings than you ever paid attention to? Would it all be too extraordinarily beautiful for one person to appreciate in a lifetime, much less a day?

Would you savor the personal interactions around you, the laughter, the older woman on a bike singing happily aloud on Euclid Avenue? Would you see people more clearly as they hurry home up Grove Avenue after a long day at work, and understand them better, without the filter of judgment? Would you experience a profound compassion for their aches and preoccupations, which the great religious figures always talked about?

Would unresolved relationships with people living just a short walk from where you're standing put you through the greatest sadness and greatest joy you've ever known — inextricably intertwined? Would you suffer deep regrets about missed opportunities? Would you let the full force of love break your heart wide open? Would you summon, from God knows where, the grace to forgive yourself at last for your shortcomings and all your fellow human beings for theirs?

Would you come to terms with the fact that our inability to comprehend all this during one lifetime is not some unconscionable, inconsolable tragedy but simply the "melancholy of our fate," as Martin Buber called it in *I and Thou*?

Would you understand at last what it means to be fully human?

Emily realizes soon enough why she was warned against a return visit.

"I can't bear it," she says, gazing at her parents. ... "I can't look at everything hard enough!"

She surrenders, saying, "I can't go on. It goes so fast. We don't have time to look at one another. I didn't realize. All that was going on and we never noticed. Take me back — up the hill — to my grave. But first: Wait! One more look. ... Oh, Earth, you're too wonderful for anybody to realize you."

Perhaps the ultimate definition of living: Too wonderful for anyone to realize, but if we could, we would realize that life is that beautiful.

And that realizing it is worth the heartbreak.

If you died and were given the chance, would you return for just one day more? To say goodbye to your town — to waking up to bustling mornings, to hearing the St. Edmund bells mark the hours of another day, to saying hello to people you pass on the street, to seeing the grass greening in the chilly wet spring on the slope leading to the top of the rise near the memorial where tulips are just beginning to open, to smelling donuts and linden blossoms wafting on the night air, to letting the porch lights warm your walk as you pass by lived-in houses, to hearing a siren or train whistle sounding in the distance, to watching someone you love walking toward you from a distance, to taking one last look at the wonderful, terrible moon out your window before drifting into dreams.

If you come across someone, someday, standing on a street corner, taking it all in, lost in their surroundings, let them be. You never know.

They might just be visiting.

And saying one last goodbye.

Or maybe it's just me.

Acknowledgments

Writing is a solitary occupation, many have noted, but producing a book is not. In this particular case, it took a village to give birth, or at least inspire it. These days, when someone asks how long it took to write a particular newspaper column, I usually respond, "About 32 years," and that is true of this book as well. So first I have to thank those who have read these weekly installments, one by one, over the last three decades, and secondly those who thought enough of them to encourage me to publish a compilation.

Thanks to Marty Berg for so carefully editing the manuscript and becoming a fan of the book in the process. Thanks to Frank Lipo, executive director of the Historical Society of Oak Park-River Forest for checking the book for historical accuracy. This is not a history book, but there is plenty of history in it. And thanks to volunteer readers Marty Swisher and Rebekah Levin for their invaluable feedback.

I asked all of the above to read the book, which is a considerable commitment of time, which I don't take lightly, specifically because I knew if they didn't like it, they would be honest enough to say so — and that is the most valuable feedback of all.

Thanks also to Mac Robinet for being willing to provide his comments for the back cover and doing so on very short notice. I regard no Oak Parkers more highly than McLouis and Harriette Robinet.

Thanks to Kevin Theis and Paul Stroili of Fort Raphael Publishing for designing the book and helping me navigate the self-publishing process.

Thanks to Javier Govea at Growing Community Media for hunting down the photos I asked him to locate in the Wednesday Journal archives, no small task considering the general disarray of our archives. Thanks to Frank Pinc, former Wednesday Journal photographer, who searched his archives and provided several of the photos that appear in this book. And thanks as well to Dan Haley, publisher of GCM, for providing support for this venture and giving me the platform (and the job) that led to it.

Thanks to artist Mitchell Markovitz for granting permission to use his work as the cover art for this book, and to Brian Kinyon for his photographic expertise in making Mitch's Oak Park poster art pop.

I also need to thank the late, great Thornton Wilder for writing *Our Town*, which provided the lens and unifying thread that pulled these disparate parts together into (hopefully) a comprehensible narrative — and to Rick Bacchi, who found and gifted me with Howard Sherman's book, *Another Day's Begun – Thornton Wilder's 'Our Town' in the 21st Century*, which provided valuable context and confirmation of the influence of Wilder's play worldwide and how it pertains to all our towns in their continuing search, conscious or not, for true community.

And finally, thanks most of all to those who trusted me to tell their stories over the past three decades.

About the Author

A storyteller, chronicler of life, and occasional provocateur, Ken Trainor has been a "free-range" community journalist and newspaper editor in Oak Park, Illinois, for the past 32 years with Growing Community Media as editor of the Forest Park Review, Austin Weekly News, and Wednesday Journal of Oak Park-River Forest (not all at once). Now semi-retired, he works two days a week rescuing the prose of harried reporters on deadline, refereeing the opinion pages, and tending the obituaries with loving care.

Born and raised in Oak Park, since 1985 he has honed his storytelling skills as a weekly columnist for newspapers ranging from Ft. Collins, Colorado to Mt. Pleasant, Michigan to Oak Park — proving with the latter that you can go home again.

He has been named best columnist in the weekly newspaper category by the Illinois Press Association four times. He has written over 2,000 columns and yet, somehow, hasn't run out of things to say.

His first book, *We Dare to Say – An Adventure in Journaling*, was produced by ACTA Publications in 2007. His second book, *Unfinished Pentecost – Vatican II and the Altered Lives of Those Who Witnessed It*, was published in 2013 and is available at Amazon.com.

CPSIA information can be obtained
at www.ICGtesting.com
Printed in the USA
JSHW010943250523
42234JS00002B/2

9 781958 943441